GLOBAL
SCRIPTWRITING

GLOBAL SCRIPTWRITING

Ken Dancyger

Focal Press
Taylor & Francis Group

NEW YORK AND LONDON

First published 2001

This edition published 2013
by Focal Press
70 Blanchard Road, Suite 402, Burlington, MA 01803

Simultaneously published in the UK
by Focal Press
2 Park Square, Milton Park, Abingdon, Oxon OX14 4RN

Focal Press is an imprint of the Taylor & Francis Group, an informa business

Notices

Practitioners and researchers must always rely on their own experience and knowledge
in evaluating and using any information, methods, compounds, or experiments described
herein. In using such information or methods they should be mindful of their own safety
and the safety of others, including parties for whom they have a professional responsibility.

To the fullest extent of the law, neither the Publisher nor the authors, contributors, or
editors, assume any liability for any injury and/or damage to persons or property as a matter
of products liability, negligence or otherwise, or from any use or operation of any methods,
products, instructions, or ideas contained in the material herein.

Library of Congress Cataloging-in-Publication Data
Dancyger, Ken.
 Global scriptwriting / Ken Dancyger.
  p. cm.
 Includes index.
 ISBN 13: 978-0-240-80428-6 (pbk)
 1. Motion picture authorship.   I. Title.

PN1996 .D365 2001
808.2′3--dc21   2001018790

British Library Cataloguing-in-Publication Data
A catalogue record for this book is available from the British Library.

CONTENTS

          Melodrama   199
          Docudrama   201
          Hyperdrama   204
          Experimental Narrative   207

16   *Big Issues Plus National Stereotypes*   209
          The Case of *Elizabeth*   209
          The Case of *Fire*   211
          The Case of *Antonia's Line*   212
          The Case of *All About My Mother*   213
          The Case of *French Twist*   214
          The Case of *Shall We Dance*   215
          The Case of *The Full Monty*   216

17   *The Search for the Global Tale*   218
          The Case of Agnieska Holland's *Olivier Olivier*   221
          The Case of Mike Radford's *Il Postino*   222
          The Case of Ang Lee's *The Ice Storm*   223
          The Case of Sam Mendes' *American Beauty*   224
          The Case of Mary Harron's *American Psycho*   226

     Appendix: Script Treatment   229
          Treatment Sample   229
          Master Scene Format   234

     Index   241

ACKNOWLEDGMENTS

Global Scriptwriting began as a notion born out of a series of workshops I conducted in various parts of the world between 1996 and 2000. What I learned from the participants nurtured the ideas now set down in this book. I'd like to thank Martin Amstell of the London International Film School; Joost Hunninger and Chris Williams of the University of Westminster in London; Jeanne Wikler, Jane Williams, and Karol Kulik of the Maurits Binger Institute in Amsterdam; Reinhard Hauff and Uschi Keill of the DFFB in Berlin; Oliver Schuette and Stephanie Bastian of the Master School in Scriptwriting in Berlin; Margit Essenbach of the Zurich Film School; Victor Valbuena of Ngee Ann Polytechnic in Singapore; and Ron Blair, Paul Thompson, and Carolyn Vaughan of the Australian Film and Television School. There are many others, you know who you are and I apologize to you for the less specific acknowledgment. Space dictates brevity.

At Focal Press I first broached this idea with the ever-adventurous Marie Lee. She became the midwife for this book and I value her ongoing enthusiasm for my work. She was aided also enthusiastically by Terri Jadick, Maura Kelly, and copy editor, Harbour Hodder, who pushed this writer as he's never been pushed before, to make this a better book. Thank you. I'd like to thank my friend Maura Nolan who prepared the manuscript for the new computer age. And I'd like to thank my friends and family who tolerated my obsession with this book wherever we happened to be—on vacation or at home. Their good nature and good humor—is it an illness?—helped me progress to the finish line. Finally, I'd like to particularly thank my wife Ida whose sense of wonder and subtle support were critical to the completion of this book. She is the silent partner who deserves co-credit in this adventure.

This book is dedicated to the next generation of my family—Emily, Erica, Richard, and Jacob. May their enterprising natures lead them to experiences as adventurous and pleasurable as writing this book has been for me.

Ken Dancyger
New York

INTRODUCTION

As you read this book, 2001 has come and gone. As Stanley Kubrick implied in his classic film of the same name, the world both progresses and reverts to its beginnings. So too with filmic storytelling. Telling stories on film has been a global art form since its beginnings. But at the outset of film, the storytellers worked outward from the perspective of their national cultures and their personal artistic predispositions. Today, they work from the opposite perspective—the globe is their palate. And to be global they are creating new forms and new approaches to classic subject matter. That is the subject of this book—how filmic storytelling has changed. But to understand those changes and to catch the sense of direction of future filmic storytelling, we need two more perspectives: the past and the present. What is beyond question is that future storytelling will be global. To understand why this phenomenon is taking place, we need to look at the factors that are driving change and the factors that are supporting those changes.

First, the factors that are driving change. The last decade of the twentieth century has witnessed unprecedented transformation in media technology, in the industrial organization of the film and television industries, and in the genuine globalization of the film and television industries. I'll turn to the last point first. We need only look at the ownership and organization of the major film studios to see such globalization. The current ownership of Twentieth Century Fox was originally an Australian company. Columbia Pictures is under the aegis of a Japanese company, and the ownership of Universal Pictures is about to shift from a Canadian base to French ownership. When one looks at the relationship between the film, television, music, and publishing industries, not to mention Internet companies, national boundaries blur even further.

Looking at the flow of talent makes the point even more impressively. Whether the perspective is the director, the writer, or the cinematographer, the flow of talent is profoundly international. It is the July 4th weekend in the United States in the year 2000. The two big films of the weekend are *The Patriot* and *The Perfect Storm*, and both are directed by German directors, Roland Emmerich and Wolfgang Peterson. The next most significant film of 2000, *Gladiator*, is directed by the British director Ridley Scott. A side note is that the stars of *The Patriot* and *Gladiator*, respectively, are Mel Gibson and Russell Crowe, both of whom are Australian. And the list goes on. The latest Demi Moore film, *A Passion of Mind* (2000) is directed by Alain Berliner from France. The last episode of the *Alien* series (1996) was also directed by a French director, Jean-Pierre Jeunet. Australian directors are responsible for *The Witches of Eastwick* (George Miller, 1988), *The Truman Show* (Peter Weir, 1998), *My Best Friend's Wedding* (Paul Hogan, 1998), *Driving Miss Daisy* (Bruce Beresford, 1991), *Six Degrees of Separation* (Fred Schepsi, 1994), and *Patriot Games* (Phillip Noyce, 1993). British directors are responsible for *American Beauty* (Sam Mendes, 1999), *The English Patient* (Anthony Minghella, 1996), *High Fidelity* (Stephen Frears, 2000), *Shakespeare in Love* (John Madden, 1999), and *Ethan Frome* (John Madden, 1992). A Dutch director, Paul Verhoeven, is responsible for *Robo Cop* (1987) and *Basic Instinct* (1992). A Hong Kong director, John Woo, is responsible for *Broken Arrow* (1997) and *Mission Impossible II* (2000). *Cider House Rules* (1999) was directed by the Swedish director Lasse Hallström. This international flow of talent to Hollywood is not a one-way flow, however. The Italian film *Il Postino* (1996) was made by a British director, Mike Radford. Volker Schlondorff, a German director, has made two of his last three films in English. Clara Law of Hong Kong made the English-language *Floating Life* (1995). Ang Lee, originally from Taiwan, has just completed his first Chinese language production, *Crouching Tiger, Hidden Dragon* (2000) after a half-dozen English-language productions. In short, the flow of talent is profoundly international.

The explosion of media technology, both at the low end and at the high end, has also expanded the trend toward internationalization. The low-tech *Blair Witch Project* (1999) was inspired not only by the horror genre, but also by the success of an idea subscribed to by a group of Danish filmmakers. Lars Von Trier, under the aegis of Dogma 95, has suggested that less is more—less artifice and less intrusion (e.g., technical-artificial music, sound effects, lighting) in the filmmaking process will generate more deeply affecting films. It remains to be seen whether Thomas Vinterberg's *The Celebration* (1998), *Mifune* (1999), and *The Idiots* (1999) prove to be as influential as Dziga Vertov's *Man with a Movie Camera* (1979) or Peter Watkin's *Culloden* (1965). Nevertheless, these films and the idea that production values are secondary to a sense of reality, has already produced the most profitable film of all time—*The Blair Witch Project*. They have also encouraged important filmmakers to experiment with the techniques of Dogma 95. Mike Figgis' *Time Code* (2000) and the opening sequence of Steven Spielberg's *Saving Private Ryan* (1999) owe much to the ideas that were generated by a small group of filmmakers working in Denmark—which again supports the notion that filmic storytelling is more global than ever. Technology and the flow of talent and capital are driving change. And developments in the pedagogy of storytelling are supporting those changes.

In the 1970s, ideas about screenwriting were generated out of the work of a number of playwrights who became screenwriters. All paid appropriate allegiance to Aristotle and his ideas on drama. Two events coincided to influence scriptwriting and its pedagogy. The first was the release of *Star Wars* in 1977, a film whose origins were in other movies as well as other popular forms: comic books and serialized stories in prose and on stage and screen. The second event was the publication of Syd Field's book on scriptwriting, *Screenplay* (1982). Between the commercial success of *Star Wars* and of Syd Field's *Screenplay*, an industry was born—the "how-to-write a screenplay" industry. *Star Wars* propelled the renewed vigor and commercial power of Hollywood film. My task, fortunately, is not to prioritize the flood of books that have followed but rather to suggest that the pedagogy those books have supplied has helped to internationalize filmic storytelling. It has provided a common language and a set of terms and approaches to story that are shared by beginning as well as seasoned professionals. Agents and executives, as well as writers and directors, talk of plot points, character arcs, and resolution or nonresolution with a confidence that was less certain pre-Syd Field. What is of interest to us in this particular addition to the literature is that writers now have distinct choices in the pedagogy. I find it useful to consider these choices on a grid.

In the center there are the structuralists, who begin with Syd Field's paradigm but who also may veer from formula into consideration of character and genre. Many of the best known script teachers and gurus dwell in this space. Most enduring in my view is the work of Frank Daniel, first at Columbia and later in the writing area at the University of Southern California. His legacy, with its emphasis on structure, remains a critical foundation in contemporary pedagogy.

To the right of the structuralists, there is a school that I link with the importance of mythology in filmic storytelling. These teachers and writers emphasize the hero, the journey, and the deep layer of archetypical behavior that marks films such as *Star Wars* and *The Lion King* (1993). This pedagogical approach owes much to the work of Joseph Campbell, especially *The Hero with a Thousand Faces* (1949).

To the left of the structuralists are writers and teachers such as myself. Here the influence of the work of Luis Buñuel, Jean-Luc Godard, and Michelangelo Antonioni, those filmic storytellers who broke all the rules, holds sway. The consequences of this pedagogical approach is to look at the work of those who break the rules to see if there is a pattern that is pedagogically useful. Since this approach will occupy a good part of the middle section of this book I needn't belabor the point. However, what I can say is that much innovation—the nonlinear story as well as feminist styles of storytelling—suggest that this area has much appeal among younger filmmakers and writers.

What is important about these pedagogical developments is that together they have buttressed the globalization of filmic storytelling. In this sense, ongoing pedagogical developments will encourage and empower writers the world over to use these tools to reach out to national and international film audiences.

As a writer I have had a tendency to include any new ideas about filmic storytelling in the book I was engaged in writing at the time. Consequently I have written about nonlinear storytelling in my book on film and video editing, *The Technique of Film and Video Editing*, 2nd edition (1996), and on my latest ideas about genre in *Writing the Short Film* (2000), a book I cowrote with Pat Cooper. This book gives me the opportunity to pull all of my ideas into a single volume and to push the exploration about global scriptwriting out of the context of all my deliberations about script. Consequently I have structured this book to be inclusive of those past ideas as well as contextual for the newest ideas in the field as a whole. The book follows a three-part structure:

1. Universal Elements of Script
2. Particulars about Scriptwriting
3. The Internationalization of Storytelling

As has been my strategy in the past, I follow a case study approach in all the chapters. In choosing these case studies I have drawn on American, European, as well as Asian films that are widely available, although some will not be widely known. Now, on to the beginning.

PART I

UNIVERSAL ELEMENTS OF SCRIPT

1

THE BASICS

In order to understand the basics of script—premise, character, structure, and all the dramatic properties of film narrative—we need to consider a number of questions whose answers will conceptualize the substance of this chapter. What is storytelling? How does it relate to our lives? And why do certain stories succeed in affecting us, and others fail? These questions are our starting point.

It's best to begin with a central term, *drama*, a term that is usually associated with the stage and with theater critics. The term itself implies conflict. If Macbeth didn't want to become king, with the sitting king as a barrier to his goal, there would be no conflict in Shakespeare's play. If the warring families in *Romeo and Juliet* got along, the play wouldn't take the dramatic shape that it does. If Othello weren't as jealous, if he weren't a Moor surrounded by Caucasians, and so on. If the senators of Rome were content to allow Julius Caesar to fulfill his ambition to be Emperor of Rome . . . well, you get the picture. Shakespeare would not have found the tragedy of Julius Caesar compelling; nor would we.

Not all conflict is a merit from the perspective of the critic. If a drama is overwrought, the critics consider the story melodramatic or operatic. When they want to suggest that a drama is flat, they describe it as flawed or cheapened. In either case the implication is that when drama is working the level of engagement between the audience and the story is ideal. It has credibility, and it has the capacity to, in a valuable way, invite us into an identification with the actions of the character and with the narrative arc of the play.

Drama, then, is a level of conflict that is shaped, as Aristotle suggests, with a beginning, a middle, and an end. That conflict may be internal, interpersonal, intersocietal, or between man and nature. The consequent clash of goals brings us into an identification with a character. If the character has will and energy, we identify with the drive. If the story positions the character as a potential victim, we fear that the character's will (and ours) will be crushed.

What needs to be said about drama is that it differs from real life. That is not to say that each of us do not have conflict in our lives. Quite the contrary. But the conflict in drama is intensified and structured for a purpose—to entertain or to capture us in a moral swamp where we can swim or sink with a character. And drama offers resolution or catharsis in two hours. Few real-life conflicts hold out such a promise.

Which brings us to the importance of storytelling in the human experience. Whether expressed in a series of cave paintings, a series of tapestries, a sonnet, an

3

epic poem, a novel, a photograph, a play, or a film, all these storytelling expressions have meant so much more than the artifacts now housed in museums or the plays read in high schools. For each generation these communiqués from one human being to his or her community have served multiple purposes. On the most basic level, an artifact is an entertainment that might promote laughter or joy from the experience. Cartoons, TV situation comedies, and soap operas have their equivalents in the travelling plays, court jesters, and clowns of former times.

Or the story might have an educational goal. Education is a broad term, and all of us throughout our lifetimes are in the process of becoming educated. New information, moral education, political education, social education—all are the valid educational goals of storytelling. Fairy tales and fables for children, or the more complex education layers of a play such as Arthur Miller's *The Crucible*, offer different types of education for their audiences.

Whether informational or moral, or educational about the social and psychological dimensions of the human experience, stories educate us in layered and complex ways. The outcome might be to improve us as all education can, or it might simply provide a cathartic experience that helps us cope with demons that would otherwise prove harmful to ourselves or to others.

I'm not suggesting that stories are the panacea for all that ails society and its members. But I am suggesting that storytelling has played an important role in helping societies function. And when those stories are seminal and important, they can have a transformative effect, as all art can. Stories can yield the understanding that brings people together, and in this sense it has and does fulfill a critical function in society.

Imagine for a moment stories told in a form that reaches across societies, across nations, and around the world. That is the power of filmic storytelling. This invention of the late-nineteenth century became the popular art form of the twentieth century. The storytellers of the twenty-first century want to tell their stories in images. Whether in film or video, those stories have become the most important and most powerful story form of our time.

THE VISUAL VERSUS THE SPOKEN

Storytelling as an evolving form followed two distinct paths—the visual and the aural. Theater today owes much to how far the aural tradition has progressed. And although film owes much to theater structurally and in basic dramatic principles, it is distinctly visual as a medium. Its use of light also owes much to painting and to photography, but its visual character goes beyond those forms. It's best to think of filmic storytelling as a form where every aspect of the form evolves out of this visual character.

Consequently, certain film genres that are particularly visual—the western, the musical, the action-adventure film—are dominated by visual action. That action may characterize, it may advance the plot, or it may simply provide the context for both. But these genres are not exclusively visual, they are simply the most predominately visual.

To illustrate the depth of the visual character of the medium a cross-section of famous and less-famous film sequences will serve. Among the most famous are the shower sequence in Alfred Hitchcock's *Psycho* (1960), the Odessa Steps sequence in Eisenstein's *Potemkin* (1925), the breakfast scene in Welles' *Citizen Kane* (1941), the gunfight toward the end of Peckinpah's *The Wild Bunch* (1969). Among the less-famous but notably visual sequences, the burial of a child's mother early in David Lean's *Dr. Zhivago* (1965), a young boy's escape from a tyrannical housekeeper in Carol Reed's *The Fallen Idol* (1948), the sniper attack in Stanley Kubrick's *Full Metal Jacket* (1987). In this last sequence, many men die on a patrol during the Battle of Hue. They die because of a single sniper. After many losses they kill the sniper, only to discover she is a woman. These sequences are powerful, dramatic evocations presented to us at set pieces.

The medium more often functions with more modest but no less visual aspects. For instance, it may offer insight into character. The visual action of the Marlon Brando character, Terry in Elia Kazan's *On the Waterfront* (1954), when he's getting to know Edie, a young woman (Eva Marie Saint), is instructive. He is a young man with lots of rough edges; she is a student in a convent school. They sit on swings making conversation. He has taken one of her gloves and as he talks he plays with her glove. From his actions we understand his desire—he wants to get close to this young woman but he doesn't know how. His awkward visual action implies that desire and that awkwardness.

Another example is an early action in Carol Reed's *The Third Man* (1949). An American writer named Holly Martins (Joseph Cotton) arrives in post-war Vienna, invited and paid for by his friend Harry Lime (Orson Welles), only to find that his friend Lime is dead. A policeman arranges his accommodations and a return to America. Holly tries to punch the policeman for insulting his friend. He is knocked out instead. The scene visually illustrates both the impulsiveness and the naivete of the writer. His refusal to believe Harry Lime is dead leads him to fight and, predictably, to lose.

Characterization in film is almost always visually captured. So, too, is plot. The murder of a brother motivates Wyatt Earp to become the sheriff of Tombstone in John Ford's *My Darling Clementine* (1946). A case of mistaken identity leads the main character to be kidnapped in Alfred Hitchcock's *North by Northwest* (1959). The placement of a damaging item in a gossip column will either move the main character up the ladder of success or lead to his ruin in Alexander Mackendrick's *Sweet Smell of Success* (1956). The key here is that it is a visual action rather than a described action (in dialogue) that is natural and useful in filmic storytelling.

This idea of visualization should pervade your thinking as you begin to write your screenplay.

Consider visualization as the first writing strategy when faced with characterization or plot advancement. The examples of wordsmith David Mamet, a playwright, writing for the screen is instructive. In terms of characterization, his screenplay of *The Edge* (1997) is instructive. The main character Charles Morse (Anthony Hopkins) is a billionaire. He is also an older gentleman married to a young model. He is jealous of his younger rival, Robert Green (Alec Baldwin), the photographer, who will photograph his wife in a natural wilderness setting in

Northern Alaska. Charles is portrayed as insatiably curious to understand and control his world. He is deeply knowledgeable about tribal artifacts as well as means of survival—creating fire without matches, keeping warm when wet. But he's never had to act on this knowledge, until he and Robert and an assistant crash land deep in the wilderness. At that point, it's all about survival.

Mamet characterizes Charles continually faced with a life-threatening challenge—a Kodiak bear, a freezing environment, no real compass to guide him to safety. In each case, Mamet visually illustrates Charles' capacity for hope and for intelligence to solve the problem and to save himself and his companions.

The visual characterization and the visualization of plot (the escape to the south) is Mamet's writing solution, his visual solution to the writing problem.

TERMS—USEFUL, CRITICAL

If directors of films think in terms of *shots*, writers think in terms of *premise, character*, and *structure*. These narrative terms, some borrowed from theater and some adapted for film, are the common language of film writing. Practitioners and producers sometimes adapt them according to their experience, so you will encounter variations in how they are used. What I present here are the terms I have found useful to writers to help them write.

Screenplay Format   Prose is presented in a novel in sentences and paragraphs. A script is presented in visual detail and dialogue organized in a distinct fashion unique to film. That format is called the master scene format (see Appendix for example). What is most common in screenplay format for film and television films is the master scene format. Although multicamera television uses its own format (visual/audio side by side), as does documentary, the format here described is the master scene script format.

This format is useful because it facilitates the reading of the script as well as the budgeting of the script. The scene numbering changes as there is a location change. This allows tabulation of personnel, cast, crew, and props per location facilitating budgeting.

The Premise   We experience a film through the main character. The *premise* refers to the particular challenge facing the main character. In certain genres such as the thriller, it is an external choice. In *The Fugitive* (1993), Richard Kimble (Harrison Ford) finds his wife dying and after her death he is accused and tried as her killer. He knows he didn't do it. How will he regain his freedom? In *Raiders of the Lost Ark* (1981), Indiana Jones (Harrison Ford) wants to find the Lost Ark. Will he? How, given the obstacles in his way? In these cases the premise is an external rather than an internal struggle.

More often the premise does refer to an inner struggle. In this case, it's best to consider the premise as the two opposite choices facing the main character. In Anthony Minghella's *Truly, Madly, Deeply* (1991), the main character has recently lost her lover to an unexpected illness. She is deeply wounded and struggles with overwhelming grief. The premise of the film is whether she will go on grieving for the rest of her life (hold on to the dead lover) or whether she will take up life, in the future, by way of a new relationship.

In Lee Tamahori's *Once Were Warriors* (1995), the main character must decide between her husband and her children. Although she lives in the illusion of a family life, her husband's attitude and his lifestyle choices (drinking and partying with his friends) are destructive to the her goals for the family. She must make a choice.

Often the premise is worked out through the exploration of two relational choices, in this case, the husband or the children. She cannot have both.

The Critical Moment   The beginning of the film story should throw us into the story. If the setup is too gentle or too slow we may not join with the story. The point at which we begin the film story should capture us powerfully. Whether this means a low point in the life of the main character, as in Sydney Lumet's *The Verdict* (1982), or the accidental, untimely death of T.E. Lawrence in David Lean's *Lawrence of Arabia* (1962), the beginning, because of its special function of propelling us into the story, is called the *critical moment*.

This point can be mysterious, or it can be rife with danger, or it can seem to be a trap or a dead end for the main character. The key here is the conflictual quality this moment has for the main character—it will be a turning point for the character's story.

The Catalytic Event   If the film story begins at a critical moment, the *catalytic event* (sometimes referred to as the *point of attack*) will propel the main character away from the trap or toward another option. In film noir the catalytic event is when the main character meets the woman who will rescue him from his state of despair. (Quite the opposite happens.) In Lumet's *The Verdict*, the drunken lawyer who is an ambulance chaser in his profession, is given a case, a "moneymaker." This case will constitute the plot of *The Verdict*. In Lean's *Lawrence of Arabia*, the young officer Lawrence is given permission to join Faisal, the leader of the Arab revolt against the Turks (again the beginning of the plot).

Main Character   The main character is at the heart of the film narrative. Not only do we experience the narrative through the point of view of the main character, every element of the narrative impacts upon the main character. Consequently the main character is key. This is not necessarily the case in other story forms and their consequent adaptation to film. In the case of the Francis Ford Coppola 1974 adaptation of Fitzgerald's novel *The Great Gatsby*, the point of view of the novel is Daisy's cousin. This perspective is maintained in the film directed by Jack Clayton. The result is a flawed film narrative because the central or main character of the film story is clearly Gatsby, the man with a past. In the Coppola screenplay, the chosen point of view distances us from what should be the main character. The consequence is respectful but not emotionally engaging.

Examples of more effectively positioned main characters are Margo Channing (Bette Davis) in *All About Eve* (1950) and Marty (Ernest Borgnine) in the Paddy

Chayefsky 1955 film adaptation of his screenplay *Marty*. These characters are right in the middle of the narrative action in each of the stories.

Character Goals   A film narrative works most effectively when the character has a strong goal. The desire for a love match on the part of the main character Rose (Kate Winslett) in James Cameron's *Titanic* (1997) is a good example. Another is the young main character's belief in a better life in the midst of his family's sufferings during the Depression in Steven Soderbergh's *King of the Hill* (1993). Another is Erin's desperate desire to take care of her children in Steven Soderbergh's *Erin Brockovich* (2000).

The benefit of a strong goal is that it creates drama. Rose must go against her mother and her rich fiancé in *Titanic*. The young boy in *King of the Hill* struggles against the economic challenges to his family, to the health challenges to his family, and to the social challenges at school. Erin Brockovich has to fight economic, social, and political opposition in order to achieve her goal. A film story can proceed where a character doesn't have a goal, as for the character in Soderbergh's *sex, lies and videotape* (1989), but your job as a writer will be much easier if all your characters have goals.

Polarities   Polarities or opposites are a very useful device to create drama or conflict. Where characters in the story have opposite goals, where they are different from one another in age, status, race, and gender, and where these differences are dramatically purposeful, you have the idea of opposites working for you in the narrative.

Erin Brockovich is uneducated and poor. The lawyer she goes to work for is educated and rich. Erin's ultimate opposite is the power company that has been polluting the drinking water of its neighbors. The power company stands at the opposite end of the power grid from Erin.

Rose's two suitors, the artist Jack Dawson (Leonardo diCaprio) and the financier Cal Hockley (Billy Zane) couldn't be more opposite. The artist is giving emotionally, fun-loving, and, in the end, self-sacrificing. The financier is materially giving but possessive, and he's not fun at all. In fact, he spends a good deal of the time being angry or aggressive, and in the end he is totally selfish rather than considerate of Rose or anybody else, for that matter.

The important point here is that opposites or polarities are very useful in the film narrative. Think of them as the dramatic train tracks for the story.

Secondary Characters   The secondary characters serve the main character in two ways. Either they help the main character, or they create barriers for or harm the main character. In certain genres the difference is strongly apparent. All those who pose a threat or are harmful to the main character in Roland Emmerich's *The Patriot* (2000) are British (with one Colonial loyal to the British added). This has great logic in a story set during the American War of Independence (1776–1783). The helpers are family, neighbors, freemen, and slaves who share the main character's goal: first to protect his family and finally to defeat the British, the Colonial power in America.

In other genres the distinction is less clear-cut. In *All About Eve*, an ambitious would-be actress and the critic who promotes her are harmers to Margo Channing, the main character. The playwright, his wife, and the director are all characters who help Margo. The distinction blurs here because at one point or another each of these characters falls out with the main character or, in the case of the playwright's wife, is actually seriously harmful to the main character. Nevertheless, in the end, she too is helpful.

The Antagonist   The antagonist is the most important secondary character. This is the character whose goal is in greatest opposition to the main character. In this sense, the antagonist is the most significant harmer. In James Cameron's *Titanic*, the antagonist is the main character's fiancé, the financier, Cal. In Joseph Mankiewicz's *All About Eve*, the antagonist is Eve, the ambitious rising star whose goal is to take over the roles of the main character, Margo Channing.

Often the antagonist is overt and obvious—Darth Vader in *Star Wars*. At other times, the antagonist might be the conflicted self. The main characters in Minghella's *Truly, Madly, Deeply* and George Stevens' *A Place in the Sun* (1951) offer examples where the main character is their own antagonist.

The nature of the antagonist will have a profound influence on the dramatic arc of the story. If it is to be heroic, the antagonist should be all the more powerful. The British Colonel Tavington in Emmerich's *The Patriot* and Javert in Bille August's *Les Miserables* (1998) are good examples. More usual however is a more realistic antagonist, such as Mr. Sheldrake in Billy Wilder's *The Apartment* (1960), or Gordon Gekko in Oliver Stone's *Wall Street* (1987).

Structure   Structure, which is essentially the shape of the narrative, is actually composed of four layers: the mechanical structure, often referred to as the three-act structure; the plot, which I called the Foreground Story in *Alternative Scriptwriting* (a book I cowrote with Jeff Rush); the character layer, which I called the Background Story in *Alternative Scriptwriting*; and the genre, or the story form that serves as the container for the structure. These layers are sufficiently important that I will define each of them separately.

Three-Act Structure   The organization of events and characters tends to be organized in a three-act structure in the classical film story. In keeping with Aristotle's beginning, middle, and end, three acts orchestrate for dramatic effectiveness the events of the story. Act I, the Setup, joins the story at a critical moment. The main character and the premise are introduced. Approximately one-third of the way into Act I, a catalytic event kick-starts the plot or another source of momentum for the story. In film noir, for example, the main character meets the woman of his dreams. The First Act ends with a turning point that takes us into the Second Act.

Act II is the act of Confrontation. Twice as long as the other acts, it tends to explore two options or choices (in terms of relationships) for the main character. There is a midpoint to the Act. Act II ends with another turning point, which takes us into Act III.

In Act III, the act of Resolution, the main character finally makes his or her choice, or achieves or fails in his or her goal. In this act, the plot as well as the character layers (which I will define in a moment) must be resolved.

Three-act structure refers to the classic film narrative. There are increasing examples of films that choose to drop resolution (Act III) (an example is Spike Lee's *She's Gotta Have It* [1986]), or which sidestep this linear structure altogether (see "The Nonlinear Story" later in this chapter). (Linear is a narrative in which the goal directed character moves through the narrative toward resolution of that goal.) However, 95 percent of screen stories adhere to this structure.

Major Plot Points   Major plot points are the turning points at the end of each act. These tend to be very strong events. The major plot point at the end of Act I opens up the story in an unexpected way. The major plot point at the end of Act II closes down the story and motivates the main character to make a choice.

The turning points in Lee Tamahori's *Once Were Warriors*, a story of domestic violence among the Maoris of New Zealand, are as follows:

It is clear in Act I that the marriage of Beth and Jake is troubled and that the mother, the main character, cares deeply about her children. Yet nothing prepares the viewer for the physical beating she undergoes at the hands of her husband. Its violence and its sexual aggression present the audience with a shocking reality check on the state of her marriage. This is the first major plot point. The second turning point at the end of Act II comes after Beth exerts a great deal of effort to keep the family together. The suicide of her oldest daughter (after being raped by her father's friend) forces the mother to face a choice—between her marriage or the fate of her children. She chooses to leave the marriage. Both turning points occur at the end of a long night of social drinking and partying at the home of Beth and her family.

The key element of major plot points in comparison to other plot points is that they are very distinct in the impact they have upon the story.

Plot Points   Sometimes referred to as *beats,* plot points are the outcome of each scene in the narrative. Each plot point will either characterize the characters or advance the plot. There may be as many as eighty plot points in a feature film.

Plot   Plot is a very important layer of structure. It refers to the external set of events (in the world) that challenge the main character and his or her goal. The voyage of the Titanic in Cameron's *Titanic,* the Battle of Hue in Kubrick's *Full Metal Jacket,* the War of Independence and its progress (or lack thereof) in Emmerich's *The Patriot*—these are the plots in the respective film stories.

The importance of plot is that it should complicate the main character's goal. Often it works in opposition to the character's goal. In this sense, plot enhances the dramatic or conflictual properties of the screen story.

Character Layer   The character layer of the screen story is on one level the direct expression of the premise of the film. Should I choose my dead lover or a new live lover in Minghella's *Truly, Madly, Deeply*? Should I choose my husband or my children in Tamahori's *Once Were Warriors*? This character layer requires that each option be fully explored in the screen narrative. This layer often dominates Act II of the structure. Because these options have to be fully explored prior to the main character making his or her choice, Act II tends to be long and dominated by characters and their relationships.

Resolution The resolution, sometimes referred to as the climax of the story, is best understood in light of the goal of the main character. In the resolution, the main character either achieves or fails in his or her goal. The goal of the main character in Emmerich's *The Patriot*, is to save his family. Given that the colonials need soldiers, his sons are expected to fight, as is he. The war and its progress mitigates against this goal. He has lost two sons and a home, but the war is won, and he now will return to the complications of that original goal, to provide a future for his remaining family members. In *All About Eve*, Margo Channing is a 40 plus year old actress. She is a star. But she is tremendously insecure about her age. She is less so as a star. But as a star she feels its her image, her talent that keeps her lover, the director, with her. Her choices are either to be a star (and forever doubt her personal relationships) or to acknowledge her age and choose what is being offered, a real relationship with the director, in essence, a family life. This will mean that she moves away from being a star whose life is dominated by the stage. She chooses personal over professional goals and in doing so her insecurity about Bill, the director, ebbs. She is comfortable in her choice; and by making the choice, she resolves the conflicting issues in her life.

Resolution that is appropriate to the linear three-act structure creates closure to the film's narrative arc. And closure for the main character means closure for the audience.

Genre Genre is the story form that contains the overall structure of the screen story. There are numerous genres—action-adventure, melodrama, the western, the gangster film, the police story, the musical, the situation comedy, science fiction, film noir, and the horror film, among others. These story forms have very particular characteristics. They differ in terms of the goals of their characters, the role of the antagonist, their dramatic shape, and the balance of plot to character layer and tone. What is important about genre is that there are distinguishing features over time that unite films within a genre (compare *Scarface* [1934] and *The Godfather* [1973], for example). There may be tonal variations over time, but the substructure within genres endures and it is that substructure that audiences identify with and value in a genre.

Scene A scene is the smallest unit within the overall structure of the screen story. Although a shot may be smaller, a shot more often will only refer to a directorial decision that is the equivalent of a single detail within the scene.

From a narrative perspective, consider the scene to be the context for the plot point, as described earlier. A scene has a purpose, and once that purpose is achieved (the plot point) the scene is over.

The Sequence   A sequence is a series of scenes within the overall structure of the screen story. The purpose of a sequence may be to advance the plot or characterize an environment or a person, and therefore may be plot- or character-driven. A good example of a character-driven sequence is the introduction of the gunnery sergeant, Hartman, and his strategy to the new army inductees in Kubrick's *Full Metal Jacket*. The purpose of the sequence is to illustrate that the goal of Sergeant Hartman is to break the individualistic spirits of the inductees. His deeper goal, as he states it, is "to turn them into killing machines." Breaking their spirits is, to his mind, the way to achieve his goal.

The Act   I have already defined the individual acts within a three-act structure. In relation to the sequence, an Act is a series of sequences that are organized along a rising action to promote the conflict between the main character and his goal, those who oppose him, those who may help him, and the plot, which will oppose him.

The Nonlinear Story   The nonlinear story has been with us since Luis Buñuel made *Un Chien Andalou* in 1929, but it's been more recently popularized and mythologized by the success of Quentin Tarantino's *Pulp Fiction* (1993). Essentially, nonlinear screen story is a story whose shape is not driven by a main character who has a clearly defined goal and who is rushing towards resolution. On the contrary, the nonlinear story may not have one main character, it may proceed where the character(s) do not have goals, and it certainly does not have resolution. Consequently, the experience of the nonlinear story is very different from the experience of a three-act film narrative. Recent examples include Paul Thomas Anderson's *Magnolia* (1999), Terence Malick's *The Thin Red Line* (1998), and Tom Tykwer's *Run, Lola, Run* (1999).

In Terence Malick's *The Thin Red Line*, the battle is over at the end of the film, but since we have followed 10 characters, some with goals, others simply wanting to survive, we don't have the conclusive sense of closure that we have in Spielberg's *Saving Private Ryan* (1999), a linear war film. The Captain has saved Private Ryan, dying in the act, but with the invocation, make your life worthy of my sacrifice. This kind of closure leaves the audience with a far different, more articulated sense of emotions than does the end of *The Thin Red Line*. Whether we conclude more poetically, or more philosophically, the ending offers us choice rather than forcing the choice upon us.

Surprise   Generally surprise is achieved in the film narrative via the twists and turns of plot and of the individual behavior of the characters in the narrative. This might mean the "humane" behavior of the serial killer Hannibal Lecter (Anthony Hopkins) toward Clarice Starling (Jodie Foster) in Jonathan Demme's *The Silence of the Lambs* (1991), or it might mean that Lucky, the leader of the Allied demolition team, breaks his leg and is therefore no longer able to lead, in J. Lee Thompson's *The Guns of Navarone* (1961). In both cases, surprise leaves the audience in a state of heightened tension about the fate of the main character. Surprise is very important to sustain audience involvement with the film narrative.

Tension   Tension is a critical factor in every scene. It is the key to our involve-ment in the film narrative. What creates tension is specific to the dramatic con-struction of each scene. Imagine two characters with differing goals. The goals may be simple; the key is that they are opposing goals. The scene itself is resolved when one character or the other achieves his or her goal. But the tension in the scene is generated from the conflict between the two characters and their oppos-ing goals. Who will achieve his or her goal? This is the question as we move to-ward the resolution of the scene. The byproduct of this question is tension, a key ingredient in your screen story and in how involved the audience will become with your story.

Energy   Energy, a critical element in every film narrative, relates to character: the nature of character, the behavior of character, the will of character, and the desire of character. On one level, energy relates to the goal of the character. If the character's nature is to be intense, this quality when applied to his or her goal will generate the kind of energy that is powerful and endlessly useful in the screen story. Plot can also generate energy.

Ridley Scott's *Gladiator* (2000) provides good examples of both types of energy. First, the goal of the main character, Maximus (Russell Crowe), is to return home to his wife and son. But to do so he must complete his responsibilities to Caesar, Marcus Aurelius (Richard Harris). As the general of the army of the north, Maximus must end the war with the German barbarians. But when he does so, Caesar poses another responsibility—to be his heir, and restore Rome to a repub-lic (it has drifted toward an absolute monarchy). Maximus, a man of duty, is torn, but he will serve. Here the plot intervenes. Commodus (Joaquin Phoenix), son of Caesar, doesn't like his father's decision. He kills his father, tries to kill Maximus, and has the wife and son of Maximus brutally murdered.

Now the goal of Maximus becomes revenge and here it is the energy of the plot that gives him his opportunity. He becomes a slave, then a gladiator, and then, as the greatest gladiator, a threat to Commodus, the new Caesar.

The tension between the will of Maximus to have revenge and justice and the barriers before him creates the powerful energy in *Gladiator*. Energy facilitates our involvement with the screen story.

Tone   The tone of a film is the nonverbal, visual surround of the story. Tone tends to direct the audience towards a particular interpretation and is often genre-specific. Because melodrama is essentially a genre about recognizable peo-ple in believable situations, the tone is realistic. In a musical, a genre of wish ful-fillment, the tone has to be fantastic or magical, a tone in which we in the audi-ence believe dreams can come true. As you might expect, the tone in the horror film has to be overflowing with danger and the feeling that anything can happen. The excessive, over-the-top tone of the horror film is the surround that helps us believe in the unleashed aggression and sexuality that are central to the horror film.

There is tone that draws us into the story, and there can also be tone that is so absurd it pushes us away from character and events in the screen story. This tone, irony, is useful in genres such as the satire and the screwball comedy, where distance is critical to the effectiveness of the screen story.

Voice   Each of us has a point of view, a filter through which we see the world. This is no less true for writers and directors who use that filter to translate their world—their screen story—for us. That editorial position I will call their voice.

When you see a number of films by a particular writer or director you begin to get the sense of their voice. Billy Wilder has a cosmopolitan cynicism that moves throughout his work. Preston Sturges had a profound sense of irony about relationships and the American dream. Quentin Tarantino is media-obsessed in his work, as is Oliver Stone. Spike Lee wants to educate his audience. Every writer and director has a voice that makes his or her work unique.

In the past ten years, voice has become more personal and more assertive, overwhelming our relationship with character and story. In the past, voice was more subtle, more subdued. This is such an important shift in storytelling that we will return to the issue more than once in the balance of this book.

Narrative Strategies   A narrative strategy refers to the particular mix of plot, character layer, and genre that a writer deploys. It also refers to variations in expectations as to how the main and secondary characters are treated in the script. For example, the expected dominant narrative strategy in melodrama is the deployment of the character layer as the primary structural component. Although this holds true for the majority of melodrama, particular stories have included a plot layer. Indeed in a film such as George Stevens' *A Place in the Sun*, the plot layer is substantial.

Taking this mix further, Nick Enright and George Miller treat their story *Lorenzo's Oil* (1992) primarily through plot layer. Consequently the genre expectation of the dominance of the character layer is in this case substantially altered away from genre expectation.

In the case of character, the dominance of the main character vis a vis secondary characters in melodrama can also be altered. In Robert Mulligan's *To Kill a Mockingbird* (1962), the main character's father, a secondary character, is more a presence in both the character layer and the plot layer of the narrative. The main character, a 10-year-old girl is present only in the character layer.

A CASE STUDY IN THE BASICS:
ELIA KAZAN'S *AMERICA AMERICA*

Elia Kazan occupies a unique place among directors. For the period of the playwrights Arthur Miller and Tennessee Williams (1940–1960), Kazan was the most important director of American theater and film. What is so valuable about Kazan to writers is that the man had a profound understanding of drama. For that reason I've chosen to focus on his work in this introductory chapter. On a very fundamental level Kazan understood that the premise, character, and plot all must be compelling in the tale. The result has been a series of films quite unlike the careers of other directors. His films have an effectiveness in their dramatic shape that had, and still have, an emotional resonance for his audience. One could say that if a young director wants to learn to direct, Hitchcock is your man; but if a young writer wants to learn how to write, study Kazan. The premise is always clear in a Kazan film. In *Gentleman's Agreement* (1947), does the main character want to be a reporter who describes experience, exploiting material, or does he want to write from experience by pretending to be a Jew? In *East of Eden* (1955), does Cal want to be a free spirit like his mother or a judgmental, rigid person like his father? In *Viva Zapata* (1952), does a man become a revolutionary because of his ideals or because he wants power? In *Splendor in the Grass* (1961), does a young man follow his heart in a relationship or does his father choose a mate for him? In each case, the choice the main character struggles with is articulated in terms of a powerful character. The result is drama at its most visceral.

America America (1963) is Kazan's own story about how his uncle came from Anatolia, a region of Turkey, to America at the beginning of the twentieth century. In order to outline fully the dramatic properties of *America America*, we begin with the premise.

Premise—*America America*

America America is the story of Stavros, a twenty-year-old Greek living with his family in Anatolia (Turkey) in 1896. His dream is to leave Anatolia and go to America. Given his age, the resistance of his family, the danger in the journey, and the expense, much must be overcome to fulfill his dream, but that is precisely what he will do in this film story.

With this brief description in mind, let's move on to the premise. The two opposing choices for Stavros are:

1. To leave in order to be free—and I mean freedom in the fullest sense. Freedom from the constraints of his family, freedom from exploitation by the Turks.
2. To stay and have no freedom—to be a slave to the political system (the Turks are in control of all the minorities, the Greeks as well as the Armenians) and to be a slave to a social system in which his father is his master.

In a sense Stavros' choices are free man or slave, and these two choices will resonate throughout the narrative in every sequence.

Character—*America America*

Stavros as a young man is ambitious and headstrong but inexperienced. He has a dream about America but knows little about it. All he knows is that he must leave. From a dramatic point of view, the impossibility of his achieving his goal and the barriers that lie before him are daunting and they create a dramatic arc of epic proportions. How can a young man with nothing but his will succeed?

What is critical from the point of view of character is that the secondary characters be emblematic of the premise—that is, they help Stavros, and yet they also are barriers to the achievement of his goal (they imprison or enslave him). How this works will become clearer as I describe the sequences. Because the characters are both enablers after being victimizers, there is no clear, single antagonist.

What is interesting about all of the secondary characters is that in their own way they are as willful as Stavros.

Structure

The act structure of *America America* is quite clear. Act I is set in Anatolia, Act II on the way to and in Constantinople, and Act III on the journey to and in America.The turning point that ends Act I is the father's decision to send Stavros to Constantinople. As the eldest, Stavros will be the first to leave. When he is established in Constantinople, he is to bring his seven siblings out and then his mother. Act II consists of Stavros' journey to Constantinople and his experience there in his efforts to secure passage to America, first working as a stevedore, then seeking to marry a wealthy woman. Act II ends with the opportunity to take passage to America in return for sexual favors for a rich American woman. Act III consists of Stavros' voyage to America, concluding with his arrival and hard work there—because his siblings and his mother are waiting.

In order to illustrate more fully the dramatic properties of the narrative, we now look at the structure in much greater detail, act by act.

Act I

Act I of *America America* begins at a critical moment. Stavros and his friend Vartan are chopping ice from Mt. Ergis to sell in their village, but the political reality is that Armenians have bombed a bank in Constantinople and an edict has gone out to punish the Armenians. Vartan is Armenian; Stavros is Greek. Both are minorities under the control of the Turks. The catalytic event in Act I is the Turkish pogrom against the Armenians in the village.

Act I has two sequences. The first establishes the relationship between Stavros and Vartan, and the second fleshes out the relationship between Stavros and his father.

In the first sequence, the premise is established. Stavros wants to go to America. He sees Vartan as an older, experienced man who also yearns for freedom. In this sequence Vartan is challenging to the authorities while passing through a Turkish encampment commanded by the Turkish Captain Memet for whom Vartan was an orderly eight years earlier. Vartan has served his time. He wants to be free. Memet will protect him if he stays with him, but Vartan insists on going home and selling his ice. He then goes to a Turkish bar to spend his earnings. Here, too, he is provocative. He dances. Stavros follows him, for Vartan is the mentor to his dream to go to America. The pogrom against the Armenians follows that very night. Stavros witnesses the events and in trying to save his family, Vartan is killed. But even in death, he represents an ideal for Stavros. Stavros attempts to return Vartan's body to the family for burial, but in doing so, he is arrested by the Turks. In this sequence, the man who wants most to be free, Vartan, is killed, and the others who are Armenian are arrested. Their fate is unclear. Surprise in this sequence comes from the behavior of both Stavros and Vartan. They are defiant in their will to hold on to their dreams.

In the next sequence, Stavros is rescued from prison by his father. The price is a bribe to the Turkish governor. But Stavros, instead of being grateful, runs off. He runs up to the hill above the village to the home of his grandmother. He smiles, but she knows what he has come for—money. She belittles him as being his father's son rather than being a real man like his grandfather—a man who knows that such a false smile would please his patrons, the Turkish overlords. The grandmother gives him his grandfather's dagger and nothing more. He runs down the hill overwhelmed with frustration.

At the base of the hill a young man who is Stavros' age asks for his help. The young man, Oaness, will reappear in each act. Like Stavros, he is obsessed with getting to America. He is Armenian and he has walked very far. His shoes are worn. Angry at being trapped in the current situation, Stavros gives him his own shoes, an act of good will and defiance, and the young man tells him he will remember Stavros. At home, Stavros finds his father to be reflective and his mother to be angry when they discover he no longer has his shoes. And then the surprise, his father has decided that Stavros will go to Constantinople with all the belongings and wealth of the family. There he will invest in a cousin's business and prepare to send for his siblings and his mother. Again, Stavros is being diverted from his own goal—America. As the family prepares Stavros for his journey, his mother describes him as a young man who can't be trusted to go to a bakery to buy a loaf of bread. He might not return. And now the father is sending him with all the wealth of the family. Is this an act of madness? The act ends as Stavros leaves Anatolia with a loaded donkey, his coat sewn with money and jewels.

Act II

Act II of *America America* is composed of three primary sequences. The first is the trip from Anatolia to Constantinople. In Constantinople, the second sequence follows Stavros in his first attempt to earn the 110 Turkish pounds he needs to pay for ship passage to America. He is freely interpreting his father's charge. First he will go to America, then he will rescue the family. The third sequence follows his second attempt to secure the needed monies—by trying to get married. The act ends when a married woman from America pays for his passage. As in Act I, the dramatic articulation of the premise works its way through each sequence. Consequently, the secondary characters who first appear to be enablers of Stavros reaching his goal, actually prove to be victimizers, and vice versa.

The first sequence, the journey from Anatolia to Constantinople, begins with the trip across a lake. Just short of the shore the oarsman begins to threaten Stavros with drowning. The oarsman takes all his money and runs off at shore. A Muslim traveler recaptures the money for Stavros. Grateful, Stavros begins to travel with his rescuer. But this traveler, Abdul, who offers Stavros his friendship and his assets (even though he has none), expects the same in return. The character who has secured Stavros' freedom and enabled him to carry on in his journey now becomes his victimizer. He asks for food and refreshment, then for Stavros to pay for a prostitute. First willingly, then more reluctantly, Stavros agrees. The man did save him. But the situation deteriorates quickly. Abdul sells Stavros' assets—his food—while he sleeps. Angered, he breaks with the man and recovers what he can.

Shortly afterwards Abdul accuses Stavros of stealing all these things—he can describe them to the Turkish authorities. The law sides with a fellow Muslim and now Stavros has nothing. Abdul taunts him, riding the donkey beside Stavros, who no longer has his coat and jewels or the donkey and its blankets. Stavros kills Abdul but recovers very little, only enough to take a train to Constantinople. He arrives with nothing of the monies his father entrusted to him. Now Stavros has no means to get to America.

The second sequence of Act II begins with Stavros meeting his cousin, Mr. Opouzoglou, a down-and-out businessman who needed the money sent from his uncle in order to rejuvenate his business. There is no alternative, according to Mr. Opouzoglou: Stavros must marry someone plain but rich to secure a future for all in his family. Stavros doesn't agree. He runs off, believing that his own hard work will secure the monies he needs for passage to America. He works on the docks as a stevedore. Here he meets a worker who befriends him. This friendship is at the core of this sequence.

The stevedore is different from all the characters we have met so far. Only the grandmother seemed spiritual and reflective about the values of life. All the other characters were practical. The stevedore is philosophical and seems fatalistic about the possibilities in life—later we find out he is an anarchist. Early in the relationship the stevedore offers Stavros food and advice, and eventually his first night with a woman. Although all of Stavros' savings are stolen by the prostitute, the influence of the stevedore on Stavros remains strong. Under that influence Stavros joins a anarchist political cell led by the stevedore. They will bomb the establishment that enslaves them in an act to secure their freedom, just as Stavros wants to secure freedom in America. The plan never has a chance. Turkish soldiers don't arrest the members of the cell—they kill them. A seriously wounded Stavros is hospitalized. There, near death, he is sent by the doctor to be buried in the sea. The death cart is heavy and Stavros falls off, saving himself as the soldiers are distracted by hauling the cart. He makes his way back to his cousin, Mr. Opouzoglou. With his second mentor, the stevedore, dead, Stavros' hopes for securing freedom through anarchy are ended.

The third sequence of the Act II, the longest, is the proposed courtship and marriage of Stavros to the plain daughter of a wealthy merchant. In this sequence, the victimizers appear to be the proposed father-in-law and the fiancée. Both represent staying within the family, within the society from which Stavros wants to be free. Mr. Sinnikoglou, his father-in-law-to-be employs Stavvros and buys an apartment for the couple—adjacent to his own. Stavros keeps his dream of freedom to himself until he literally bumps into Oaness, the young man from Armenia to whom he gave his shoes. Now he offers a meal and a shared dream of going to America. But Oaness' cough has grown worse and he is less sure of being able to actualize his dream.

Next, under pressure from his fiancée, Domna, Stavros confesses his dream and tells her not to trust him. She wishes she were prettier for him. She doesn't understand why he wants to go to America, but she doesn't present a barrier. Like the other women in this narrative, she is a "slave" in the power grid of family where men are masters. In this sense, like all the women in the story, the grandmother and later Mrs. Kababian (she will pay for his passage to America), the fiancée is a kindred spirit to Stavros' dream to be free. (Only his mother resists this enabling role.) Enter the Kababians of America. Stavros meets Mr. and Mrs. Kababian at the shop of his father-in-law-to-be. He is a Greek who made good in America; she is his wife, twenty years younger. It is clear that Mrs. Kababian finds Stavros attractive, and she promotes the notion of an affair. Their implied agreement is that she will help Stavros get to America. This proves to be Stavros' means to reach America. He tells his fiancée, apologizing for leaving her, but he can't give up his dream. He tells her he will never find another woman like her.

Act III

Act III of *America America* is composed of two sequences and a resolution. In the first sequence, on the ocean liner en route to America, Stavros rekindles his relationship with Oaness who travels with seven others, their passage paid by an American businessman in return for two years service as shoeshine boys. In this sequence, the affair with Mrs. Kababian proceeds until it is discovered by Mr. Kababian. The second sequence concerns itself with Kababian's revenge— Stavros will be sent back to Turkey on his arrival in America. Within sight of Ellis Island, he must cope with this new threat. In the resolution, Stavros reaches America, and an epilogue describes how he repays his obligations to his family.

In the first sequence, Stavros is on the ship, finally enjoying the expectation that he will achieve his goal. In this sequence, he again shares his dream with Oaness, but the health situation for Oaness has deteriorated. His cough is severe. In this sequence the enabler-victimizer premise is also played out again—this time with Mrs. Kababian as the enabler and with Mr. Kababian as the victimizer. Upon discovering the affair, Mr. Kababian aggressively attempts to destroy Stavros's dream. He will have him sent back. Stavros assaults Mr. Kababian, now assuring he will be sent back because of the criminal charges Mr. Kababian, a rich American, will file. The sequence ends with Stavros in a hopeless situation.

The next sequence takes place outside Ellis Island. In the hospital, their physical health status is assessed in preparation for entry into the United States. Stavros and Oaness are told by the doctor that their fate is set but tenuous. Oaness must appear to be healthy to American officials or he will be sent back. Stavros will be sent back because of the Kababian charges. Although unable to swim, Stavros says that no one will rob him of his dream and he will swim to shore. In the morning, American health officials inspect the human cargo and Oaness passes (heeding Stavros' advice to imagine himself in a relaxed place, not overwhelmed with stress). And now it's time for Oaness to repay his debt to Stavros. Oaness jumps into the ocean to commit suicide on Stavros' behalf. He drowns so that Stavros can take his identity among the eight indentured young men. Mrs. Kababian sends him a straw hat and fifty American dollars to help him begin his new life. The sequence ends when an American official accepts that the drowned man was Stavros and that Stavros is Oaness. He renames him Joe Arness. Stavros kisses American soil as he steps off the ferry from Ellis Island.

In the epilogue, Stavros is working in a shoeshine parlor for the businessman who supposedly brought him from Constantinople. He rushes on to another customer saying, "Hurry up, people waiting." As the narrator, Elia Kazan tells us that Stavros indeed brought over his siblings and his mother, but that his father died in Anatolia. Stavros achieves his goal after the most challenging of journeys. He is free.

From a dramatic point of view, the premise has worked its way through the screen story. Whether or not Stavros' claim to his fiancée at the end of the second act—"In America I will be washed clean"—will come true is another story. In the course of achieving his goal, Stavros has killed, stolen, lied, been shot and used, and manipulated others. He has traveled far from the inexperienced, naïve young man we met at the beginning of Act II.

Notable as well is how in each sequence a surprise in plot or character either moves Stavros closer to or further from his goal: the military attack on the anarchists' cell; the threat of Mr. Kababian; the suicide of Oaness—each of these events twists the action away from what we expect. These surprises or plot twists amplify the tension and exemplify how using dramatic principles effectively serves us in a powerful way through a screen story.

IMAGINATION AND SUCCESS IN THE SCREENPLAY

There are a number of questions that arise out of the description of the operation of the drama in Kazan's *America America*. These questions run through the mind of writers all the time so it's best that I make them explicit. They are, in good part, questions that you should pose for yourself when you are writing a screenplay.

What Is a Mechancially Good Story versus a Creative Story?

Many stories are mechanically well structured. Emmerich's *The Patriot* is an example of a mechanically well-structured story. In such a story all the elements are manifest. The main character Benjamin Martin, played by Mel Gibson, has a clear goal—to protect his family, his reason being that he is a widower. He has a past as a brave, fierce warrior. And the plot, the progress of the War of Independence, will create challenges to his goal. The primary vehicle of the plot's opposition will be a British officer, Colonel Tavington, a proper antagonist. He kills two of the main character's sons. For a man who wants to protect his family, this is sufficient reason to enlist and fight fiercely for the Colonial side. Every time the plot development wanes in energy, there is a new threat to Benjamin's family: the attempt to capture his children, the burning of a church filled with worshippers who include Benjamin's daughter-in-law. These threats are always made by Tavington.

Finally, the story has a resolution, a decisive battle that is punctuated by the hand-to-hand combat of the main character and the antagonist, concluding with Tavington's brutal death at the hands of Benjamin Martin.

What I'm suggesting here is that *The Patriot* is a mechanically well-constructed screen story. But I'm also implying that it is not a particularly creative story. What would constitute a more creative story? What might be useful to consider are issues of character and plot that might yield a sense of what would constitute a more creative story.

Let's turn first to Mel Gibson's own movie *Braveheart* (1995), a story that is also about a war of independence, in this case, the thirteenth century Scottish rebellion against the British. With respect to the issue of character, the main character, William Wallace, becomes the leader of the Scottish rebellion and his antagonist is King Edward of England. Here, both the main character and the antagonist play central roles in the narrative. This is not the case in *The Patriot*. A second point about the main character and the antagonist in *The Patriot* is that both are stereotypical characters—the good parent versus the evil, cruel enemy. In *Braveheart*, the characters are more complex: Wallace is presented as a son, a lover, a brilliant, fierce warrior, and a leader with considerable political acuity; Edward is presented as a father, a king, and a ruthless leader. Each is complex, and although Edward is the antagonist, we understand and on some level perhaps even feel sorrow for him (his son and successor is not even a shadow of the father). This complexity of character makes behavior more layered and at times surprising.

In terms of plot, *Braveheart* deals with political, economic, and military issues, so that the challenges to the main character and his goal are complex and at times surprising. The result is a more powerful and a more emotional struggle on the part of the main character to achieve his goal. The experience of *The Patriot* is more predictable and consequently mechanical rather than complex or surprising.

Other examples of more creative stories about similar issues include another story from the screenwriter of *The Patriot*, Robert Rodat's screenplay for *Saving Private Ryan*, Stanley Kubrick's *Paths of Glory* (1958), and Ed Zwick's *Glory* (1989). What characterizes each of these screen stories as creative is their approach to character and plot.

Each of these screen stories is a war film. The role of the main character in the war film is to survive. The main character in *Saving Private Ryan*, Captain John Miller, wants to survive but in the end gives his life to save Private Ryan so he can go home. But Miller puts the question to Ryan and to us, the viewer, make the personal sacrifices in war (his life) mean something. He embodies responsibility, personal and national. This behavior raises *Saving Private Ryan* above the usual war film.

So, too, the goal of the main character in *Paths of Glory*. Colonial Dax is a brave solider and an outstanding lawyer. In the plot of the World War I narrative, three of his men are charged with cowardice by the French general who ordered Dax and his men on an impossible mission. The three will set an example for the regiment—not to fail in their mission. In this story, the antagonists are the French generals who persecute their own men. Colonial Dax seeks justice as well as survival for his men. His failure reflects not so much on him as it does upon the enemy within—the General staff. This turn of events surprises, shocks, and creatively elevates a screen story about trench warfare into an anti-war classic.

What Is an Imaginative Story?

Imaginative stories are always creative rather than mechanical. But they have something more: they surprise us. This doesn't always mean a pleasant surprise. In Peter and Bobby Farrelly's *There's Something About Mary* (1998), the story is essentially about first love. The main character, Ted (Ben Stiller), fell in love as a teenager and now, as a thirty-something adult, he decides that Mary (Cameron Diaz), his first love, is the only one for him. He pursues her via Healy (Matt Dillon), a private detective, having been encouraged in this endeavor by his best friend, Dom (Chris Elliott). The imaginative dimension, the surprise in *There's Something About Mary*, is that both the best friend and the private detective are in love with Mary. In fact, almost every man who comes into contact with her becomes a stalker. This aggressive love—as opposed to the idealistic love of adolescence—is the creative dimension of *There's Something About Mary*. The first general point I'm making about the imaginative story is that it surprises us.

The second point about the imaginative story is that the main character has to exhibit a boldness that we rarely encounter in screen stories. By boldness I'm not referring to James Bond boldness or Clint Eastwood–Dirty Harry brashness. Rather I'm thinking about the main character in Paul Mazursky's *Enemies: A Love Story* (1989). He's a man with a wife, a mistress, and a former wife. What is a man to do in these circumstances? I'm also thinking about the main character in Joseph Mankiewicz's *Five Fingers* (1952), by day a valet, by night the greatest spy who plied his trade in World War II. And I'm thinking about the main character in Nikolai Mikhalkov's *Burnt by the Sun* (1995)—a general, a father, a husband, a politician, and a patriot, all energetically manifested in one man in Stalin's Soviet Union of the 1930s. These characters make life bigger than it is; they are imaginative characters.

What Makes Stories Succeed or Fail?

Much speculation has suggested that it is stars that make films succeed or fail. An equal amount of speculation about the success or failure of films has revolved around marketing campaigns and decisions—the dates of release, the number of theaters, and so on. There are enough examples to make the case on either side of the argument. Fortunately, this book is about narrative issues, so we can sidestep these arguments. The issue I don't want to avoid is what makes certain stories succeed and others fail from a narrative point of view. When I speak of success, I should point out that I'm looking for examples where a film has been embraced critically and commercially. I'd like to point out that this approach has its own minefields. For example, I believe that Spielberg's *Amistad* (1997) is no less powerful a narrative than his *Saving Private Ryan*, and yet the latter was a towering success and *Amistad* was a critical and commercial failure. Thus acknowledging the fragility of the term success, let's move into the issue.

The first observation I would make is that successful films are films where the main character's goal and therefore his or her dramatic arc is as great as possible. The larger the reach and the greater the consequent resistances, the greater the impact upon us, the audience. A negative example begins to make the point. In Scorsese's *Bringing out the Dead* (1999), the main character is close to the end of his rope. He is a depressed, guilt-ridden paramedic in New York City. We enter the story late in his day. Throughout the narrative, he wants to leave the profession. And in the end, he settles for a good night's sleep. There is much desperation here but very little character arc. *Bringing Out the Dead* represents the baseline of what you don't want for your character if your story is to succeed.

Examples of characters with a large dramatic arc include the main character in *Shall We Dance* (1997), a narrative in which a conservative man from a conservative society (Japan) decides that what he needs to change his life is dancing lessons. Another example is the main character in *Gladiator*. He's a man at the top of his profession (as a general). He is offered the emperorship by the Emperor who feels the main character will restore needed values to the empire. The Emperor's son disagrees, kills the Emperor and attempts to kill the main character, but fails. He does succeed in killing the main character's family. The main character's goal then is to take revenge. How can a man, albeit a gifted soldier, achieve revenge against the emperor of the most powerful empire in the world? The goal seems impossible, and the dramatic arc of the character will be great indeed. So the first ingredient of success in a screenplay is the significant scale of the goal of the main character. Other good examples here would be the main character in *Tootsie* (1982), whose goal is to be a successful actor by pretending he is a woman. Another good example is the main character in *Saving Private Ryan*, whose goal is to preserve as many lives of the men in his command as possible, while undertaking a mission to save one man on the killing fields that were France during the D-Day invasion. The goal is all but impossible.

A second prerequisite for success is to find a structure that stretches and challenges the character's goal in imaginative ways. How does a housewife trapped in a bad marriage find liberation, a situation complicated by her own prudery? The answer, of course, is through sexual liberation in Soderbergh's *sex, lies and videotape*. In M. Night Shyamalan's *The Sixth Sense* (1999), how can a character, desperate to save a child from his demons, use all his skills as a psychologist to do so, when the psychologist is in denial about his own death? In John Sayles' *Lone Star* (1996), the main character is the sheriff in a small Texas border town. The majority of the population is Mexican-American or African-American. He is white. The plot of the film is a murder investigation in which the main suspect is the sheriff's dead father, the much revered former sheriff. If this were not enough of a structural challenge, the main character rekindles a love affair with a Mexican-American woman. His investigation uncovers that she is his step-sister. Shades of *Chinatown*! Thus the second element of success is to use the plot and character layers of the structure to powerfully amplify the difficulties the main character has in achieving his goal.

A third characteristic of the successful screenplay is the energy level of the language. In part this will come from the impossibility of the main character's goal. Consider here the main character in Sam Mendes' *American Beauty* (1999), or the two main characters in Billy Wilder's *Some Like It Hot* (1959), or the main character in Mike Leigh's *Secrets and Lies* (1996). There is something loud about all of these characters. But it's more than that. It's a life force, a desire or desperation—whatever its source—that gives the successful narrative a drive that is unusual. The main character in Mike Newell's *Four Weddings and a Funeral* (1993) has it, as does the main character in Danny Boyle's *Trainspotting* (1995). The main character in Lewis Gilbert's *Alfie* (1965) had it, as did Scarlett O'Hara in Fleming's *Gone with the Wind* (1939). I will touch on this issue in Chapter 2, "Character," when I discuss issues of identification.

My point regarding successful narratives is that there are certain qualities that are critical. There are others beyond the character's goal, the level of structural challenges to that goal, and the energy of the main character, but I will take up those other issues in Chapter 4, "Genre," and Chapter 5, "Tone."

THE SHORT FILM AND THE LONG FILM

Before we leave this chapter I need to differentiate the long film from the short film. Because the long or feature film is the principal narrative currency of film narrative, and because early filmmakers learn their craft from making short films, these differences need to be made overt.

A good starting point is to state the obvious: You can't tell the same story in less than thirty minutes that can be managed in more than ninety minutes. This has implications for character, structure, and form.

The second point I'd like to make is that the short film has much in common with the photograph, the painting, and the poem. Not so the long film, which has much more in common with the novel, the play, even the short story. In this sense, the short film tends to be more literary, and more allegorical, than the long film, which relies more heavily on a tradition of realism.

A third point is that the structural shape of the short film is not only shorter, it looks different. The short film has the equivalent of a very short Act I and then, depending upon whether you are deploying resolution or not, what follows will be Act II (no resolution) or Act III (resolution). The feature film, as we have outlined, proceeds along a three-act structure.[1]

The last point I'd like to make about the differences between the short and long film is that the short film has a greater affinity to story forms that have literary origins, such as the fable. Although there are long films that are fables, there are far more fables among short films. Other literary forms that are favored in short films include the experimental narrative and the poem.

DRAMA VERSUS DOCUMENTARY VERSUS
EXPERIMENTAL NARRATIVES

The dramatic notions discussed so far are applicable to the long-form film, or the feature film. There are dramatic properties to the documentary and to experimental narratives, but there are significant differences that it is useful to point out at this stage. The long-form feature film is characterized in the majority of cases by a goal: a main character struggles for his or her goal against an antagonist and against obstacles posed by the plot in a linear dramatic arc from catalytic event to resolution. As viewers, we experience the story through that main character.

At the opposite extreme from the dramatic feature film is the experimental narrative, a story form that emphasizes style over content. It is likely that the character will not have an apparent goal, that the character will be reacting to another person, situation, or environment, and that there certainly will not be a plot. Consequently, the whole issue of linearity, or of cause and effect, will not be relevant. The dominant quality of the narrative may be a mood or the voice of the writer or director. If the drama is content- and character-driven, the experimental narrative is mood- and voice-driven.

The documentary, on the other hand, lies between the drama and the experimental narrative. It too has dramatic properties, but as a form, a main character is not as important as the voice of the author (writer-director). In terms of structure, the documentary looks more like an argumentative case that is being developed rather than the dramatic arc of a character. There are subcategories of documentary: the personal documentary, the social/political/educational documentary, and the cinema vérité documentary. Each implies a different level of intervention by the writer-director; each implies a different balance between an information line and an emotional line; and each has different implications regarding the issue of voice. But as a form, the documentary values educational goals over entertainment goals when compared to the drama.

What is important at this point is that you, the writer, realize at least in a preliminary way how different each of these forms is from the others. Now that some of the basics have been addressed, let's move on to the more specific issue of character.

NOTES

1. A full discussion of all these issues is presented in P. Cooper and K. Dancyger, *Writing the Short Film*, Second Edition (Focal Press, 1999).

2

CHARACTER

Who is the character I need to tell my story? Who is the character that will help an audience enter the story? What is the relationship of character to plot? What is the relationship of character to story form? And who are the secondary characters that will help amplify the dilemma of the main character? All of these issues are the substance of this chapter. First, the issue of character positioning in story.

OWNERSHIP OF STORY

In a novel, character can be located anywhere in the story—even on the sideline of the story or outside the story—and the story can still work. This is because multiple points of view are not an exception (nor are they the rule) in the novel. The form tolerates more than one point of view. Not so the screen story. In film, we enter the story through the main character. The result is that the main character has to reside in the story; indeed, it's best if the main character is in the middle of the story. Ownership implies point of view but also a position that articulates the premise. In Franklin Schaffner's *Patton* (1969), although the D-Day invasion is the most significant military event of the day, in terms of scene construction, we stay with Patton and within his marginalized position at that time during that war. Were we to focus on the events of D-Day, we would have left Patton's story (and point of view) and begun to be more focused on World War II itself. To do so would alter the emotional link and understanding we experience by staying with the main character's perception. In the film story we need to stay with the main character to sustain the emotional build necessary in the film story.

The issue of ownership, however, goes beyond scene selection and organization. It is important that the main character's subjective sense and interpretation of what he or she is experiencing permeate the narrative. We have to see the main character in the scene, and we have to see the scene as the main character sees it. For example, the main character in Hitchcock's *Vertigo* (1958), a traumatized detective, falls in love with a woman he is following (for her protection). Following her for her protection is all a deception, but the main character is in a state of obsessive love and everything is distorted by that obsession. That feeling permeates the scenes so that we experience the woman and the world of the story through that obsession, just as the main character does.

THE MAIN CHARACTER AND THE ROLE OF A GOAL

Having located the character in the story, the next issue is to pull us, the viewers, through the screen story. The character can be charming, even charismatic, an issue we will return to, but that's not enough. What carries us through the story is the goal of the main character and the resistance to that goal.

Whether the goal is a relationship, as in Jonathan Demme's *Something Wild* (1987), or the goal is an accomplishment, as in Sylvester Stallone's *Rocky* (1976), the drive and the desire fuel our relationship with the main character. The goal also creates the dramatic arc that shapes the film. An example of the relationship of goal and arc is Ingmar Bergman's *Autumn Sonata* (1978). In that screen story, the main character's goal is to reestablish positively her relationship with her mother whom she has not seen for seven years. The body of the film, from the catalytic event, the arrival of her mother, to the film's resolution, the departure of her mother, forms the dramatic arc—the exploration of the possibility, whether mother and daughter can have an accepting, supportive relationship. By the time of the resolution, the depth of the mother's narcissism has precluded the main character from ever achieving her goal.

SOURCES OF RESISTANCE TO CHARACTER AND GOAL

In Regis Wargnier's *East West* (1999), the main character, who is French, goes to the Soviet Union in 1946 with her husband, a Russian expatriate, and their son. Very quickly Marie discovers that the Soviet Union is not a worker paradise or any other kind of paradise. For her it is a large punitive prison and she's trapped in it. She spends the rest of the narrative trying to get out. Her goal, then, is to return to France. The sources of resistance to her goal could be characterized as the political, social, and economic system she has entered. But that description does not emotionalize the resistance to her goal. To make the struggle vivid, other characters must resist and become barriers to her goal.

Beginning with the authorities, the Soviet KGB officer who tears up Marie's French passport early in the film is a primary source of resistance. He reoccurs throughout the film and is a presence at moments of great opportunity and danger late in the film (the Odessa sequence). He embodies the power but also the harshness of the state. Closer to home, the manager of the building for the government (and who also covets Marie's husband) is a threat to the main character. But here the threat is on a far more personal level. These characters live in separate rooms in the same apartment. The main character is vulnerable because the closed doors of her home do not protect her from a character who has great power over her. The greatest resistance, however, seems to come from Alexei, a doctor and an attractive, ambitious man who seems to embody the anxiety of a trapped man. Their difference of opinion on the issue of returning to France and her outspokenness leads to a fracture in the marriage, and he takes up with the woman across the hall. The husband's very personal resistance to the main character's goal makes her struggle emotionally overwhelming, and yet, because of the level of these sources of resistance, her goal and the dramatic intensity of the goal becomes ennobled, almost epic. In the end Marie is free, but the journey to freedom in France has ended her marriage and damaged her health.

THE SOURCE OF GREATEST RESISTANCE:
THE ANTAGONIST

The greater the antagonist, the greater the dramatic energy of the story. Norma Desmond (Gloria Swanson) in *Sunset Boulevard* (1950) and Magwa (Wes Studi) in *Last of the Mohicans* (1992) are memorable antagonists. The consequence of their presence is to make the efforts of the main characters in those stories—Joe Gillis (William Holden) in *Sunset Boulevard* and Hawkeye (Daniel Day Lewis) in *Last of the Mohicans*—noble and equally memorable. The antagonist is a very important character in creating energy and involvement with the main character and his or her dramatic arc. What happens when the source of greatest resistance is the self, when the main character is his or her own antagonist? The result can be as powerful, but the focus of the story will differ—it will be shifted to a more interior level. An example will clarify the issue.

In Damien O'Donnell's *East Is East* (1999), the main character, George "Ghengis" Khan is a Pakistani immigrant to England. He wants his children, who have grown up in England, to follow the ways of his mother country. For George that means he arranges their marriage for them rather than allowing them their own choice of mates. The arrangement has social and economic ramifications for the main character, but it has no cultural meaning for his children. They have grown up in England and they view their father as a tyrant, a tyrant they are afraid of. The complication in this story is that the mother of his five children is British and Caucasian. The children are mixed, but he denies these facts. They must listen to their father. In this story, then, the main character is his own antagonist. He denies his children the same choice he himself made, and in his stubborn denial, he almost destroys his family.

The point here is that the willfulness of George to force on his children his beliefs—beliefs that he himself transgressed—makes him a monster to his children. But in doing so, and thus bringing the family to the edge of destruction, the main character must face his own prejudices, his own hypocrisy. The result is a powerful exploration of character. George Khan is almost larger than life because of his exercise in will. He also presents us with an internal struggle—between the values of the mother country and the values of the host country—in one character. *East Is East* is certainly not the only example of a main character who is both protagonist and antagonist. The main characters in Anthony Minghella's *Truly, Madly, Deeply* (1991) in William Wyler's *Jezebel* (1938) and Billy Wilder's *Ace in the Hole* (1951), all exemplify characters with similar dramatic profiles.

The key element to take away from this section of the chapter is the notion that your antagonist provides the greatest resistance to the main character's goal.

Whether you use an external antagonist or an internal antagonist, make it a powerful antagonist. It will help dramatize the main character's goal.

CHARACTER CONSTRUCTION

So far our concern has been the positioning of the character in your story and the consequent movement of the character through the story. Now we turn to the nature of the character. Who is your character and how do you develop qualities that will be helpful to you in the screen story? Here we are talking about construction.

Writers, it is true, base characters on people they know, people they have met, and TV and movie characters they have experienced. And sometimes they base a character on themselves. This is all well and good as a starting point. But as an end point, you don't want to end up with a set of characters who are all variations on you. With construction, a useful starting point to begin with is the stereotype. Because stereotypes are recognizable to all, they are useful to the writer. The high-minded physician, the lawyer as word gymnast, the anal accountant, the high school jock, the college nerd, the queen of the prom, the angry feminist, the spiritual priest, all are readily recognizable stereotypes. More recent additions that are already stereotypes are the working mother, the New Age man, the iron man, the violent sports star, and the spoiled rock star.

To begin to make a character interesting you want to work off this recognizability factor. The stereotype becomes the base for construction. The next step is to use physical characteristics and behavioral characteristics as variables. Think in extreme terms, what I refer to as dominant characteristics. If you give a character a dominant physical characteristic and a dominant behavioral characteristic, characteristics that differ from the stereotype, you are beginning to move in a productive direction. The athlete who is very short; the priest who is an addictive personality; the rock star who is high-minded; the accountant who is a rock musician in his mind; each of these characters begins to move away from the stereotype.

The next step in the construction is to choose at least one dominant quality that is dramatically purposeful. The blind detective, the marathon runner who has lost a leg to cancer, the housewife who has written a best-selling novel, the African-American son who is told by his parents, one white, the other African-American, that he is adopted—these are all examples where the dominant physical or behavioral characteristic can be central to the screen story. It is very useful if one of the dominant qualities feeds powerfully into the story.

An example of characters who work with a stereotype, move beyond it, and make a dominant quality purposeful are both of the main characters—the black detective and the white sheriff—in Norman Jewison's *In the Heat of the Night* (1967). Another excellent example is the collection of characters in Billy Wilder's *The Apartment* (1960). (Although here only the two principals, C.C. Baxter and Fran Kubelik, veer away from stereotype.) A third example is the three principals in Sydney Pollack's *The Firm* (1993).

MYTHS ABOUT CHARACTER

You've constructed characters that will be dramatically useful to your story. They have a goal and they have opposition. Now is the moment to dispel five popular myths about character (in case one of them is irresistible to you).

Real People and Dramatic Characters

Many people will tell you that your characters have to be real, that if they are not there is something lacking or false in your screenplay. This isn't necessarily the case. The first myth about character is that good characters are real characters.

In a sense the best way to understand this paradox is that real characters, the people you know, can be complex, intriguing, charismatic, but they function in their world as opposed to a dramatized world. In a dramatized world characters function in dramatic situations, but more importantly, they function with a dramatically purposeful goal. In this sense, both the character and the situation are more constructed, more intentional, more purposeful dramatically. A real character is a good starting point for character, but where you want to get in your screenplay is to a character who is more dramatically useful.

Character and Behavior

The second myth about character is that if your character is intense and expressive in their behavior, the character will be beneficial to the screenplay. Although it's true that intense people generate energy, it is not necessarily the case that the energy will be dramatically purposeful. The behavior that is useful to the story is behavior that functions within a relationship with other characters. That behavior, when it functions in conflictual opposition to other characters or when it functions with goals that are in opposition to the goals of others, is behavior that contributes to the dramatic arc of the story. My point here is that behavior abstracted from dramatic intention is in itself not helpful, even if it is intense and expressive.

Main Characters and Secondary Characters

The third myth is that the main character should be the most appealing of the characters in your screenplay. The main character may prove to be, but it is equally valid if the main character is the least appealing character in the screenplay. The role of Shakespeare, played by Joseph Fiennes, in John Madden's *Shakespeare in Love* (1998) is a good example of this. All the other characters in the narrative are more interesting than Shakespeare, even though his case of writer's block is the critical moment where we join the story.

Indeed, how the interplay of the main character and the secondary characters proceeds is one of the critical elements of the construction of the screenplay. Essentially, as I described earlier in the chapter, the main character should be in the middle of the story. The secondary characters break down into two groups—

helpers and harmers. The group that represents the helpers (three to four in the feature film) represents one option in the premise. For example, the helpers in *Shakespeare in Love* are those characters who help Shakespeare to write *Romeo and Juliet*. They are the producer, the financier, and the actors—particularly Lady Viola (Gwyneth Paltrow), the woman acting as a man who inspires Shakespeare. The harmers, those who oppose or pose a threat to the main character and his goal, represent the other option in the premise. As with the helpers, there tends to be three to four of them in a feature film. In *Shakespeare in Love*, the harmers include Shakespeare's rival for the attention of his muse, her fiancé, Lord Wessex (Colin Firth), as well as those authorities who have the power to shut down his production, thereby undermining his product, the production of *Romeo and Juliet*.

The bifurcation of secondary characters into helpers and harmers only makes sense in relation to the main character, his or her goal, and the premise of the screen story. Rather than viewing the main character as abstracted from the other characters, it's best to see the main characters and the secondary characters as the heart of the drama, and that each part needs to be considered in relation to the other parts.

Character and Plot

The fourth myth is that you can consider the primacy of plot over character in order to assure the success of your screen story. Although plot is a very powerful device, here too it's best to consider plot in light of the main character's goal. Only if there is a conflictual relationship between the two is plot useful to your screen story. Joseph Ruben's *Return to Paradise* (1998) provides an excellent example of how character and plot effectively work together. The main character in *Return to Paradise* is Sheriff (Vince Vaughn), a young man who vacationed with two other young men in Malaysia. He is working class; the two others, Tony and Lewis (David Conrad and Joaquin Phoenix), are privileged—educated and rich. In Malaysia, they enjoyed life: smoking hashish, chasing the local women, being Americans in Paradise. The main character and one of the others leave, and the plot revolves around the arrest of the third for possession of hashish. The problem is that he had enough hashish to be considered a trafficker and the consequence is that he is sentenced to death. The plot follows the legal appeals to prevent Lewis' execution. The only way to prevent his execution is to get the other two boys to return and for them to accept responsibility for the possession (by doing so, the amount each has will drop the charge). They will each have to serve three years in prison in Malaysia.

The premise for the main character is the following set of options. The first is to be selfish and not go back; your friend will die, but you will preserve yourself. The second option is to take responsibility for the possession of hashish, serve your time, and accept responsibility, thereby saving the life of your friend. Selfishness or responsibility, this is the moral quandary in which the main character finds himself.

It is the urgency of the plot—the trial and potential execution will all take place in six days—that puts pressure on Sheriff whose goal in life is taking care of himself. The secondary characters, particularly Tony and the lawyer for the young man facing execution (who is also his sister) put special pressure on the main character; but above it all it is the plot that challenges the values of our main character.

In the effective screenplay, this is how plot works. If plot is divorced from the character and his or her goal, it does not overshadow character, it simply becomes a backdrop.

Character and Form

The fifth myth is that character can exist exclusive of story form and its demands on character. This is no more the case than plot existing exclusive of character. Character, its nature and its goal, should function within story form expectations. Not to do so is to undermine the story form. When a film noir character has as his goal to thrive and to overcome victimization within a film noir world, to succeed would mean that the story was no longer part of the film noir genre. To be a film noir main character the fate of the character is to be a victim.

The corollary is that the character who does function within the story form strengthens the effectiveness of the story form. The main character in Peter Medak's film noir *Romeo Is Bleeding* (1993) is a corrupt policeman, Sergeant Jack Grimaldi. His goal is to have accumulated enough money off of his criminal activity that he will be able to have a family and the love of both his family as well as his extended love interests. Instead, as one would expect within the genre, his activities end up destroying the very people he is working for—his family and his mistress. Although the evocation is dark, the character's spiritual and pragmatic hopes should not be realized if the story form is film noir. He doesn't want to be a victim. In fact, he vigorously tries to avoid being a victim, but in film noir the main character is destined to be a victim, and so his fate in this story form is sealed.

ISSUES OF IDENTIFICATION

In the screen story it is useful (but not always necessary) for us to identify with your main character. We now turn to how to secure this identification.

Character and Human Behavior

Compassion, self-preservation, selfishness, and selflessness—these are human impulses we all recognize. In order for us to identify with your main character, it is important that we recognize your main character. But for a film character these qualities must be powerful, even if they are not admirable. What I referred to earlier as the "dramatic" as opposed to "real" is what is needed here. It's not enough that Mr. Smith in Frank Capra's *Mr. Smith Goes to Washington* (1939) is an idealist. He is the ultimate idealist, the proselytizing idealist. It's not enough that the main character in Jane Campion's *The Piano* (1992) be passionate about music, she is passionate about every aspect of sensual life—and she is mute, so her expression has to be physical.

Two examples will illustrate how human behavior can be harnessed to the dramatic arc of the narrative. Bille August's *The Best Intentions* (1992) is a film with a screenplay written by Ingmar Bergman about the marriage of his parents. We are introduced to his father, Henrik Bergman, at the opening of the story. Henrik visits his grandfather. The scene that follows presents information about Henrik: he is studying to be a priest; he and his mother have been ostracized by his wealthy grandparents (for marrying beneath the family); the grandmother is in the hospital dying; and the grandmother wants to see Henrik to ask for his forgiveness. We also learn that if Henrik complies with his grandfather's request, he will be rewarded financially and neither he nor his mother will face financial hardship again.

The response of Henrik is surprising. He refuses his grandfather's request to see his grandmother, but he does so with a powerful outpouring of hostility. He essentially damns both his grandparents and leaves. The scene characterizes him as a young man with enormous hostility to the rich, and as someone who will proceed in life with a chip on his shoulder. The fact that he will be a priest further complicates his character; this paradox makes him more human (as opposed to idealized) as a character.

This paradoxical quality links to the dramatic arc of the story in the following manner. Bergman's mother, Anna, who becomes Henrik's wife, is rich and willful, yet she is open as a person (the opposite of the main character). In status and nature they differ and, of course, the arc of the story is that this marriage is doomed to failure.

William Wyler's *Dodsworth* (1936) offers a second example. Dodsworth, a successful businessman from the Midwest, retires. He travels to Europe because his wife Fran wants to expand her horizon. Although she has a grown, married daughter, she wants to recover her youth. Whether this is denial or a genuine search for renewal, the challenge to Dodsworth is to retain his relationship with his wife. As our main character, this effective man in the sunset phase of his life is challenged to change by the actions of his wife.

What is clear is that Dodsworth lóves his wife, is content with his life. Whether he is confident or limited in his horizon (as his wife claims), he is presented as a happy man who is challenged by his wife's unhappiness. She is younger than he and her embrace of Europe as a center for culture, for change, and for a setting to transcend "American provinciality" shakes the main character. His all-too-human response—depression, anger, and resignation—mark him as a man faced with believable human dilemmas: aging, "the impermanence" of relationships, the sense of loss, and the human capacity for change, all mark his character and this narrative as humane and feeling.

Character and Passion

A second characteristic that invites identification with the main character is passion. Passion can be interpreted in diverse ways, and I want to use it in the widest terms. Passion is about a feeling in a character that will enable us to identify with a character. It's about emotion over reason, this moment over the future. Passion is about not thinking about consequences—it's raw and immediate. Juliet, the main character in Peter Jackson's *Heavenly Creatures* (1993) for whom friendship is more important than anything else in the world, does not concern herself with consequences. Nor does Dr. Larch in Lasse Hallström's *Cider House Rules*. He will do whatever it takes to protect the orphans under his care, including performing abortions—to prevent another orphan from coming into a life of desperation and desertion. So too the main character in *Saving Private Ryan*, Captain John Miller. He will do anything to avoid losing the life of another member of his company. But passion can also take a character into a pattern of thinking that has disastrous consequences for him or herself or for others. Consider Colonel Nicholson who decides to build a bridge for his Japanese captors in David Lean's *Bridge on the River Kwai* (1956), and T.E. Lawrence in Lean's *Lawrence of Arabia* (1962), who decides to take on the garb of the Arabs he leads in the Arab revolt. He loses himself in the cause with considerable personal consequences.

The key issue about characters who are passionate is that we identify with their urgency, their commitment, their capacity for belief. Their passion, of course, has considerable dramatic consequences. The passion takes them into conflict with others at an intense level. The resulting dramatic energy is useful to the dynamics of the story.

Character and Desire

Another quality that facilitates our identification with a character is desire, and as with passion, we have to consider desire in the broadest terms. It can be many characters' desire for Mary in Peter and Bobby Farrelly's *There's Something About Mary* (1997), or it can be the main character's desire for an improvement in the standard of living of her family in Ang Lee's *Sense and Sensibility* (1996), or it can be the desire for justice in Steven Soderbergh's *Erin Brockovich* (2000). Or it can be the desire of a character to fulfill his lifelong ambition to be a screenwriter in Billy Wilder's *Sunset Boulevard* (1950). Whatever the source of desire, that sense of yearning and frustration can fuel our identification with a character.

Desire, passion, and human behavior all can help us to recognize a character and facilitate our identification. But in order to lock in our identification with the character, a variety of technical options allow us to identify more deeply with the character. I've written about many of these tools elsewhere[1] but I will revisit those options here.

Self-Revelation

One device that is often used in theater, and is no less useful in film, is self-revelation. When characters display insight about their behavior and share that insight with us, we relate to the character more readily. When Doc McCoy, the main character in Sam Peckinpah's *The Getaway* (1972) is freed from prison, his wife Carol picks him up. They have not been together for three years, and he expresses his sexual anxiety. This moment is very out of keeping with what we know about the character; he is a bank robber with a considerable reputation.

The revelation humanizes him and makes the relationship with his wife the focal point of our sympathy for him. Although he is a criminal, this is the vulnerability that enables us to identify with him. The fact that so many other criminals are trying to betray him makes that identification stronger. As they try to victimize him, our identification with him deepens.

Self-Awareness

When a character is self-aware, it is easier for the identification process to move ahead. In a sense the main character usually proceeds in exactly the opposite manner from the main character in Harold Ramis' *Groundhog Day*, a screen story where the character is totally victimized by the plot precisely because he doesn't understand what's happening to him. A character who is self-aware, is much easier to identify with.

The main character must be reflective, even oversensitive to an inner drive. By being overly sensitive he or she is attuned to that sense of self that determines action. An example of this characteristic is the main character in Zoltan Korda's *Four Feathers* (1939). The main character, Harry Faversham, grows up in a late-nineteenth-century military family, and he is expected to be as great a soldier as his father. He moves from adolescence to adulthood feeling that he is a coward. As an adult he chooses to resign his commission at the moment when his regiment will be shipping out to Egypt to join the war against the Sudan. His three closest friends in the regiment, as well as his fiancée, each give him a white feather signifying his cowardice—hence the title. He spends the balance of the narrative trying to make them admit they were wrong. This involves going to the Sudan, pretending he is a Sudanese slave, and infiltrating the battle lines. At great risk to himself he proves his valor. But he admits to a family friend that inside he felt himself to be a coward. This level of self-awareness fuels not only his sense of self, but the actions he undertakes. And it is this level of self-awareness that ingratiates Harry Faversham to us. His self-awareness humanizes a character who in the average action-adventure film would seem a cartoon character, and the consequence is that we identify with him.

Heroism

Heroism, as presented in romantic epics such as Mel Gibson's *Braveheart* (1995) and Anthony Mann's *El Cid* (1961), is by its nature attractive but distant. We admire the character and care about his fate, but it's too far from us. In order for the audience to come closer to the character, the character has to be more accessible. If this happens, the heroism can be more deeply meaningful, more human, and more affecting. To create this type of heroism, writers often resort to what I call the reluctant hero, such as the captain in Spielberg's *Saving Private Ryan* or the colonel in Kubrick's *Paths of Glory*. Jean Valjean as presented in Bille August's *Les Miserables* (1998) is a good example of a hero we can easily identify with. First Valjean is a freed convict whose first act is to steal from the bishop who offers him shelter and a meal for the night. Caught, Valjean is surprised when the bishop confirms "the gifts" he carried off with him. And the bishop surprises him further when he adds two silver candlesticks to the gifts for Valjean. From the influence of this event, Valjean attempts to live his life in grace, to give to others as the bishop gave to him. And he is successful until his true identity is discovered by the policeman Javert. Thus begins the twenty-year pursuit of Valjean by Javert.

Valjean eludes capture, saves a young girl, raises her as he promised her dying mother he would, rescues the girl's lover, and even rescues Javert from death at the hands of Parisian revolutionaries. Valjean puts himself at risk for others. These acts together present the portrait of a main character as a genuine hero, in the most human sense. It is this characteristic that enables us to identify so *strongly with Jean Valjean.*

Charisma

The charismatic character is almost impossible to resist. Identification is inevitable. But what are the attributes that make the character irresistible? Charisma implies attraction, although it's often mistaken for a kind of perfection—physical or behavioral. Actually, the attraction must be present, but charisma is more akin to an energy field, generally created by a personal intensity. That intensity may be belief-based or goal-based. It tends to have layers of physical, sexual, and aggressive energies. Political leaders such as Ghandi, spiritual leaders such as Pope John Paul, and economic leaders such as Alan Greenspan all share a sense of power that is charismatic. Power, and its possession, is an inherent characteristic of the charismatic character.

An example of such a character in a screen story is the main character in Shekar Kapur's *Bandit Queen* (1995). The main character of *Bandit Queen*, Phoolan is introduced to us as an eleven-year-old girl. She is spirited, but since she comes from a poor, low-caste family, she is sold into marriage to help out the family. Her husband is an adult. Initially, Phoolan is compliant, but she quickly objects to being a physical servant to her mother-in-law and a sexual servant to her new husband. She runs away, back to her parents. The story moves to eight years later and Phoolan, now a woman, is sexually harassed by the upper-caste young men of the village. One of them assaults her in the field. She is not compliant. Consequently she is accused by him of having attempted to seduce him. The elders of the village, with the assent of her father, agree to ban her from the village—the reason, immoral behavior that will corrupt the young men of the village. She leaves and quickly falls in with criminals. Here she finds a supportive mate. Eventually, after his death, she becomes the leader of the criminal band, but not before she has been captured, raped, and humiliated by competing criminal elements. Men always take advantage of her womanhood and her caste status.

This true story is powered by the charisma of its main character. She is motivated by a profound sense of the injustices in her life, particularly by the behavior of the significant men in her life. She is angry, but her power comes from the feeling that she is acting for all women in her situation. She exhibits the outrage and the sexual power that unite with a sense of religious fervor. She is a charismatic main character.

Tragic Flaw

The issue of a tragic flaw has long been used by playwrights to develop empathy for their characters. Willie Loman in Arthur Miller's *Death of a Salesman* (1952) and Macbeth in William Shakespeare's *Macbeth* (1971) are good examples. But how does this failure in a character encourage us to identify with the character? In order to understand the operation of the tragic flaw, we must look more fully at a character whose flaw is critical to our involvement with him or her.

Michael Mann's *Heat* (1996) is a screen story with two main characters, and each of whom has a tragic flaw. Vincent Hanna (Al Pacino) is a Los Angeles detective and Neil McCauley (Robert de Niro) is the leader of an armed robbery gang. Each has his goal—apprehension of criminals, and successful robberies, respectively. But it is their tragic flaws that make both of them easy to identify with.

In the case of Hanna the detective, he is a workaholic whose work habits destroy his personal life. He has to be too cold, calculating, and competitive to succeed against the criminals, and the result is destructive to his marriage. The very quality that makes him a success as a detective destroys his effectiveness as a human being.

This paradoxical quality is reversed in the criminal. McCauley is cold, cruel, and calculating as a criminal, but as a person he is loyal and emotional. In the end, he allows that emotionality to override his criminal judgment. It costs him his life.

In both cases, these men have an exaggerated quality that corrodes the quality of their lives. The excess of that quality is their tragic flaw. And just as excess aggression makes Jake LaMotta a champion in his professional life and a failure in his private life in Scorsese's *Raging Bull* (1980), the same can be said for Hanna and McCauley. Their flaws make them human, and as a result, we care about each of them.

The Private Moment

When a character confesses something to us, having displayed a public or social side that is the opposite, we feel privileged. We have been let in on a secret, befriended, and the result is an identification with the character.

Michael Lehmann's *The Truth about Cats and Dogs* (1996) focuses on a pet psychologist Abby (Janeanne Garofalo) who is open and affectionate and committed to pets, but who has trouble with people. As a radio talk show host she is confident. In her private moments she displays her vulnerability and her lack of confidence in her physical appearance. A plot of pretending to be someone else ensues when she becomes interested in a man Brian (Ben Chaplin) but is too lacking in confidence to own up to her feelings. She asks Noelle, an attractive neighbor (Uma Thurman), to pretend to be the pet psychologist in relation to Brian.

The main character's confession of insecurity and loss of confidence about her physical appearance makes her a vulnerable character who has shared her vulnerability with us. Consequently, we identify with Abby as she runs away from her attraction to a man. In the end, her confession and a shared attachment to a large dog, will bring them together, but not before every effort is made to avoid the relationship.

We have looked at the position of the main character in your story, the issue of character construction, and the issue of how you can move us into a position to identify with your character. To close this chapter I thought it would be useful to look at two differing approaches to character, one an interesting plot-driven storyteller, and the other, an unusual character-driven storyteller. The issue here is to look at the level of characterization necessary in each approach.

CHARACTER IN THE PLOT-DRIVEN FILM:
THE FILMS OF JOSEPH RUBEN

Character tends to be stereotypical in the plot-driven film. The characters in *Armageddon* (1997), *Titanic* (1997), and *Die Hard* (1988) exemplify this approach. That is not to say that the characters are not fun or that the film is not exciting. But from the point of view of what you can learn about using character in a plot-driven film, we have to look to other examples—the work of John Ford, Howard Hawks, Joe Mankiewicz, Billy Wilder, and Fred Zinnemann, for example. More recently filmmakers such as Ang Lee (*Wedding Banquet*, 1994), Shekar Kapur (*Elizabeth*, 1998), Quentin Tarantinoo (*Jackie Brown*, 1998), Peter Weir (*Fearless*, 1993), and Bernardo Bertolucci (*Beseiged*, 1999) have worked effectively to integrate more complex characters in their plot-driven films. In the case of Joe Ruben, I'll refer to three of his films to suggest how the integration of complex characters works in his plot-driven films. The films are *Sleeping with the Enemy* (1991), *True Believer* (1988), and *Return to Paradise* (1998).

What marks each of the main characters in these different genre films by the same filmmaker is that the character is struggling in a plot that poses for each of them a moral dilemma. In a sense, struggling with the plot is a test for each of them. What kind of a person are they? And in each case the test of the plot proves that the characters are better or more moral or worthy than they thought themselves to be. More specifics will flesh out how Joe Ruben's main characters rise above characters who usually populate the plot-driven film.

Sleeping with the Enemy is a thriller, a genre in which ordinary people are caught in extraordinary circumstances, circumstances that will destroy them unless they not only take evasive action, but also find a solution that will provide a permanent solution to those circumstances. In this case the main character is Laura Burney, a woman who finds herself in an abusive marriage. She feels that if she doesn't get away from the marriage her husband will kill her. She fakes an accidental death, but eventually her husband finds her and it becomes a fight to the death. The main character, a romantic, a person who doesn't think enough of herself, allows her abusive husband to impart his possessiveness and violence upon her. Only when she is convinced that he will kill her does she fake her death and run away. It is clear that Laura Burney has done nothing to deserve this situation. She is decent but naïve. The moral dilemma is whether naivete deserves a violent death. Her answer is no.

The plot consists of the pursuit of a woman who is running for her life. The next moral dilemma for this character is whether she will kill to escape from her pursuer. To survive, Laura Burney will kill. This is her moral choice in *Sleeping with the Enemy.*

True Believer is essentially a police story with a lawyer, as the main character who fulfills the police role. In the police story the plot follows a crime-investigation-solution shape. Here the moral dilemma is that the lawyer is sought out to defend a murderer, a man who has just killed someone in prison, where he has been sentenced due to an earlier murder. The moral dilemma for the main character, Eddie Dodd (James Woods), is that he used to be a lawyer for the dispossessed, the liberal causes no one would touch. Now he is a lawyer to drug dealers. In the plot, Eddie Dodd is asked to defend an imprisoned Chinese man. The man has killed a fellow prisoner, a murder witnessed by many convicts and guards. This case poses the issue—either to return to a case where there is the possibility of defending someone worth defending or to carry on cynically practicing law and benefiting those who should be in prison. But Eddie Dodd confounds us when he says that both groups deserve the best representation available. He stands by his interpretation of the law rather than a divisive view of clients into two groups, deserving and nondeserving. Eddie Dodd also confounds our expectations when he constantly breaks the law in his own behavior. Whether it is his drug-taking or his willingness to break and enter in his search for critical evidence, Eddie Dodd is presented to us as a flawed man of principle. He is a bundle of contradictions, all of which together create a complex character. But Ruben makes sure that Eddie Dodd, as with Laura Burney in *Sleeping with the Enemy,* is tested by a plot that challenges him to rise above his limitations as a person. And as Laura Burney does, Eddie Dodd rises to the challenge and regains his self-respect.

In *Return to Paradise,* the main character is also faced with a moral choice. I refer you to the section earlier in this chapter entitled "Character and Plot" for a discussion of this issue in *Return to Paradise.* I would only add here that as in the other two examples from Ruben's work, the main character in *Return to Paradise,* Sheriff thinks less of himself initially. Through the plot he learns that he is a different person than he believed. He is morally tested, and, to his own surprise, he meets the challenge. The use of the plot to pose a test for the character both challenges and humanizes each of these characters.

THE CHARACTER-DRIVEN FILM:
THE FILMS OF LASSE HALLSTRÖM

Characters have an appealing complexity in the character-driven story. The issue here is that the narratives may not gain the additional conflict and consequent energy that comes from plot. Energy and conflict then must come from other characters whose goals are in conflict with the main character; from the dialogue; and from the nature of the main characters themselves. An added component that can help fuel the dramatic character is the situation in which the character finds him or herself. The situation, whether it be oriented to life-stage, sociological, or geographical issues, has much bearing on the level of drama and our level of involvement with the screen story. Filmmakers who are importantly associated with character-driven stories included Jean Renoir, Francois Truffaut, Rainer Fassbinder, George Cukor, and Preston Sturges. More recently John Sayles (*Lone Star*, 1997), Warren Leight (*The Night We Never Met*, 1995), Anthony Minghella (*The English Patient*, 1996), and Erick Zoncka (*Dreamlife of Angels*, 1999) have created excellent character-driven screen stories. To dig deeper into the nature of character in character-driven films we turn to the work of Lasse Hallström. The three films we will examine are *My Life as a Dog* (1987), *What's Eating Gilbert Grape* (1991), and *Cider House Rules* (1999). When one looks at these three films a number of features about the main characters are notable. The most obvious quality is that the characters in each of these films are in a rather limited life situation and, as a result, they have no horizon. So for each of these characters the screen story becomes a means to get out of the trap life has dealt them. The second quality one notices is that the main characters tend to be individualistic and eccentric within their worlds—their relationships, community, and society. The third quality that the main characters share is their decency. They are, in essence, good people, even though their life circumstances have marginalized them. The fourth quality they share is a passive external posture (other characters easily influence them) that is paired with a raging desire on the inside—a desire that is very difficult for them to express or even understand. Finally, all of these main characters are surrounded by characters even more extreme than they are themselves: extreme in their despair and extreme in their desire. Turning now to the films themselves, we will examine how situation and character energize these character-driven screen stories.

My Life as a Dog, the Swedish film that established Hallström's international reputation, unfolds as a biography of twelve-year-old Ingmar. On the cusp of adolescence and filled with energy, Ingmar must deal with the illness of his mother, his separation from his dog (Ingmar must live with an uncle), the death of his mother, and the death of his dog (he has been destroyed because no one wanted to care for him). Although this sounds like a remarkably depressing tale, in fact, there is a great deal of humor in the story.

Ingmar is neither antisocial nor isolated. He has a "girlfriend" who is his own age in his hometown, and there is a girl in his uncle's hometown who is attracted to Ingmar. Her character is instructive about Hallström's approach to character. Saga is a tomboy, a person taken up with sports—soccer, boxing—and her way of relating to Ingmar is to beat him. Later, when their relationship progresses, she puts on a dress and he is shocked by the change in her appearance and behavior.

Her transformation is symptomatic of the sexual prism all the characters present. Ingmar's mother is a beautiful, sexually charged presence. So too is Ingmar's uncle, Gunnar. As an adult, Gunnar is "young" and sexually charged up; he pursues a fellow worker. The fellow worker Berit follows her artistic dream by posing nude for a local sculptor. But the sexuality would be prurient if it were not attached to a particular value in all of Hallström's characters: sexuality is their life force in the face of limited life circumstances and a bleak environment. And for Ingmar, the life force of sexuality represents an antidote to the death (of his mother and his dog) that pervades his young life.

In *What's Eating Gilbert Grape*, the main character Gilbert (Johnny Depp) is also faced with a life of enormous limitations. His mother is morbidly obese, his sisters are self-absorbed, and his brother is mentally challenged and self-destructive. All of this family challenge is juxtaposed with the ultimate challenge—Gilbert's father hanged himself in the basement of the family house. Gilbert, the oldest male, must hold all this together in a small, dead-end town in the Midwest where he works as a clerk in a grocery store that's being put out of business by the local supermarket. For a young man, Gilbert faces a limited life with no choices and enormous responsibility. And his sole personal relationship with a woman is with a married woman. Gilbert, then, is a man with enormous, almost impossible responsibility and no prospects for change. He is trapped in a destructive circumstance. Will he replicate his father's exit plan? No.

The possibility for change in this limited life begins with the arrival in town of a young woman named Becky (Juliette Lewis) who, unlike Gilbert, has met adversity and overcome it. She is filled with hope—with the life force—and it is her relationship with Gilbert that begins his transformation from being trapped to being free.

In *What's Eating Gilbert Grape*, no relationship is more challenging to Gilbert than the relationship with his mentally challenged brother Arny (Leonardo diCaprio). His brother is always in physical trouble. He climbs the town water tower continually. Gilbert is always in danger of losing Arny through self-destruction. The brother is demanding and unpredictable, and Gilbert is trapped. He is his brother's keeper. Will this obligation ruin him or save him? This is a constant question in this narrative. This is the case in Gilbert's relationship with his mother too. Gilbert is the responsible one, the savior in a family populated with self-destructive people. Hallström, using humor and acceptance as he did in *My Life as a Dog*, captures desperation and hope and keeps us caring about Gilbert, and whether he has a future with any horizon. Indeed, the power of the trap is so strong that we identify with that sense of being trapped in life, with overwhelming responsibility, and with the desire to be free. All of those dimensions echo in Hallström's characters.

In *Cider House Rules* (1999), based on the book and screenplay by John Irving, the central character is Homer, played by Tobey Maguire, an orphan who is now a young adult, working in the orphanage in which he was raised. Although Homer is not formally educated, the medical director of the orphanage, Dr. Larch, played by Michael Caine, has trained him in all matters medical. Dr. Larch has also designated Homer to be his successor.

Although the children adore Homer, the role designated for him by Dr. Larch is the trap that encloses Homer. He has no life experience outside the orphanage, and so when an opportunity to leave arises via a successful and grateful recipient of an abortion, Homer runs away from the trap and out into the world. He fares as well in the world as he did in the orphanage. But what he discovers is that life outside has its own traps and limitations. In the end, after Dr. Larch's "accidental" death, Homer returns to the orphanage to take up where Dr. Larch left off. Homer accepts a life of responsibility, never having been able to shake off his sense of responsibility to others. Homer is a man trapped by his own decency.

In *Cider House Rules* it is Dr. Larch who is far more extreme than Homer. He breaks the law to perform abortions for women who have nowhere else to turn; he is addicted to ether (his reason being that he needs anesthesia to sleep); and he lies to the Board of Directors of the orphanage about Homer's credentials—forging the documents. And yet Dr. Larch's decency, his sense of responsibility for the children in his care and his sense of duty toward women in society, all create an overwhelming sense of pain in this character, pain that explains and justifies his transgressions. His life, its limitations and its dedication, create the context for and the central influence on Homer's life.

In each of these films, the main characters are faced with a quality of life issue. In each case, the situation is a trap for the characters. How they reconnect with the life force tends to depend on another, more extreme character. And in every case, humor is used to make these characters and their situations less grim than they might be otherwise. Hallström points out in his work that character-driven stories can be intense, engaging, and enjoyable if appropriate narrative strategies are enlisted. One of these strategies—structure—is the issue we turn to next.

NOTES

1. K. Dancyger and J. Rush, *Alternative Scriptwriting: Writing Beyond the Rules* (Focal Press, 1995).

3

STRUCTURE

Structure is the narrative strategy that has dominated thinking and writing about script for the past twenty years. My goal in this chapter is neither to support nor attack those notions that have held sway in the universities and in the profession. Rather, I acknowledge structure as a critical narrative strategy, as I pointed out in Chapter 1, "The Basics." In this chapter and in Chapter 4, I will explicate this endlessly fascinating but all-too-mysterious strategy and set it in the context of an important set of choices for the writer.

Structure is essentially four macroelements. They are the three-act structure, plot, the character layer, and, finally, genre. Genre is sufficiently large in scale that I will address this layer of structure in Chapter 4. In this chapter I will address the microelements of each of the other layers of structure—the three-act structure, plot, and the character layer. To think about structure visually, imagine these three layers as layers of a cake, and that the cake is contained in a larger container, genre. The proportions of the last two layers—how they look—will depend on the container or the genre. They will differ in proportions depending on the genre. In the classical screenplay (90 percent of the films produced) those proportions will be organized in a three-act structure, and it is to that three-act structure that we first turn.

THREE-ACT STRUCTURE

The three-act structure, organized along two general principles—a beginning, middle, and an end, and along an arc of rising action—essentially provides a linear shape to the structure. Within that linear arc, there are certain characteristics implicit in the structure: that the focus of the narrative is the main character; that the premise of the narrative, two opposing choices for the main character, will provide the emotional spine for the narrative; that if there is a plot it will challenge the main character and his or her goal; that the character layer will articulate the two choices implicit in the premise; and that the story will move to closure or resolution. All of these elements will be organized within the three-act structure. Naturally, the success of these narrative elements will depend upon whether we care about the fate of your main character, an issue addressed in the preceding chapter.

Our task, then, in understanding the three-act structure is to assure that all of the microelements of the three-act structure are working effectively. It is to these elements of the structure that we now turn our attention. We will look at those elements act by act.

In terms of length, consider the following model for a two-hour feature film: Act I, 30 minutes; Act II, 60 minutes; Act III, 30 minutes. This proportion, 1:2:1, tends to capture the balance of the acts in the three-act structure.

ACT I

Act I is the act that essentially sets up the story. In this act, we have to introduce the main character and his or her goal, the premise, the plot, and the character layer, and we have to do so in a manner that quickly and effectively engages the viewer in the screen story. That engagement will depend upon a number of decisions—where we join the story, and how we propel the story in the most dynamic manner possible.

The Critical Moment

The optimal point to join the narrative is a critical moment in the story. It is vital that the beginning of the screen story sharply introduce and propel us into your story. Of course there is some variability in the urgency of the beginning of a story, but for the most part the effective screen story finds an effective entry point. Some examples will illustrate how this operates.

Joe Johnston's *October Sky* (1998) is the story of a young man, Homer, growing up in Coalwood, West Virginia in 1957. The premise for this young man is will he be a coal miner like his father, or will he aspire to a different calling (as encouraged by his teacher). The critical moment when we join this story is the news of and response to the successful launch of Sputnik by the U.S.S.R. Since the boy will try to create for himself an alternative option to coal mining by deciding to build a rocket, and later enter the National Science Fair, the launch of Sputnik has direct relevance to this goal.

In David O. Russell's *Flirting with Disaster* (1996), the main character Mel is facing an identity crisis. His first child has just been born and he is unable to name the boy, because he doesn't know who he is himself. The critical moment then becomes the point at which he decides to find his birth parents. If Mel can find his birth parents, his identity crisis will be over and he will be able to name his son. The balance of the story will address finding his parents, the response of his adoptive parents, the consequent state of his marriage, and the results of finding his real parents.

In Patrice Leconte's *Girl on the Bridge* (1999), we are introduced in a psychiatric interview in a hospital to a nineteen-year-old young woman, Adele, who is disappointed in life. She's made many poor relational choices and she is in despair. The critical moment is that she decides to take her own life by jumping off of a bridge. She is saved by an older man who is walking on the bridge. He tells her he is looking for an assistant. Where better to find one for a knife-throwing act than among potential suicides on a bridge? The balance of the story will be about their professional and personal relationship; in essence, how these two people save one another.

The last example I include is from another French film, Claude Chabrol's *The Beast Must Die* (1969), also released under the title, *This Man Must Die*. In this screen story, the critical moment is a hit-and-run accident. In a small seacoast village, a young boy is fishing. He finishes and returns home through the village. As he does so, he is struck and killed by a driver travelling through the town. The main character in the story is the boy's father, Charles Thenier, who has decided to find and kill his son's killer. The problem, he doesn't know anything about the killer. The balance of the story will be the main character's search for the killer, his discovery of the killer, and his decision to kill him—now that this killer's true nature is known.

The key issue in this opening element of Act I, the critical moment, is to propel us into the screen story.

The Introduction of the Main Character and His or Her Goal

Joining the story at an appropriate moment is paramount to the effectiveness of the screen story. The next issue in Act I is to introduce the main character and his or her goal. The critical moment when we join Mimi Leder's *Deep Impact* (1998) is the identification of a comet heading toward earth. We will learn later, at the point of the catalytic event, that the comet is potentially destructive (an "Extinction Level Event"), but in between these two points we will be introduced to the main character and her goal. The main character is Jenny Lerner, a young reporter for CNBC who is looking for a story that will further her career. She wants to be an anchor to the news show and aggressively pursues that goal. Unwittingly, she comes across the story of the comet and its likely trajectory towards earth (the plot). If the comet hits and destroys the earth, her goal will be at best temporarily achieved.

In Nora Ephron's *Sleepless in Seattle* (1993), we join the story at the point when Sam has lost his wife to cancer. This untimely and painful loss has left him to raise his seven-year-old son alone. The pain is so great that he uproots from Chicago and resettles in Seattle. His goal in this screen story is to overcome his sense of loss, but he doesn't know how. The plot his son comes up with is to find his father a wife via a nationally syndicated radio talk show. Here the main character will succeed in his goal, but the efforts of all the parties—his son, his friends, and the power of media—will be heroic, for his sorrow, after all, is heroically deep.

In John Boorman's *Beyond Rangoon* (1995), Dr. Laura Bowman, the main character, is also looking to overcome loss. The critical event is the murder of her husband and son in Boston. A doctor, she is now completely disinterested in her work. Her sister takes her on a trip to Asia. Her goal is to escape from the horror and grief that has filled her life. She doesn't know it, but the journey that has taken her to Burma will also be filled with horror and grief, due to a national tragedy, the military takeover of the Government, playing itself out in that country. Her experience in Burma is the plot of the film.

The Introduction of the Premise

The next issue to address in Act I is the introduction of the premise. In *October Sky*, as I mentioned earlier, the premise for a young boy is whether he wants to be a coal miner like his father or something different like a scientist (as encouraged by his high school teacher). Clearly these two choices for a working class boy from a coal mining town in West Virginia are worlds apart. It's as if he's seeking an impossible alternative. This level of extreme choice enhances the dramatic elasticity of the entire story and offers a key element to the success of the premise. Were the two choices closer together—if the boy, for example, came from an academic family—the drama would flatten out. We would consider the choice to be a scientist well within the realm of possibility, as would the choice to follow in his father's footsteps (an academic). The greater the gap between the two choices in the premise, the greater the dramatic character of the screen story.

In Mimi Leder's *Deep Impact* the two choices for the main character, Jenny, are to be soft, pliant, and a victim like her mother (who was left for a much younger woman), or to be hard, selfish, and manipulative in the name of the self, like her father. How this character layer plays itself out in the story is that in Act I, the reporter aggressively pursues her career ambitions, like her father. It doesn't matter who gets hurt—they are simply weak, like her mother. So in Act I, the premise is introduced in scenes between Jenny and each of her parents, and each represent a clear choice for her. Will she be her father's daughter or her mother's? And given the spin of the plot, the destruction of the earth, will the reporter preserve herself (selfish, fatherly option) or save others through personal sacrifice (mother's option)?

In Patrice Leconte's *Girl on the Bridge*, the premise for Adele, the main character, is to carry on as she has been, degraded and disappointed in relationships—a choice that has brought her to a suicide attempt—or to change her ways and view a relationship as nurturing, caring for the other, and going beyond a single sexual encounter. By examining her relationship with Gabor, a knife-thrower who ostensibly is looking for a partner, the main character discovers a kindred spirit, a man with whom she enjoys great success. Only when she leaves him for another man does she understand that she had a unique experience with him. In the end she finds him on a bridge, and we learn that when he saved her, he was there to kill himself. Now she saves him on a bridge where he is ready to take his own life again. They need one another and she has made her choice for life.

The Catalytic Event

Generally the catalytic event occurs ten minutes into the first Act. The purpose is to ratchet up the dramatic momentum in the screen story. In Maggie Greenwald's *Ballad of Little Jo* (1993), a western, the main character is a woman, Josephine. She is clearly an Eastern woman of breeding who now finds herself in the man's world of the nineteenth-century West. The premise of the film crystallizes around the catalytic event. That event is the attempted rape of the main character. On the road west, she is offered a lift by a merchant. He is in the business of buying and selling. She helps him market his wares (in repayment for the ride). When approached by two soldiers, the merchant accepts their offer—$50 for the purchase of Josephine. To the merchant and the soldiers she is a woman, a chattel. To avoid this abusive treatment, Josephine cuts her hair and scars her face, in order to pass as a man. Her clothing and her demeanor are those of a man, she undertakes this deception to protect her true self. She wants to be left to make her way. Only as a man can she do so in this dangerous place called the West.

The catalytic event raises the temperature of the screen story. In *Deep Impact*, the catalytic event is the discovery by the main character that there will be an Extinction Level Event, the knowledge of which is being withheld from the public. This knowledge can benefit the career of Jenny in her rise to the top as a reporter, but it bears the seeds of her destruction as well.

In *October Sky*, the catalytic event is the main character's decision to build a rocket, just as the Russians have. Homer's intention is to enter the National Science Fair, his first step away from the option pressed by his father, to be a coalminer.

In *Beyond Rangoon*, the main character, Laura, finds herself to be more than a tourist in Burma (Myanmar), even as she looks backward mired in loss and grief. She goes to a rally where, unbeknownst to her, her handbag is stolen. Without a passport, and because of her attendance at a political rally of dissidents, she is not allowed to leave Rangoon with her sister and the tour group. This detention in Burma is the catalytic event that kick-starts the threat to the main character. As Laura becomes more involved with the dissidents, her life is in danger and the pressure on this character to make choices between remaining grief-stricken or joining life will increase.

The Introduction of Plot

Plot, the external events that are the backdrop for the narrative should have a direct impact upon the main character and her goal. A good example of how plot works is the Titanic voyage upon Rose's wish for happiness in a relationship. In a film such as *Beyond Rangoon*, it is plot, external events, that will pressure the main character to choose in clear and emphatic dramatic terms. *Beyond Rangoon*, as a thriller, is constructed as a chase. That chase begins with the catalytic event in Act I and ends with the resolution in Act III. In *Beyond Rangoon*, Laura's loss of her passport means she is trapped in Rangoon. The plot will essentially follow the repressive military as it exercises its will. That force will first trap Laura and then endanger her. Their threat to her will accelerate and eventually it will be a matter of life and death. In the thriller, the main character overcomes the threat. She will escape. But the plot, with its twists and turns, will put great pressure on the main character and her goal.

In *October Sky* the plot also begins with the catalytic event: Homer's decision to build a rocket in order to enter the National Science Fair propels a plot that exhibits the twists and turns alluded to in *Beyond Rangoon*. Will Homer and his friends, the sons of coalminers, be able to build a rocket? Who will help them scientifically, technologically, and financially, and in terms of their morale? If they build this rocket and it flies, they have to enter and win the local science fair first before they qualify for the national competition. And if they win the local science fair, can their work be effective at the National Science Fair? This is the plot trajectory that begins with the catalytic event, and which will only be completed with resolution and the answer to the question, did they make it, and if they did, what does it mean?

Jonathan Mostow's *Breakdown* (1997) provides another example of how plot can be introduced. *Breakdown*'s main character is Jeff Taylor, a man travelling with his wife cross-country for a new job. The choices in the premise of this thriller are that he will achieve his goal, make it across the country intact with his car and his wife, Amy, or he will not. The critical moment when we join the story is that an incident on the road leads to his new car's breakdown. His wife hitches a ride to the nearest phone at a café and he waits for her return. The catalytic event is her disappearance; Amy is kidnapped. This event takes us into a plot by kidnappers who are looking to extort money from the main character. The plot will end when he retrieves Amy and secures their safety. For this plot to work, he must discover if his wife has been kidnapped, by whom, why, and how he can secure her life and preserve his.

My last example of the introduction of plot in Act I is Hitchcock's *Strangers on a Train* (1951). In this screen story the critical moment is the meeting of two strangers on a train. The main character has relationship problems. As a famous tennis player, Guy's problems have been publicized in the newspapers. The other character, Bruno, the antagonist, makes a proposal, and this is the catalytic event that begins the plot. Bruno proposes a swap. He will kill the Guy's wife, if Guy will kill his father. Since neither crime is motivated, they will constitute perfect crimes. This proposal begins the plot that will only be resolved when the main character is cleared of the murder of his wife and when the threat of the antagonist, Bruno, has subsided (the death of Bruno).

In those screen stories where there is a plot, its introduction in Act I is vital. As a counterexample, look at Robert Young's *Dominick and Eugene* (1988). Here the plot is introduced in the second half of the film. Its lateness in being introduced blunts its effectiveness and actually undermines its dramatic credibility. It's best that you introduce plot in Act I.

The Introduction of the Character Layer

The writer's next obligation in Act I is to introduce the character layer. The relationship options that articulate the premise constitute the character layer of the structure. I should add that so far you, the writer, have had many obligations in Act I. They needn't appear in the order I have written about them, but they should make their appearance in Act I. The most predictable of those issues, the critical moment and the catalytic event, are the factors that have the most predictable placement in Act I—at the beginning of the act and at about the 10-minute point. The other factors, such as the character layer, can be present early in Act I or later. Character layer can also fill Act I entirely, as in George Steven's *A Place in the Sun* (1951).

The character layer essentially articulates the premise in terms of two relationship choices for the main character. In *October Sky*, the impulse to remain in Coalwood doing the same as all the males have done for generations is represented by Homer's father. In fact, his father is always presenting himself as a barrier to Homer's goal to build a rocket. It is his father who cuts off support for the rocket-building materials or locations, and if he does provide help he does so begrudgingly. Throughout the screen story, Homer's father represents the option of "don't change." The second option, to seek a different life, or to change, is represented by Homer's teacher, Miss Riley. Throughout the screen story, she is the character who encourages him in his dream: the creation of a rocket that will gain him and his colleagues' entry into the local Science Fair and then the National Science Fair.

In *Beyond Rangoon*, the options for the main character, Laura, are to maintain her grief, or to place her grief in context as a profound loss and then move on to allow life and the sustenance of life to become her dominant choice. These two options are represented by her sister and by an elderly Burmese taxi driver (formerly a highly regarded professor). The sister represents America, family, and loss; the taxi driver represents a culture where loss is part of life. The taxi driver has an inner life and an inner peace that external instability and violence have not disrupted. The sister is represented in an external manner, implying that escape and denial leave the trauma untouched and all-powerful. The taxi driver's inner peace, whether we consider it as cultural or religious, offers Laura an alternative option, a way to reconnect with the life force within.

In *Sleepless in Seattle* (1993), the two choices in the premise are to remain alone (in mourning) or to reconnect in a relationship that will restore the main character, Sam (Tom Hanks), to a sense of wholeness and, potentially, happiness. The option to stay alone is explored extensively in Act I, in which we see the main character as a father but not anything else. The second option to connect with a woman is the option represented by the radio listener from Baltimore, Annie (Meg Ryan). She hears the plea from the main character's son, Jonah, and although she has a fiancé, she instantly relates to this man whom she has never met who is lonely and sleepless in Seattle. The first option will be further fleshed out in Act II when the main character is fixed up with a woman who is clearly interested in him, but disliked by his son. He might as well be alone if this is to be his choice (according to his son).

In *Girl on the Bridge*, the main character, Adele, faces two choices—to carry on sexually with anyone who is nice to her, and then find herself disappointed and alone. In Act I, the first option is represented by a man she meets on the train heading south to a new career and perhaps a new life. She has sex with this man in the washroom. The incident is disrupted by the second option, Gabor, the knife-thrower who rescues her from the abusive first option. There on the train he offers her the second option—a job with him. He represents purpose, continuity, career, and perhaps success. In both options the men take control of the situation, but in the second option she never becomes a victim of her rescuer. Throughout the film she is always a victim of those men who represent the first choice.

The key element to remember about the character layer is that it speaks specifically to the premise of the screen story.

The Turning Point

The Act I turning point or first major plot point should be a powerful event that opens up the screen story. The turning point closes the introductory phase of the screenplay and transitions into the body of the screenplay. It should be powerful enough to close the introduction and to transition into the major portion of the screen story.

In *Beyond Rangoon*, the events in Act I have been menacing, but they haven't been as conclusive as the killing that is the turning point at the end of Act I. During the opening act, we see the motivation for the trip to Asia: the killing of the husband and son of the main character, Laura. We see the motivation for the trip, the sister's insistence that escape—a trip—will be good for Laura, and we also see the restlessness and depression of Laura, the sleeplessness that leads her to witness a political rally of the opposition to Myanmar's military leadership. We see her lose her passport and her behavior towards the authorities that leads to her being left behind in Myanmar (Burma). And we see her meeting the taxi driver who takes her on a tour. They visit a former student and his family; they are political dissidents. These dissidents offer to help fix the taxi whose collapse has led to the visit. It is the head of this family, Min Han, who offers to lead them to safety when a state of emergency is declared, and it is Min Han who is killed at a checkpoint near the rail station where the main character is dropped to return to Rangoon. When she sees the killing, she rejoins the taxi driver (to save him in her own way), and the chase is on. What determines the divide between Act I and Act II is that in Act I, the main character seemed to flirt with self-destruction. The killing of the young family head at the end of the opening act demonstrates in a palpable way that the main character is in real danger—her life is now at risk. This is the change that ratchets up the temperature of the narrative in Act I. It's now a matter of her life or death.

The turning point in *Strangers on a Train* also involves a killing. Up to this point in the narrative the antagonist, Bruno, only threatened to kill the wife of the main character, Guy. After a very public argument between Guy and his wife, Bruno follows the wife with her male companions to an amusement park. She sees him and believes he's yet another male admirer. He follows her to the Isle of Love and there he strangles her to death.

This event is the turning point, because in a sense it's the point of no return. It makes Bruno a psychopathic killer, instead of an inappropriate neurotic, and it makes Guy, the main character, the leading suspect, a man with a motive (his wife had that afternoon refused to give him a divorce). Suddenly the story has changed from a bad joke to a real and dangerous situation. As it should be with the turning point, the stakes have just gone up considerably.

In *Girl on the Bridge* the turning point is the first performance of Adele, the main character, and Gabor, her knife-throwing rescuer. The knife-thrower, who is part of a circus act, offers to throw blind in order to secure the job. Enticed by the possibility of bloodshed, the management agrees and the act proceeds. The knife-thrower places a curtain over Adele and throws a dozen knives. He succeeds, she lives, and their career together is launched. They go from being penniless to being flush with money and success. The question in Act II is, will this success grow or will it fade as so much has been disappointing for Adele. What is important here is that the potential bluff element of Act I (that Gabor may simply be leading her on for sexual favors) has evaporated, and reality has replaced fantasy. This is a new possibility for the main character.

In *Deep Impact*, the main character, Jenny, discovers at the point of the catalytic event that there will be an Extinction Level Event: a comet will strike earth. In the presidential press conference that follows, the turning point is revealed—that the comet will hit earth in one year's time, but that the U.S. will launch, together with the Soviet Union, a space mission they have entitled Operation Messiah. The mission of that flight is to destroy or at least to divert the route of the comet so that the earth can be saved. This note of hope is the turning point at the end of Act I. The comet and the effort to stop it will now dominate the plot of *Deep Impact*. And the question of whether the earth can be saved will have to be answered by the plot. The question of whether the main character can have her career ambitions in television met is dependent on the outcome of this turning point, the launch of Operation Messiah.

Before we move on to a discussion of Act II, let me reiterate the issues of essential to Act I: (1) to begin at a critical moment, (2) to introduce the main character and his or her goal, (3) to introduce a catalytic event to kick-start the screen story, (4) to introduce the plot, (5) to introduce the character layer, and, finally, (6) to introduce a turning point that will open up the possibilities for the story. It goes without saying that issues of time, place, and general atmospheric issues are also addressed in Act I. Now, on to Act II.

ACT II

Act II is the act of confrontation or struggle and because it is twice as long as the other two acts, it requires particular tools that essentially deepen the dramatic tension of the screen story and raise the ante for the main character in his or her struggle to achieve his or her goal. A way to understand Act II is to consider the elements that have been established in Act I, the plot and character layers, as now twisting into a tighter net around the main character. The turning point at the end of Act II will provide a twist that will allow the character to either get out of the net, or to be—metaphorically speaking—strangled by the net.

As we look at Act II, I will emphasize a strategy called triangulation, and a structural element called the midpoint, a dividing line between the two major elements in Act II. In order that the net of learning be cast as wide as possible, I will turn to different film examples than those I discussed regarding Act I. I do, however, suggest that you can deepen the ideas discussed in this section if you take up those films I used to discuss Act I and apply the ideas we will now discuss to those earlier films.

Triangulation

Triangulation is a technique that creates greater dramatic conflict. Given the length of Act II, the challenge of raising the level of conflict—and consequently ratcheting up our involvement with the screen story—is the main challenge of Act II. Triangulation can proceed through the character layer itself or through the triangulation of the plot layer and the character layer. This is how it works: consider in both cases that the main character is the apex of a triangle.

In the case of the character-driven story where there is no plot, the main character will explore two opposing options or relationships in Act II. Each option represents one side of the premise and the triangle. In Minghella's *Truly, Madly, Deeply*, the goal of the main character, Nina, is to hold on to her sense of loss regarding a dead lover. The premise is whether she will "stop living" and embrace loss and grief as her standard of living (and consequently have no future), or will she seek out a new relationship and, by doing so have a future, a family. These two choices are the corners of the triangle for Nina in this screen story. In the turning point that ends Act I, Nina's grief is so great that she is able to call back her dead lover. In the first half of Act II, Minghella explores her relationship with the dead lover in present time. He is a ghost and it takes Nina a while to accept this new reality. In the second half of Act II, Minghella explores her relationship with a new, living person. To fuel the sense of triangulation, these two men have to be and are opposite beyond one being dead and the other alive. At the end of the act, something will occur that forces Nina to choose.

In Lee Tamahori's *Once Were Warriors*, the main character is a mother, Beth, a Maori woman with five children. Her goal is a harmonious family life complete with a home and a future. The barrier is her husband, Jake, who is a self-centered bully. He wants to sexually possess his wife and sees her devotion to her home and the children as a spoiler for him. Act I ends when, after a drunken party at their home, he beats her mercilessly and rapes her because she wouldn't do his bidding (make eggs for one of his friends). The triangulation explored in Act II is on one side her relationship with her children. The two eldest, both male, are in trouble. She is caring and makes an effort to help them. The other relationship that is explored is the relationship with her husband. She tries and he tries to reconcile, and for a short time it works. As in the first example, what is key is that the two options are mutually exclusive and opposite. This is not a family where she is going to be able to have both. She will have to choose between her children and her husband.

What takes up the screen time in Act II is that these relationships or options have to be fully developed. To make the options credible requires time making Act II much longer than either of the other acts.

A second kind of triangle is the opposition generated in a screen story that has a character layer and a plot layer. Mike Van Diem's *Character* (1996) exemplifies this triangulation. In this family melodrama, the main character is the child, Jacob. In Act II he has grown into adulthood. In Act I the premise is whether he will grow up to be like his parents, cold and rejecting, or whether he can find a means to transcend their influence. In Act I the boy seems trapped. A small plot of self-improvement is introduced. Jacob finds books to read in English. She has no interest in talking or being with Jacob and so he reads, thereby getting away from his mother and her coldness. Act I ends with the boy being rejected by his father. He has been arrested for stealing bread. He tells his jailers his name is Dreverhavan, his father's name. His well-known father is summoned but denies knowing the boy. His father's rejection breaks Jacob's interest in connecting with his father. Like the relationship with his mother, Jacob is thrown on to his own resources.

Act II breaks down into character layer and plot. In the character layer, Jacob explores an alternative to his parents. At work in a law office, he has a mentor, a man who couldn't be more opposite to his father; the man is giving and supportive of Jacob. He also meets a woman, Miss te George, the assistant to the head of the firm. She is cultured and kind. Both of these characters are from a higher class than his parents, and both are opposite to the parents in their emotionality and in their emotional availability to the main character.

The other contributor to the triangulation in *Character* is the plot of self-advancement. In this plot, Jacob first borrows money to start a business and is then sued into bankruptcy. Later he applies for and secures a job in the law firm that was suing him. Then he again borrows money to further his studies in order to become a lawyer. He does finally become both business manager of the firm and a graduate lawyer. But at each step he's had to borrow the money needed from his father. It is his father who sues him twice. Again, a form of tough love from his father.

The triangulation here comes from the tension between the character layer in Act II (the opposite of his parents) and the plot. His career advancement in the plot is dependent on his father's money.

Another example of triangulation between plot and character layers is Andy and Larry Wachowski's *Bound* (1996). The main character here is Corky, a female ex-convict. The premise of the film is her life situation—can she survive or will she be a victim? In Act I, a relationship that promises survival presents itself: a love relationship. She is pursued by Violet, the mistress of Cesare, a mafia couple living next door to the apartment Corky is renovating. Her employer is also a member of the mafia. Act I is taken up by Violet's pursuit and then successful seduction of Corky. The turning point initiates the plot. Violet proposes that she and Corky steal laundered mob money and run away together. In Act II, this plot will be fully developed, and the option of stealing the money from Cesare will be worked out. The complication is that Cesare is also Violet's lover.

At the level of the character layer, the issue for the main character is whether she will have a solid and ongoing romantic relationship with the mistress, or whether she will be betrayed by the mistress and used to get the money. The tension between the plot and the character layer fuels Act II.

Triangulation is the key to making Act II work. In the character layer, the question is whether Violet will betray Corky. In the plot layer, Corky is helping Violet betray Cesare. The pivot is Violet. Will Corky be betrayed by her once the plot is successful and they have stolen the money (with Cesare blamed for the theft)? Here the tension between the plot layer and the character layer works as triangulation to fuel our involvement with the narrative. What is critical is that this tension keep us with the story until the character makes a decision that ends Act II and carries us toward resolution.

The Midpoint

The midpoint in Act II splits the act and transitions from one option in the triangle to the next. For example, the midpoint in *Truly, Madly, Deeply* is that point where the main character's second option, a living potential lover, makes his first appearance. That appearance has to be notable, to make an impression on Nina and on us. In this screen story, the main character is in a café with a pregnant friend, Maura. The pregnant friend, who is Chilean, is learning English from the main character. She is in the café to see another expatriate, a waiter who used to be a doctor in his native country. He takes her blood pressure. The owner of the café comes out and accuses the waiter of wasting time, offering free coffee to his friends, and finally of stealing from the proprietor. After some anti-immigrant remarks and a heated exchange between all of them, a young man stands up, commands everyone's attention, and performs a magic trick. He has deflated the overheated argument, but more importantly, he has vividly introduced himself to the main character and to us. He now becomes the living option.

In *Once Were Warriors*, the family, including the father, has set out to visit the second son, who is in juvenile detention. They have rented a car. The boy is desperate to have them visit, and the mother, our main character, feels that this is a new beginning. The father decides en route to stop at a bar for a drink or two with his mates. He never emerges from the bar. He gets drunk, and the family never gets to visit the son in detention. The hoped-for reconstitution of the family falls apart because of the father's need to drink and bond with his male friends. By doing so, once again he has sacrificed the needs of his family.

The midpoint in *Bound's* plot-dominated Act II presents a point of no return for the characters. The condition for the survival of the relationship of Corky and Violet depends upon Corky engineering a theft of laundered money from the mafia. The price for doing so is the relationship with Violet. The man who possesses the money at the beginning of Act II is Cesare, the mobster who lives with Violet, the mistress. The plan is to steal the money from Cesare before the boss from Chicago arrives the next day to pick it up. Corky and Violet orchestrate the theft in the first half of Act II. But in order to escape, they concoct a lie, that Violet saw Johnnie, the son of the mob boss, arriving from Chicago and leaving the apartment. Once Cesare knows the money is stolen he will conclude that Johnny, a rival, took it to have Cesare blamed and then killed. Violet and Corky had expected Cesare to run away, but he doesn't; he stays to confront Johnnie and allow the father to learn the truth. But talk quickly accelerates to argument when the mob boss arrives, and this argument takes us to the midpoint. Cesare kills Johnnie, his father, and the bodyguard. Now he has broken with the family. He doesn't have the money, but he does have Violet. The plan has not gone as Corky expected.

Turning Point

If the turning point that ends Act I opens up the story, the turning point that ends Act II, the second major plot point, closes the story down. This turning point must be as powerful an event as the turning point that opened up the story. Consequently, it is not transitional, as the midpoint tends to be, but rather more punctuating.

In *Truly, Madly, Deeply* the turning point has to move the main character, Nina to make a choice between her dead lover and the new living man in her life. Here I must restate a point I can't overemphasize—These two choices have to be equally strong. If they are not, there isn't any tension around the choice. If there's no tension, the choice is obvious and undramatic. In *Truly, Madly, Deeply*, there are two strong choices. The turning point is the birth of a child. Nina's Chilean friend (and client), Maura, is in the hospital to have a child, and she calls Nina to be with her. As with all births, there is anxiety, but once the child is born, the new mother passes the child to Nina. The moment is one of discovery. With a sense of wonderment, Nina repeats three words, "A new life." It is as if she is at that instant transformed, and we know she has made her choice for a new life, for a future husband and children, for a living future as opposed to living in the past with her dead lover (no future, and of course, no children).

The turning point in *Once Were Warriors* is equally directive. Beth, the wife and mother who has been struggling in Act II with the choice between her husband (and the family ideal) or her children. The midpoint—the husband's noncooperation in their family trip to see their incarcerated son—posed another crisis. The teenage daughter is now disillusioned with both her mother and her father. And now Beth is alone. One son is in jail; the other has joined a gang. Her one support in the family, her daughter, now rejects her. The turning point that ends Act II is the last straw for Beth. After another night of partying that parallels the party near the end of Act I, a friend of the father rapes the daughter. Belittled by her father shortly after the rape (he rips up her personal journal), the daughter commits suicide, hanging herself in the yard of the family home. For Beth, this tragedy forces the issue—she must save the rest of the children from their father and his abusive cruelty and selfishness. To preserve her family, she will leave him. The suicide of her daughter brings the main character to her choice.

The turning point in *Bound* twists the plot away from the outcome sought by the main character, Corky. Act II has been dominated by the plot to steal money from the mob, to leave Cesare as the fall guy, and to escape into a relationship with the mobster Cesare's mistress, Violet. At the midpoint of Act II, Cesare has killed the mob boss who came to pick up the laundered money. He now is primed to be the fall guy. But instead of running away, he stays in search of the money. When he sees Violet on the phone he suspects her. He redials the number she had called and through the thin walls, he hears that the call has been close. He assaults Violet, and through the same thin walls Corky hears that Violet is at risk. She rushes to rescue Violet and is caught by Cesare. Her capture is the turning point that ends Act II. Act II began with a plot to steal money in order to have a relationship and freedom. Act II ends with that plan in collapse. Cesare is no longer the fall guy; Corky and the relationship she desired are all now at risk. The getaway plan has collapsed. The story will now shift to the question of survival, and survival on what terms.

ACT III

Act III is the act of resolution, the act where we find out if the main character achieves his or her goal. It's the act where the character layer resolves, and the act where the plot is resolved. Once resolution has taken place, the three-act screenplay is over.

An additional point that needs to be made is that Act III tends to be longer and more complex in plot-driven films or plot and character layer films. It can be as short as fifteen minutes in a character-driven film such as Billy Wilder's *The Apartment* (1960), and it can be as long as forty-five minutes in a film with both layers, such as Spielberg's *Saving Private Ryan* (1999).

Since resolution is the linear result of the screen story that began with the character seeking out a goal at a critical moment in the story, I will use two examples from our Act I discussion and two examples from our Act II discussion. As I suggested at the beginning of the Act II section, it would be useful for you to track the other examples as well, and to watch the structural follow-through on those screen stories not addressed in this section. In terms of the films I do address, I will look at examples that are strictly character-driven as well as examples of screen stories that have both plot and character layers.

Turning first to the more complex examples of resolving both plot and the character layer, let's look at *October Sky*. The main character, Homer, is faced with two choices: a life like his father's, as a coalminer, or something different. His goal is to build a rocket to win a science fair on the national level in order to create the bridge to a new life as an adult. In Act III he has to win the science fair as well as permission from his father to have another life. At the turning point, Homer has to work in the coal mine to earn money (his father has been injured). He has "become" his father, but he does win the local science fair. Act III is about getting permission from his father to be different from his father. This character layer is further complicated by the hospitalization with cancer of his mentor, his high school teacher. He decides in Act III that he doesn't want a life in the mines and that he can compete at the national level. Supported by fundraising in the town and the support of other coalminers aside from his father, he goes to the national competition. There some of his equipment is stolen and only through the help of townspeople, now including his father, is the needed equipment replaced. In the plot layer he wins the national science competition. Back at home he will launch a rocket to show the townspeople his achievement and his gratitude. This time his father does attend to share and, in his own way, support his son. This public acknowledgement by the father of the main character resolves the character layer: the son has his father's permission to be different from his father, and the son credits the father. Both are equally willful.

In *Girl on the Bridge*, the turning point that moves us into Act III is that Adele once again (on a cruise) chooses an inappropriate man. She will leave her rescuer/ employer, Gabor, for what she believes is love (after one night). Act III is about the catastrophe that befalls both Adele and her knife-throwing rescuer, Gabor. Both fall from success: she in Greece, and he in Turkey. Each is adrift and headed for failure, particularly Gabor. His luck is over. He finds another partner. He wounds her. He tries to sell his knives, but he cannot. He has fallen from the heights to the depth of despair. He now acknowledges where he was at the beginning of Act I. He climbs out on a bridge to kill himself, but he doesn't succeed. Adele has returned to rescue him, and by doing so, she acknowledges that she is rescuing herself. Together they had luck, they had hope, and they had a relationship that contained the despair that lurked at the corner of each of their lives. Together now, the screen story ends on a note of hopefulness.

Act III in *Truly, Madly, Deeply* is brief (as one expects in a character-driven story). At the turning point that ends Act II, Nina chose life. Now she has to communicate the choice to the two men in her life. She has to alert the living one, Mark, that she wants a relationship with him, and so in Act III she opts to spend the night with him. And she has to say goodbye to her dead lover, Jamie, who has by now been joined by numerous other ghosts. She does say goodbye, and the ending suggests she is going to move in with Mark. She has made her choice— hopeful but bittersweet.

Act II in *Bound* ends with the main character in trouble. The plan that was intended to liberate her and Violet, has left her a captive of a violent man who was supposed to be the fall guy. In Act III, the plot, the robbery of the laundered money, has to be resolved. How will the main character go from being a victim to being free of Cesare and in possession of the money? She does so through the efforts of Violet and the lurking threat of Mickey, the mob enforcer, who is as much a threat to Cesare as he is to the main character. In the end, Violet kills Cesare and she and Corky imply to Mickey that Cesare ran off with the money. In the end, Corky and Violet get away with it—they are in possession of the money. The character layer quickly resolves. As the plot is worked out, we see that the main character is not betrayed by Violet; in fact, Violet saves her. And so the main character's desire for a relationship works out such that she is not victimized, one of the possibilities, but instead find the affirmation and security she sought. This is the opposite of traditional film noir endings where the main character is a victim. Andy and Larry Wachowski have altered the genre expectation in *Bound*.

The Plot Layer

Since I have already addressed the three-act structure in detail, including the introduction of the plot layer, I will not repeat that discussion here, but rather supplement this section with a number of remarks about the plot layer.

Plot is very often used as a blanket term for story. In fact, plot is quite specific in its characteristics. And the term story is inclusive of other elements beyond plot. It's useful to think of plot as something that happens out in the world—a sports event, a voyage, a battle, a crime, as opposed to an interior or psychological or personal dimension as we discover in the character layer.

The second notable characteristic about plot is that it can go on without the main character. That is not to say that plot doesn't influence the character, it does. And it must, for the story to work; but it can go on beyond the perspective or personality of the main character.

The third point is that there are movies that are plot-dominated. Action-adventure films such as *Star Wars* (1977) and *Die Hard* (1988) are examples, as is the thriller *Fatal Attraction* (1987). But films function best when there is a mix of plot and character layer. Mark Pellington's *Arlington Road* (1999) is a good example of a thriller with a strong mix of plot and character layers. On the other hand, Steven Soderbergh's *Out of Sight* (1998) is a screen story whose genre implies more plot than character layer, but Soderbergh decided to reverse the proportions. The character layer is far more prominent than plot in *Out of Sight*. Generally, however, the proportion of plot to character layer is established by the genre. Each genre has specific characteristics, and the audience knows what to expect as a result. There will be much more discussion of this issue in the next chapter.

Finally, plot that works in the screen story is deployed to create an even greater barrier to the main character and his or her goal than there would be if there were no plot.

The Character Layer

The character layer, as I mentioned earlier, is the working out of the premise of the film via two opposing relationships. As with all screen-story relationships, credibility in each case requires screen time. As I also mentioned, both options should be strong, essentially as strong as the other, so that dramatic tension can be maintained.

This describes the mechanical look of the character layer of the screen story. But it doesn't yet capture the central quality of the character layer.

The character layer is about psychology, about human behavior. If plot is about the outer or real world, the character layer is about the inner world, the emotional world, the subjective world. This is the critical feature of the character layer; without it, we wouldn't be moved by the screen story.

There are screen stories that are entirely character layer: *Truly, Madly, Deeply* is one, *Once Were Warriors* is another. These can be very powerful, but as I suggested earlier, screen stories function best when they have both plot and character layers.

Now let's move on to the fourth layer of structure, story form or genre.

---------------------------------- 4 ----------------------------------

GENRE

Genre or story form is the fourth layer of structure. As the container for the other levels, genre is both more recognizable to the audience and more critical for the writer looking for a connection with audience.

Genre as a way of understanding story evolved out of literary criticism, where the metacategories—comedy, tragedy, and romance—were used to understand the shape of stories as well as to be able to highlight the manner in which different writers brought their own particular insights to those forms. We've come far in our consideration of genre as it applies to screen stories. Screen stories evolving out of other dramatic forms—popular fiction, for example—has yielded the western, the gangster film and film noir, and the horror film. Vaudeville has yielded the character comedy, and traditional theater has added the situation comedy and the romantic comedy. Radio has contributed the melodrama, and more recently television, together with journalism, has contributed the docudrama. The spectrum of genres is wide, and we'll turn to it shortly.

To my mind consideration of genre should be useful to the writer. To be useful we have to be precise about genre. What is less useful is to include generic story frames such as the road film, the buddy film, or the stage play as genres. They are simply too general, and consequently their usefulness is limited. Rather than call *Road Warrior* (1981) a road movie, I'd call it an action-adventure. Rather than call *Thelma and Louise* (1991) a road-buddy movie, I'd call it a melodrama. Rather than call *Four Weddings and a Funeral* (1993) a filmed stage play, I'd call it a romantic comedy or situation comedy. Because a friendship is crucial to a story or a journey makes up the plot of a screen story, are not enough to identify the story form. Something more specific, such as the nature of the struggle and who is doing the struggling, will determine the genre of the screen story.

In order to understand genre and how it works, we will look at the role of character and of structure. What is striking about genre is that within a particular genre there are constants—specifically, the dramatic shape, and the nature of the protagonist-antagonist struggle that lies at the heart of each genre. There is of course some room for the writer's individuality as well as for fashion, the shifts in social values and interest. These attitudes will present themselves in genre films, and they will differ over time. But I am getting ahead of myself.

THE AUDIENCE

Film is a popular art, and in the popular arts, writers and directors ignore audience at their peril. Genre films have appealed to audiences since the beginning of filmic storytelling. When I speak of genre I'm talking about five groups of genres. They are:

Genres of Wish Fulfillment
1. Action-Adventure
2. The Musical
3. Science Fiction
4. The Western
5. The Historical Film

Genres between Wish Fulfillment and Realism
1. The Biographical Film
2. The Sports Film
3. The Romantic Comedy

Genres of Realism
1. The Melodrama
2. The Police Story
3. The Gangster Film
4. The War Story
5. The Situation Comedy
6. The Thriller

Genres between Realism and Fear (the Nightmare)
1. Farce
2. Satire
3. Hyperdrama (the adult moral fable)

Genres of the Nightmare
1. Film Noir
2. Screwball Comedy
3. The Horror Film

I cluster the genres in this manner because of audience. Audiences have differing goals when they see particular genres. Genres of wish fulfillment—action-adventure from *Captain Blood* (1935) to *The Perfect Storm* (2000)—have always been popular. They are plot-intensive screen stories where the main character will be a hero. He or she will achieve great feats, and that part of us that identifies with his or her achievements will feel rewarded. His or her heroism is our heroism. The audience for adventure films has not diminished in sixty-five years; if anything, it has grown.

There is another area of our lives, the darker area, where the nightmare dominates. Here our fears and fantasies meet and we anticipate the worst. The worst is what happens in the horror film. My point here is that different genres appeal to people for different reasons. And at different times in people's lives, and at different times in the life of a larger audience—societies and nations—different genres will have their appeal.

Writers and directors know this and adapt the form to the fashion of the day. The war film made during World War II, *The Sands of Iwo Jima* (1949), for example, presents a heroic vision of the soldier, the main character, whereas the post-Vietnam War film, *Apocalypse Now* (1979) is utterly ambivalent about the main character. The reasons have everything to do with the prevailing social attitudes toward war at the time each of these films was made. This element, too, is taken into account as a genre film is presented to an audience at a particular time.

And what of the issue of audience fragmentation? Not every segment of society is drawn to the same genre. Although two films may have as their subject matter crime in the African-American community, John Singleton uses the action-adventure story form in *Shaft* (2000) and Spike Lee opts for melodrama in *Clockers* (1995). Different treatments of similar subject matter will appeal to different audiences within the larger audience.

And what about the audience for realism? What I must say is that the realism-oriented genres—situation comedies, melodramas, and police stories—dominate television. They have also been enduring and ongoing in the feature film. They are not, however, as popular or as financially rewarded as the genres of wish fulfillment or of the nightmare. This has not discouraged writers and directors from making more realistic films.

Finally, the audience for genre films has been from the beginning international. Although the western was an American creation, German filmmakers have long had an attraction to the form and been prolific in the number of westerns they have made. So, too, the Italians. The French have been attracted to the gangster film. The Japanese pursued the horror film as aggressively as Indian film has pursued the musical.

ISSUES OF THE DAY

Issues of the day can be readily absorbed into the story form. Those issues can be social, political, or economic, or they can be less specific and essentially reflect the prevailing attitudes of the time. Whichever the choice, their absorption reflects the malleability of genre. It also reflects the level of desire to reach out and capture the audience.

When Hitchcock was making his 1930s thrillers *39 Steps* (1935) and *The Lady Vanishes* (1938), the films were entertainments, so their relationship to actual world events, particularly Germany's march toward primacy, albeit temporary, in Europe was more than elusive. These films about spying and British espionage in the middle of Europe were about as far from reality as they could be. At the end of the far less innocent 1960s, the thriller was the form of choice in Alan Pakula's *The Parallax View* (1974). Here the plots and schemes of the antagonists were as overstated as Hitchcock's plot and schemes of the relevant governments was understated. But this is in keeping with the views of politics and government in the sixties. John Frankenheimer's *The Manchurian Candidate* (1962) and *Seven Days in May* (1964) are in line with Pakula's film.

Today technology has replaced government as the enemy that was pictured in the 1960s and early 1970s. Now the thriller is represented by films such as Irwin Winkler's *The Net* (1997) and Tony Scott's *Enemy of the State* (1999).

With respect to the western, the view of the genre echoes the changes in the thriller. The West in John Ford's *Stagecoach* (1939) and William Wyler's *The Westerner* (1940) is an environment where the moral high ground lives in the setting and in the behavior of its inhabitants, particularly the protagonist. This is not the case in Sam Peckinpah's *The Wild Bunch* (1967) or in Ralph Nelson's *Blue* (1969). Here the environment is violent and promotes violence in the characters who live in this land. The two later films reflect social attitudes prevailing during the Vietnam War. This unheroic, dark view overwhelms the essentially pastoral elements of the western genre. Even a more conservative western, such as Mark Rydell's *The Cowboys* (1972), reveals a darkness totally unexpected in the genre.

Moving ahead twenty-five years to the early 1990s, Clint Eastwood's *Unforgiven* (1992) reflects the values and sentiments of the 1980s—every man for himself. No longer heroic, the main character is motivated by material necessity and is no longer noble. He is essentially a vindictive killer rather than "the Knight" so often echoed in the earlier westerns. The 1990s western is far from the morality play that is such an essential part of the classic western.

The gangster film has gone through parallel metamorphoses, from the portrait of ambitious immigrants in the 1930s films such as Howard Hawk's *Scarface* (1934), to the portrait of the gangster as an innocent, juvenile delinquent and a victim of the social and economic system in Arthur Penn's *Bonnie and Clyde* (1967), and finally back to the criminal as psychopath in Brian di Palma's *Scarface* (1984) and *The Untouchables* (1988).

All genres have displayed this degree of malleability, but because of the deeper nature of genres and their meaning to the audience, particular genres have, from time to time, come to greater prominence while others have essentially gone into hiding. This, too, has everything to do with the society of the day. The 1990s, for example, were dominated by the action-adventure film in the area of wish fulfillment. Musicals and westerns were a rarity. And in the area of the nightmare, film noir and screwball comedy were rarely represented. Even the horror film was presented as a satire of the horror film—*The Scream* series being a good example—just as the Spaghettii westerns (take-offs of the western) came to great prominence in the 1960s. Why was the 1944-1955 period so powerfully dominated by film noir? Why was the 1934-1940 period so powerfully taken with the screwball comedy? Why were there so many musicals, made from 1935 to 1950? Why were so many of the great westerns made in the 1950s? The answers to all these questions lie in the nature of the society of each period. Whether it was the Depression and the need to escape that led to the explosion of the movie musical, or whether it was the loss of innocence that followed War War II and the Bomb that prompted the interest in film noir, society, its nature and its concerns, permeated the genres and contributes to the genres to which the public feel attracted in particular eras.

What is most important in this discussion is that genres are flexible to issues of the day and, where they are not, concerns of the day will create a demand for particular genres and inhibit the demand for those whose nature is out of sync with the ethos of the day.

THE ROLE OF CHARACTER IN GENRE

One of the defining characteristics of genre is the presentation of the main character and the presentation of the antagonist. In order to understand character in genre, it's best to capture the sense of the main character through his or her goal. And goals will differ in the different genres.

In the realistic genres, there are defined and expected roles for the main character and for the antagonist. In order to understand those roles, we have to link goals to the thematic core of the genre. The thematic core of the police story is that crime cannot go unpunished. Consequently, the main character of the police story, generally a policeman or a detective or an official investigator (such as a district attorney in the army in Simon West's *The General's Daughter* [1999]), has as his or her goal: the apprehension of the perpetrator of a crime. When we look to how the issues of the day have influenced the genre, the policeman in the 1930s police story was a hero. In the anti-authoritarian 1960s, he became the anti-authoritarian *Dirty Harry* (1972), who not only had to deal with the criminal but also with the interference from City Hall. By the 1980s, City Hall and corruption were the antagonists in Sydney Lumet's *Q&A* (1990), and by the 1990s, the police story became obsessed with the humanization of the all-too-human policeman (no longer the hero). Jonathan Demme's *Silence of the Lambs* (1991) is a good example of this trend. This does not detract, however, from the main character's goal: to catch the criminal. For the most part, that criminal is the antagonist in the police story.

Turning to the gangster film, this genre is essentially the story of unbridled ambition that sees as its goal the fulfillment of the American dream. In the early gangster films the gangster was an immigrant: Italian, Irish, or Jewish. More recent gangster films have added Cuban immigrants (*Scarface* [1983]), Russian immigrants (*Little Odessa* [1994]), and British visitors (*The Limey* [1999]) to the repertory. The most famous gangster film, *The Godfather* (1972), has added a generational feature, and we have watched three generations of the Corleone family fulfill their dreams. The antagonist in the gangster film is whoever stands in their way. It might be a rival gangster or a corrupt policeman, or it might be a family member. Thematically, however, the gangster film is consistently the story of characters seeking ways to improve their status materially, and the means of improvement are always illegal.

In the war film, the goal of the main character is to survive, and it is the enemy who is the antagonist. Although particular filmmakers such as Robert Aldrich have specialized in an antagonist that is a superior officer (*Attack* [1957]), a different class (*The Dirty Dozen* [1966]), or simply an ally (*Too Late the Hero* [1969]), most war films do focus on the enemy as the antagonist. Oliver Stone looks at the enemy both within and outside (*Platoon* [1986]), as does Stanley Kubrick (*Full Metal*

Jacket [1987]). This only makes the goal of the main character, to survive, more unlikely.

The thriller presents the goal of the main character differently than the realistic genres to date in that the characters in the police story, the gangster film, and the war film have what I would call either a professional or a material goal. In the thriller, on the other hand, the character has a residual goal, arising out of the situation they find themselves in. They are in essence an ordinary person caught in extraordinary circumstances. They do not understand these circumstances, but if they don't take action, they will become a victim of those circumstances. It may have to do with their work in government intelligence as in Sydney Pollack's *Three Days of the Condor* (1976). Or it may be a case of mistaken identity, as in Hitchcock's *North by Northwest* (1959). In either case, understanding those circumstances and developing a coping strategy, an escape, and a plan to find out who created the conflicting circumstances will lead to a solution and to the survival of the main characters. Their goal, then, is to survive, and their antagonist is whoever is chasing them.

The melodrama is different from the previous realistic genres in that the main characters have a particular kind of struggle that is generated out of their goal, which is to change their life circumstances or experiences. The problem is that they are powerless, in the sense that they are young or old or female or poor or a minority person within a powerful majority community or society that excludes them. They want to improve themselves, and the barrier to improvement is the power structure. The goal then is self-improvement, and the antagonist is the representative of the power structure that is a barrier to that self-improvement. *Cider House Rules* (1999), *Character* (1998), *Sense and Sensibility* (1997), and *Erin Brockovich* (2000) are all examples of melodramas that focus on the struggle for power—and, implicitly, happiness.

In genres of wish fulfillment, the goal of the character relates to an impossible task that, if achieved, will make the main character a hero. In the action-adventure, it may be the recovery of a lost ark (*Raiders of the Lost Ark* [1981]), or saving the world (*Armageddon* [1998]), or more simply saving a building full of hostages from a group of ruthless terrorists (*Die Hard* [1988]). In each case, the task is difficult, almost impossible, and the character who stands in the way, the antagonist, must be more than capable. The more powerful the antagonist, the more heroic the efforts and the accomplishments of the main character will be. Every Luke Skywalker needs his Darth Vader, at least in the action-adventure genre.

In the western, the goal of the character is also an external goal—to complete a cattle drive, avenge a family loss, or rid a town of its outlaws. But the struggle in the western is a struggle between opposing sets of values. The western hero represents moral values, pastoral values, and primitive values; and the antagonist represents civilization, materialism, and a loss of individuality. The antagonist in the western represents civilization—the sheriff in *Unforgiven* (1992), the banker in *Stagecoach* (1939), the outlaw brother in *Winchester 73* (1950).

In all of the genres of wish fulfillment (except the musical) the main character is presented as "the knight" with a set of ideals that will carry him or her into ritual opposition and combat with the representative of the forces of the other side.

The struggle in science fiction is a variation on this struggle. Again the conflict is about values, but rather than primitivism versus civilization as in the western, the struggle in science fiction is between technology and humanity. The main character represents human values and the antagonist represents technology (or the byproduct of technology). As in the western, the goal of the main character is specific—to rescue humans from a distant planet in *Aliens* (1986), or to destroy rebellious replicants (humanlike robots) in *Blade Runner* (1981), or to prevent an invasion from outer space in *The Day the Earth Stood Still* (1951). But this goal, as in the western, is simply a pretext for the engagement in a struggle of values. By succeeding, the main character in science fiction is a hero, as in the western. The antagonist aligns with or misuses the forces or benefits of technology to undermine human values. And as with the western, the struggle proceeds in a ritualized fashion.

In genres of the nightmare, the goal of the character is far less noble than in the genres of wish fulfillment. In film noir, the main characters are at a particular point in their lives, a desperate point, and the only thing that will lift them out of despair is a relationship. Thus the goal becomes a relationship. In fact, they have judged poorly, blinded by desire or by a self-destructive impulse, and the person they have chosen destroys them. The antagonist, then, is the object of desire. The case of film noir, such as Billy Wilder's *Double Indemnity* (1944), proceeds in this way, as does Luchino Visconti's *Ossessione* (1942) (based on James Cain's *The Postman Always Rings Twice*), so the main character is in fact a victim of the lover-antagonist.

Just as the situation comedy is melodrama with laughs and a happy ending, screwball comedy is film noir with laughs (albeit nervous) and a happy ending. The goal of the main character is to avoid a relationship, and the goal of the antagonist is to have a relationship with the main character. The antagonist succeeds. Preston Sturges' *The Lady Eve* (1941), Howard Hawks' *Bringing Up Baby* (1938), and Peter Bogdanovich's *What's Up, Doc?* (1972) are all examples of screwball comedy.

In the horror film, the main characters want normalcy, but they don't accept their dark side. In Brian Di Palma's *Carrie* (1976), it is the inner aggression of the main character that unleashes destruction. In Reuben Mamoulian's *Dr. Jekyll and Mr. Hyde* (1932), it is drug-taking that unleashes the character's inner aggression. And in Steven Spielberg's *Jaws* (1975), it is human disrespect for nature that unleashes the terror of the shark on a small town.

THE ROLE OF STRUCTURE IN GENRE

When we speak of structure in genre, implicitly the question devolves to plot or character layer or both, or to what proportion of each is appropriate in each genre. In order to understand structure in a meaningful way, it's best to link the issue of structure to the dramatic arc of a genre. To exemplify how this works the simplest genre to look at is the police story. The dramatic arc of the police story is crime-investigation-apprehension. This is essentially the plot layer of the police story. In order to deepen the police story, or to give it a modern spin or an old-fashioned spin, or an unusual point of view, a character layer is added. It's not necessary to add a character layer. Police stories such as Jules Dassin's *Naked City* (1948) and Peter Yates' *Bullitt* (1968) are effective police stories without benefit of a character layer. Ridley Scott's *Someone to Watch over Me* (1987) deepens the genre with its class-oriented character layers. Will the main character stay with his working-class wife or take up with the upper-class woman he has been assigned to guard? In Jonathan Demme's *Silence of the Lambs*, the character layer explores the premise of whether a female FBI detective will be a victim (like the victims of the serial killer Buffalo Bill), or whether she will be a victor (like Hannibal Lecter and Jack Crawford in the screen story)?

If a character layer is introduced to this plot-driven genre, what are the consequences? Will it enhance the film or will it slow down the advance of the plot? These are the structural issues. But what to hold on to is that the dramatic arc of the police story is crime-investigation-apprehension.

Turning now to the other realism-oriented genres, the gangster film follows a dramatic arc of a rise and fall. The plot follows the rise of a Tony Lamonte or Vito Corleone or Michael Corelone, and then their fall. Most gangster films do have a character layer, one which is always realistic: the family relationships of Michael Corleone in *The Godfather*, the mother fixation of Cody Jarrett in Raoul Walsh's *White Heat* (1949), the immature love of Clyde for Bonnie in Arthur Penn's *Bonnie and Clyde*. Unlike the police story, the effectiveness of the gangster film seems to rely on the character layer, and consequently it is a genre that has and should have both plot and character layers. We turn now to a more detailed look at this dynamic.

THE CASE OF MICHAEL MANN'S *HEAT*

Michael Mann's *Heat* (1995) is actually a combination of two realistic genres—the police story and the gangster film. Both screen stories follow the classical plot of their respective genres. The police story follows Lieutenant Vincent Hanna (Al Pacino) as he investigates a series of large-scale robberies. He is after "the crews" who are responsible, and in the end he will apprehend "the crew." The gangster film's plot follows the rise and fall of "the crew," particularly of its leader, Neil MacCauley (Robert de Niro). Both stories have a strong character layer that has to do with family and with relationships. Mann makes a point of not differentiating between the policeman and the gangster, in the sense that they both need relationships and that those relationships are complex. It is not the case that these men are as effective in their personal lives as they are in their professions. Quite the contrary, their personal lives are flawed.

The plot layers here are classic; they conform to the genre expectations. And the presence of strong character layers do not move us away from our experience of each genre. What is different in this film is the dramatic treatment of the protagonist-antagonist relationship. Our expectation is that the main character of the police story, Vincent Hanna, will have as his antagonist the gangster Neil

MacCauley, and that conversely, the main character of the gangster film, Neil MacCauley, will have as his antagonist the policeman, Vincent Hanna. They are protagonist and antagonist, and yet the existence of the character layer in each humanizes these two rivals. And even though the plot dictates that Hanna kill MacCauley, we don't experience this resolution as a victory. The character layers in each make the two men human, complicated, and vulnerable. They point out their similarities rather than their differences, and in the end we view them as "brothers" rather than as antagonists. Circumstance has made them who they are. Both are professionals, habitual in their work, and society has determined that one operates within the law and the other outside the law. And so one has the power of the law on his side, while the other is a threat to the law. These men admire one another rather than despise one another. This is Mann's editorial position—that in the 1990s there's not much difference between the police and the criminals. Both are organized brotherhoods pitted against one another. This moral blurring is not untypical of the gangster film. We see it in John Huston's *The Asphalt Jungle* (1950). We see it in Raoul Walsh's *High Sierra* (1941). Nor is this the first all-too-human policeman we have experienced. Clint Eastwood's character in Richard Tuggle's *Tightrope* (1984) comes to mind. But Mann's notion of equivalence between policeman and gangster is the new perception, the 1990s perception.

The same is true for the war film. At its core, the dramatic arc of the war film relies less on plot and far more on the character layer. The plot is always centered on a battle, an incident within a battle, or even an entire war. But it is the character layer that yields meaning to the screen story. In *Saving Private Ryan* (1999), the issue for the captain, John Miller, the main character, is that there is duty and then there is the preservation of the lives of the men in his command. The implied goal is to save as many of his men as he can. But orders during a war, particularly on D-Day, mean death. The assignment that precipitates the main character's journey concerning the issue of the preservation of life versus duty is the assignment to save Private Ryan, a young man who is at the battlefront and who has lost his three brothers in the war.

In Oliver Stone's *Platoon* (1986), the question in the character layer is whether any human values remain during the violence of war. The epitome of this notion is the murder of one American by another in the same outfit. Because of the outcome of the relationships in *Platoon*, war itself becomes "the antagonist," because of the violent values it promotes.

The character layer in Terence Malick's *The Thin Red Line* (1999) presents us with the assertion that it is human life that you stamp out in war. Whatever the circumstances, whether they are heroic or cowardly, it's all about dying. This more philosophical position is less emotionalized than Oliver Stone's treatment of war in *Platoon*, but it is also powerful.

The dramatic arc in the thriller is a chase after the main character by the antagonist. This is principally the plot. Generally, the character layer in the thriller is modest and simply provides a humanization of the main character, as it does in Andrew Davis' *The Package* (1989). But it provides little more than coloration. The thriller is essentially a plot-driven genre.

The most complex of the realist genres is the melodrama. The dramatic arc of the melodrama is an interior journey around the issue of power and the place of the main character in the world of power. If the main character is a child, the arc tends to be either a loss of innocence or a coming of age. If the main character is a woman in the world of men, the arc is also a loss of innocence or a coming of age. In a sense, the same arc is the journey for a minority person in a majority culture, and for an elderly character in a culture obsessed with youth.

In terms of structure, melodramas tend to be principally dominated by the character layer. There are many melodramas that proceed with only a character layer. *Truly, Madly, Deeply* and *Once Were Warriors* are two examples, as I discussed in Chapter 2, "Character." There are also melodramas that proceed with modest plots, in films such as Elia Kazan's *East of Eden* (1955), and there are melodramas with significant plots, in films such as George Stevens' *A Place in the Sun* (1951). For the most part, however, the melodrama is dominated by its character layer.

It's important to note that melodrama and its reliance on the character layer forms a principal dimension of the sports film and of the biographical film. Think of the plot as the career of the sports or biographical figure, whether it be Martin Scorsese's *Raging Bull* (1980) or Robert Mulligan's *Fear Strikes Out* (1957), which dramatize the careers of boxer Jake LaMotta and baseball player Jim Piersall, respectively. The melodrama layer in *Raging Bull* has to do with LaMotta's personal relationships with his wives and his brother. The very quality that makes him a champion in the ring (aggression) is the same personal quality that destroys these personal relationships. In *Fear Strikes Out*, the instability of Piersall's personal life stems from his relationship with his father. In both cases, the characters are looking to strengthen or gain power in the world of personal relationships, but the challenge is formidable.

In the biographical film, the career is again the plot—the general in Franklin Schaffner's *Patton* (1969), the rebellion leader in David Lean's *Lawrence of Arabia* (1962), the painting career in Vincente Minnelli's *Lust for Life* (1956). The melodrama layer is found in how the failure of relationships undermines or compromises the sense of achievement experienced by the subject. What makes all of these films unique is how the character layer humanizes all of these characters. Each had a talent, but not a very happy life.

In order to get a fuller sense of how the melodrama operates, we turn to the example of Michael Mann's *The Insider* (1999).

THE CASE OF MICHAEL MANN'S *THE INSIDER*

Michael Mann's *The Insider* (1999) takes an unusual approach to the melodrama. Thematically, the dramatic arc remains the struggle of the powerless main character against the power structure. In this case, there are two main characters, a scientist, Dr. Jeffrey Wigand who has been dismissed from his position as Vice-President for Research at a major tobacco company, and a producer, Lowell Bergman, working on *60 Minutes* at CBS. The power structure is corporate America as represented by the tobacco companies and the CBS corporate hierarchy. They provide the antagonists for the screen story.

How Mann's approach differs from traditional melodramas is in its structure. The traditional melodrama relies principally on its character layer, and it may or may not have a plot. Michael Mann treats this melodrama principally as a plot rather than a character-driven screen story. This has been done before. Euzhan Palcy treated her story of South African apartheid, *A Dry White Season* (1989), as a thriller, as did Christopher Morahan in his melodrama, *Paper Mask* (1991). By treating the story as a thriller, the plot layer becomes critical and the character layer lessens in importance. The dramatic arc in *The Insider* (1999) specifically becomes about the price the characters are willing to pay to tell the truth. The underlying assumption for both characters is that telling the truth is for the greater good of the society at large. The oppositional dynamic throughout becomes characters who want to tell the truth versus characters who willfully misstate, lie, or are a barrier to the truth.

The plot layer begins with Lowell Bergman, who is finding stories for *60 Minutes*. That is his goal. Jeffrey Wigand is someone he approaches to be an expert witness. Consequent to his being fired by a tobacco company, Jeffrey Wigand has signed a confidentiality agreement and so resists talking to Lowell. But corporate, threatening behavior towards him and his family prompt Jeffrey Wigand to entertain speaking about what he knows.

The plot proceeds through threats about his interview and toward CBS, and on to his deposition by the state of Mississippi, who is filing a lawsuit against the tobacco companies. In the process he loses his family, only to learn that CBS no longer wants to broadcast the interview as shot for reasons of concern surrounding the imminent sale of CBS. The fear is that a company sued by big tobacco is a company worth less than a company with a clear profitability horizon. The threat from big tobacco has been effective. Betrayed, Lowell Bergman leaks the story to the *New York Times* and eventually the original interview is aired. Jeffrey Wigand's family life has been ruined and Lowell Bergman quits his job.

The sense of menace and powerlessness that pervades the Jeffrey Wigand story is paralleled by the sense of commitment and loss of confidence that underlies the Lowell Bergman story. What we are left with is that for the community to gain, individuals have to put everything at risk, yet inevitably they lose a great deal.

By presenting *The Insider* as a plot-driven story, Mann leaves only a small space for the character layer. Here the most crucial relationship is between the two main characters. They are the only ones who have been truthful with one another. Jeffrey Wigand loses his family. Lowell Bergman gives up his professional relationships with his colleagues—he cannot stay in a compromised situation.

By replacing the character layer with plot, Michael Mann has used the dynamic quality that the plot layer can yield to make the story of these two men larger. At one point, Lowell Bergman characterizes Jeffrey Wigand and his family as ordinary people under extraordinary pressure. Michael Mann puts extraordinary narrative pressure on the narrative by using plot rather than character. By doing so he raises this screen story to a melodrama of tragic proportions.

Turning now to the genres of wish fulfillment, I will focus on two genres where the dramatic arc is intriguing. I've already alluded to the struggle at the heart of the western—primitivism versus civilization. How does this polarity use structure to articulate this struggle?

THE CASE OF MICHAEL MANN'S
THE LAST OF THE MOHICANS

In Michael Mann's *The Last of the Mohicans* (1992), the main character has a foot in both camps—primitivism and civilization. Hawkeye is a white man who was raised by the Mohican Chief, Chingachgook. The values he understands are both the primitive and the civilized. But he has a clear preference for the primitive. In the western, primitivism represents pastoral values, moral values, honesty, and individuality. Civilization represents materialism and organizational life with its hierarchies. Hawkeye, called Nathaniel in this version of the James Fenimore Cooper novel, embraces these pastoral values and lives by the moral code they imply. As with the classic western hero, Nathaniel is capable with weapons and has masterful survival skills. And as with the classical western screen story, the plot will unfold in a manner sufficiently ritualistic to give the screen story the moral message of the genre—that civilization is a threat to the virtues of primitivism, an ideology that thrives in an environment called the West.

The Last of the Mohicans has a structure dominated by plot. It is set during the Seven Years War (1756–1763) in Northern New York State, an area contested by the British and French and their respective Indian allies. The plot of the film revolves around the ongoing warfare and the efforts of Nathaniel and his Indian father and brother, the last two living members of their tribe, the Mohicans, to rescue two British women from being captured and killed by the enemy. The British officer who is escorting them also plays an important role in the plot. But it is the character layer that reveals the depth of the clash of values. Nathaniel has powerful and empathic relationships with his Indian family and with Cora, one of the British women. She embraces his values of individualism, morality, and freedom to choose. The other relationships, which relate to civilization, are represented by Major Hayward, the escort, and by British Colonel Munro, Cora's father. Their authoritarian and imperial behavior is part and parcel of the values that have unleashed the Seven Years War and prompted the Indian allies such as the Hurons, particularly the bitter Magwa, to undertake vengeful action in response to the power politics (civilization) and the discontent it has unleashed in the Colonies.

The character layer, although not as prominent as the plot, is fully articulated to triangulate and fuel the plot. In this sense, *The Last of the Mohicans*, although made in 1994, clearly returns to the classic western form with its view of the main character as a knight-hero. The genre presentation is reminiscent of the presentation of earlier western heroes and their struggles to preserve primitive values. Cecil B. De Mille's *The Plainsman* (1936), William Wyler's *The Westerner* (1940), and Sam Peckinpah's *Ride the High Country* (1962) come to mind.

THE CASE OF FRANKLIN SCHAFFNER'S
PLANET OF THE APES

The dramatic arc of science fiction, technology versus humanity, goes to the core of Franklin Schaffner's *Planet of the Apes* (1968). Like the main character in Mimi Leder's *Deep Impact* and the main character in Stanley Kubrick's *2001: A Space Odyssey* (1969), Taylor must choose between the values of technology or humanity. The plot of *Planet of the Apes* is straightforward. Taylor, a human astronaut, has crash-landed on a planet where human beings are treated like animals and where the masters are apes. The apes exhibit "human" behavior and the humans exhibit "animal" behavior. The plot involves the efforts of Taylor to escape from his captors. He does escape, only to learn that the planet he has landed on is actually Earth in the future. He makes this discovery when he finds a piece of the Statue of Liberty floating in the bay.

The character layer of the story has to do with Taylor's relationships with a few of his captors, who are very human, and with the leadership, who are very antagonistic—Taylor is a threat that must be eliminated. Because the leadership knows the truth about the human past, who destroyed the earth with their weapons of mass destruction, they believe they must suppress the humans' impulse to dominate, to oppress, and eventually to destroy.

Although the plot is dominant, the nature of the characters—animal and human—feed directly into the technology-humanity issue. Consequently, it is the character layer that articulates the fundamental struggle at the core of the science fiction film.

Turning now to the genres of the nightmare, we notice a schism between the structure of film noir and the structure of the horror film. The horror film is a genre in which the main characters are victims. Their humanity will not help them overcome their hubris, and consequently they face the ultimate punishment. The dramatic arc, essentially a chase, is plot-driven. Film noir, a genre in which the main characters are also victims, relies more on betrayal than pursuit, and consequently the path to destruction is more a character-driven path than a plot. But because the dramatic arc of destruction is so very different, let's examine the following two examples in detail.

THE CASE OF RIDLEY SCOTT'S *BLADE RUNNER*

Although Ridley Scott's film *Blade Runner* (1981) blends two genres, science fiction and film noir, it is the film noir layer that will be our focus here. Think of mixing genres as apportioning structure via genre. The science fiction layer in line with genre expectations fills out the plot, and the technology-versus-humanity struggle proceeds around the efforts of the main character, Deckard, to track down rebellious replicants (lifelike robots) here on earth. The film noir layer dominates the character layer of the structure. The dramatic arc in film noir is the effort by the main character to save himself through a relationship. The object of desire for Deckard is Rachel, a young woman who works closely with the scientist who is responsible for the creation of the replicants. Rachel is his latest model. She is a replicant who has been imbued with so many human qualities that she believes she is human.

Thus Deckard has chosen as the woman whom he believes can save him, a woman whose life span will be no more than a half-dozen years. The knowledge that he has made a limited choice introduces a dimension of consciousness into the usually less conscious self-destructive impulse of the film noir main character. But this only makes the nightmare worse. To proceed with the knowledge of the destruction of the one relationship that can give the main character hope, is torture indeed (unless Deckard himself is a replicant, as some versions and interpretations of the film have claimed). In either case, the dramatic arc conforms to the film noir expectations in spite of the more optimistic spin of the plot layer.

THE CASE OF JOHN FRANKENHEIMER'S *SECONDS*

In John Frankenheimer's *Seconds*, the main character, a middle-aged man, believes he can be reborn, as a younger man, and given a second chance at life. He is wrong, and in the end he is destroyed for the effort.

At its core the horror film is about pursuit. You can be chased by the devil (*Rosemary's Baby* [1968]). You can be chased by your own demons (*The Shining* [1979]). Or you can be chased by your overflowing desire (*Dr. Jekyll and Mr. Hyde* [1932]). In each case, the pursuit articulates itself in a plot-driven experience. But at its core, the dramatic arc of the horror film is about the unconscious—which we don't know, acknowledge, or accept, but which resides within us and needs to be suppressed. The goal of the character in the horror film is to taste the forbidden fruit, whatever it may be. And for doing so, the character is punished.

Is the horror film only a dream? Many will say that dream life is every bit as real as conscious life, and that in the dream world there is no judge and jury, just energy, desire, aggression, and sexuality. These are the forces unleashed in the horror film.

In Frankenheimer's *Seconds*, the main character, Arthur Hamilton, wants to be young again, to be reborn. The company that organizes his accidental death creates a new life for him. When he discovers that his new life as Tony Wilson is a "creation," that its inhabitants are employees of the company or reborn like himself, he demands to return to his old life. At last he understands there is no going back, and this time he will make his life count, he won't make the same mistakes. That's not how the company sees it, and they kill him to provide a corpse as a stand-in for the next reborn. He is killed because he had the hubris to believe in rebirth. He is a victim of his own desire.

Although relationships are developed in *Seconds*, all are in the company's interests and therefore they are part of the plot. Only the main character's relationship with his wife is part of the character layer. It is modest and empty and consequently acts only to illustrate how little he will give up if he agrees to be reborn. As his wife says in Act III to the main character reborn as Tony Wilson, "[My husband] was dead long before that fire in his hotel."

WORKING WITH GENRE

What I hope I have conveyed is that genre is a very important tool for the writer. Genre provides a narrative shorthand for the audience. When they see a gangster film, they know it will have a rise and fall shape and that thematically it's about a character who wants to get ahead in the world. Genre also provides flexibility—to the issues of the day and to the writer's own viewpoint. Genres have story shapes that have appealed for deep reasons to their audiences over a long period of time. All of these points are advantages. Many filmmakers have been attracted to genre filmmaking. Joel and Ethan Coen have worked in the gangster film, film noir, the action-adventure film, and the police story. Steven Spielberg has worked in the action-adventure film, science fiction, the war film, melodrama, and the horror film. Brian De Palma, Michael Mann, Lawrence Kasdan, and Sydney Pollack, all have worked formally in classic genre films. All of this is preface to the notion that you have to know how to work with genre if you are going to work against genre, the subject to which we now turn.

WORKING AGAINST GENRE

When Michael Mann opted to use a plot layer over the character layer in his melodrama, *The Insider*, he was opting to work against genre. The result was a surprisingly fresh treatment of the genre. Essentially this is the purpose of working against genre—to freshen an old story or to make an old story frame new.

The choices when working against genre are to alter a motif of the genre—such as the nature of the main character, the nature of the main character's goal, the nature of the antagonist—or to alter the expected structure, as in *The Insider*, or to alter the tone. Any change will in a sense change the total experience. I will begin to detail these choices in the next paragraph. The second choice for the writer is to mix genres as Michael Mann did in *Heat*. Here too there are ramifications for our experience of the story.

The most obvious choice here is to work with the main character, particularly in the area of his or her goal. I've already mentioned the material goal of William Mooney in Clint Eastwood's *Unforgiven* (1992). Another example is Neil Jordan's *Mona Lisa* (1985). The main character in the gangster film tends to be ambitious about fortune and possibly fame. George in *Mona Lisa* wants his family back. He's not materially driven, and the result is a very unusual narrative. In Bruce Beresford's western, *Black Robe* (1991), the main character is given a spiritual goal. As a result, he is at odds with the physicality of the primitive. In this sense, he becomes more antagonistic, the representative of civilization, than the hero, who identifies with the pastoral values (primitivism) of the West. As a result, we experience the film as a lament for what was lost as a result of the "Black Robes," or the priests.

Another motif that can be altered is the structure. We have looked at the examples of a number of melodramas where plot superseded the character layer. In a film such as David Mamet's *Homicide*, a plot-driven police story is totally altered by a character layer about identity. The usual balance is reversed as the scale of the character layer overwhelms the police story.

Or you can simply alter the resolution from the expected one. Paul Schrader doesn't destroy the main character at the end of *Light Sleeper* (1991). In film noir, that destruction is expected; instead, the main character is redeemed, saved in a relationship. This altered experience introduces hope into one of the darkest genres, and again we experience the narrative in a surprising way.

Finally, the issue of tone, which we will discuss in detail in the next chapter. The expected tone in the gangster film is realism, but Steven Soderbergh introduces considerable irony in *Out of Sight* (1998), just as Barry Sonnenfeld did in *Get Shorty* (1997). Perhaps the most extreme example of altering expectations with respect to tone is Joel and Ethan Coen's *Fargo* (1996). In the police story, the tone tends to be realistic, but in *Fargo* the humor and the use of irony distance us emotionally from the pregnant sheriff as she proceeds to solve the crime of kidnapping and murder.

The larger-scale alteration of genre is to actually mix two genres. This works best when one genre occupies the plot layer and the other genre occupies the character layer. We've already looked at the example of Ridley Scott's *Blade Runner*. Other examples include Steven Spielberg's *Schindler's List* (1995), with the war against the Jews as the war film, and Schindler's effort to save the Jews as the layer of melodrama. Another example is John Sayles' *Lone Star*, with a police story as plot and melodrama as the character layer. A fourth example would be Woody Allen's *Crimes and Misdemeanors* (1989), with a plot-driven melodrama and a character-driven situation comedy.

The challenge with a film that mixes two genres is that each genre has to be set up, and that takes time. Will the audience have the patience for the additional story? Will it confuse them? What we do know is that mixing genres has become popular and seems to have become more mainstream now. Consequently, it's important for writers to understand each genre very well, a prerequisite to making two genres work.

TONE

Tone is the visual and verbal detail that directs us toward meaning. The writer and director also use those details to direct us toward the meaning they intended. How that direction is conveyed to us in a larger sense has to do with the use of character, structure, and form. Both the micro and macro decisions that influence meaning is the subject matter of this chapter.

In order to look at the issue in a way that will maximize our sense of it, let's break down tone to two functions—credibility and editorial direction. I will continue to refer to the credibility function as *tone*, but I'll call the function of editorial direction *voice*—the voice of the author of the screen story.

What captures tone with a broad brush is its relationship to genre. Let's relate original intention with genre—wish fulfillment, realism, and the nightmare. What is the tone that will most readily capture these underlying intentions?

When we look at the genres of wish fulfillment, there should be a lightness to the tone, because this is a genre where the main character, against considerable odds, gets what he or she wants. This means that the visual and verbal details should contribute to this sense of possibility. Think for a moment of the tone of musicals from *Grease* (1978) to *The Sound of Music* (1965), or the tone of *Star Wars* (1977) and *Indiana Jones and the Last Crusade* (1989), two action-adventure films. In each case, the important dramatic goal, the heroic struggle by the main character to overcome insuperable obstacles, means an optimistic tone, almost romantic tone, that makes credible the achievement of the main character.

For the realist genres, the police story, the gangster film, the war film, and the melodrama, believability in the situation and the characters sets the boundaries for the tone of these genres. The tone most observed in these genres is the kind of detail found in films such as *Serpico* (1974) or *Prince of the City* (1981) or *The French Connection* (1971): the details build up the case for believability. This is the impulse behind successful TV series like *Hill Street Blues*, *NYPD Blue*, and *Law & Order* as well. Emotional believability is behind the TV melodramas such as *Thirtysomething* and *Once and Again*. In all of these cases, language, appearance, and behavior must conform to the principles of recognizability and believability.

At the outer edges of these genres, filmmakers add their own voices. Francis Ford Coppola in *The Godfather* (1972), Ridley Scott in *Someone to Watch over Me* (1987), Jonathan Demme in *The Silence of the Lambs* (1991)—these filmmakers add an operatic dimension to the genre-specific realism. They are adding metaphor. It doesn't always work, but when it does, as in *The Godfather*, the story is enlarged beyond the story of one character and one family—it becomes the story of a society.

With regard to the genres of the nightmare, they require an overheated feeling that makes the unthinkable inevitable. Whether you consider this tone expressionistic or baroque, it is over the top, excessive. In order to have a feeling for this nightmare tone in particular, we turn to film noir, and the example of *Romeo Is Bleeding*.

THE CASE OF PETER MEDAK'S *ROMEO IS BLEEDING*

Romeo Is Bleeding (1993) is a film noir story where the main character is a policeman. Sergeant Jack Grimaldi is desperate because he can't deny himself women or money. Although married, he never has enough love or sex. He needs a mistress, and he needs money. Not that we see him spending or enjoying the money—he hoards it. He makes the money by informing for the mob. He tells them where people they want to kill are being hidden.

Everything in his life begins to unravel when the person the mob wants to find and kill is one of their own—a killer named Mona Demarkov. She is seductive and endlessly dangerous. The mob boss Dan Falcone, because he is unsuccessful in killing Mona, threatens Jack. Will Jack survive betrayal and counterbetrayal? In the end he does survive, but he loses everything he valued—his mistress, his wife, the money, his job, even his identity.

This plot and summary cannot do justice to the tone that makes this screen story emotionally credible. This is a film about desire, about a character who can never have enough. And so his judgment is poor. As he says, he is motivated by his heart and, as a result, he always listens to the wrong voice in his head.

What is critical is to believe the level of his sexual desire, the constancy of his desire. This dimension, set of relationships, of the story, whether focusing on his wife Natalie, his mistress Sheri, or his target/lover Mona, is highly sexualized. Their scenes are all about desire.

The other aspect of the tone is the violence of the film—people are killed, mutilated, and buried alive. This heightened violence is not isolated from the sexuality. In one scene, Mona chops off her own arm so that a body will be identifiable as hers. Jack, the main character, has accidentally shot his mistress, whom Mona had dressed up in a wig so that she would be mistaken for Mona. The amputated arm will confirm the body's identification as Mona. Shortly thereafter, Jack and Mona make love. This scene is not the only scene that mixes sexuality and violence.

The third input to the tone of film noir is a literary quality that is manifest in the language: it tends to be philosophical and fatalistic. When Don Falcone talks to Jack, giving him no choice but to kill Mona, the conversation devolves to if there's any difference between a murderer and a pacifist who find themselves in the cell next to each other. The difference is none—they are both in jail.

But perhaps the most important contributor to the tone of film noir is the pervasive sense of betrayal. No relationship can save you. Jack kills Sheri, Mona betrays Jack, Jack betrays his wife, Jack betrays his colleagues and the police, and betrayal is rampant within the mob. At its heart, film noir is about a character who wants to be saved; he chooses a relationship that will save him, but the person he has chosen betrays him—she makes love to him and then tries to kill him. He has sent away his wife for protection never to connect with her again. He has accidentally killed his mistress. And, finally, to preserve himself, he kills Mona. At the end he is alone in what seems a state or perpetual loneliness.

To sum up, the tone of this film noir is highly sexualized and violent, relationships are overridden by desire, and personal chaos and betrayal quickly follow.

THE CASE OF THE FILMS OF ANG LEE
AND STANLEY KUBRICK

If tone is created by the use of visual and verbal detail that are in keeping with genre expectations, voice is created by using tone to a particular and often more personal purpose. This may mean altering tonal expectations. Specific examples will illustrate this and move us on to a fuller discussion of voice.

Every filmmaker has a point of view that both attracts them to material and with which they translate the material. Voice is the screen storyteller's prism. Ang Lee made *The Wedding Banquet* (1993), a situation comedy about a Taiwanese main character, Wai-Tung, who is in a gay relationship with a Caucasian male. His parents want him to marry and have grandchildren. Their visit to New York prompts a ruse—to pretend to be engaged to a Chinese tenant in one of his buildings. She moves in and they become a platonic threesome. The story twists again when, on their wedding night, he actually impregnates his "pretend" wife. Now he is in a real threesome, and the film ends accepting sexual and racial variations. They will continue to be a threesome.

The tone, which is realistic, as we expect in a situation comedy, has an undercurrent of acceptance and of embracing the outsider, whether he or she is a racial outsider or an outsider in sexual preference. This acceptance and plea for tolerance can also be seen in the family life and generational conflict in Ang Lee's *Eat/Drink/Man/Woman* (1994). The same dimension is vivid in Lee's *Sense and Sensibility* (1995), a story adapted from Jane Austen's novel of the same name and set in early-nineteenth-century, British, upper-class society. And the same voice speaks clearly in *Ride with the Devil* (1999), a Civil War story focusing on a young man whose father came from Germany but who identifies with the values of the American South. In each case, the voice is the same: accept and tolerate the outsider and your community will be better for it.

Voice is not always so specific as in the case of Ang Lee. As in the case of Stanley Kubrick, the range of subject matter over the course of his career is very great. Is there any identifiable voice? I think so. Thematically, Kubrick is attracted to screen stories where individual behavior is examined in the light of a different or majority behavior. As so often is the case in the melodrama, the character, because of his marginal position, is powerless—think of the slave Spartacus; or Joker, the private in the U.S. Army in *Full Metal Jacket*; or the poor Irishman Barry Lyndon. In each case, whether the power structure is Rome or the U.S. Army or the British upper class, the main characters are trying to exercise their rights or claim some power in the light of the power of the organization or society. This theme extends to include the sexually individualistic in the case of Humbert Humbert in *Lolita* (1962), the creatively frustrated in the case of Jack in *The Shining* (1979), or the moral colonel in *Paths of Glory* (1958).

To see how the same voice can be culled from such a broad band of material is to see how critical Kubrick is being of the sexual mores of small-town America in *Lolita*, or of the consequences of power politics in army life (as opposed to just fighting the enemy) in *Paths of Glory*. Kubrick is critical of the same power politics on a global scale in *Dr. Strangelove* (1963), and he is critical of the power politics of technology in *2001: A Space Odyssey* (1969). In a sense, Kubrick celebrates the individual and individual differences as does Ang Lee, but he cautions us that the individual pays a price for being part of an organization—often, too high a price.

Ang Lee and Stanley Kubrick present two polarities of voice around similar themes. To understand how voice has developed, we need to look at earlier examples as well, filmmakers who preceded Bergman's obsession with guilt, anxiety, and identity, or Fellini's playful obsession with the same issues. I now turn to three disparate storytellers who provide a range of voices—John Ford, Fritz Lang, and Billy Wilder.

THE CASE OF THE FILMS OF JOHN FORD, FRITZ LANG, AND BILLY WILDER

In the case of John Ford, what is apparent in his fifty years of filmmaking is that he was obsessed with particular themes: the immigrant, the West, the poetic character of love and commitment, and the celebration of those institutions that support and discipline the individual to be what he can be—particularly the Army. *She Wore a Yellow Ribbon* (1949), a film that focuses on the last days of a captain in the army prior to his retirement; *My Darling Clementine* (1946), the iteration of family responsibility and love set against the career of Sheriff Wyatt Earp; and *The Searchers* (1956), the obsession with primitivism versus responsibility (civilization) in post-Civil War Texas—all of these stories create a portrait of a land and a time that is imagined and poetic, where the individual struggle is a celebration of the forces of life in the face of constant challenge, tragedy, and loss. The vigor of Ford's voice finds its best expression in the western, that pastoral place where poetry is a natural fit. Whichever of Ford's films one looks at, whether it is made in 1925 or 1965, the voice is apparent and powerful.

We find a very different voice in the work of Fritz Lang. If John Ford is a filmmaker who celebrates the past, Fritz Lang is a filmmaker who looks at the dark side of the past, the present, and the future. In his films about the past, Lang did make two westerns, and so the comparison to Ford is telling. In both the *Return of Frank James* (1940) and *Rancho Notorious* (1952), commitment, love, and the land are as present as they are in Ford, but the emphasis is different. Frank James is looking for revenge for the murder of his brother; for the characters in *Rancho Notorious*, the land is an escape from the dangers of what lies outside the boundaries of the ranch. Both of these films focus on violent outlaws as their main characters, and their perspective is completely different from the army captain in *She Wore a Yellow Ribbon*. In Lang, a gunfight is necessary for personal survival; in Ford, the gunfight or Indian battle is a moral struggle.

But the issue of morality is more central in Lang's works that are set in the present. In his German production *M* (1931), the main character is a child molester and child murderer who eludes the police, but who cannot elude the underworld of the community. They see him as a threat to their world, and so he is caught and tried by his fellow criminals. What this says about organized law abiding society is powerful. The world is upside down. This same view pervades Lang's American production *Fury* (1935), where an innocent man is arrested and almost burned alive by his law-abiding captors. He escapes to torment the decent citizens of the town that has spiritually destroyed him.

There is no relief in Lang's futuristic film *Metropolis* (1926). Here the workers are regimented and imprisoned in an underground world. Their savior, a female Christ figure, leads them in bloody revolt against their technological masters. But there is throughout the film the feeling that the workers are exchanging one master for another. This view of an immoral world with its corners of moral ambiguity speaks to anxiety and fear. There is no respite in Lang's world. This is the voice of Fritz Lang.

Somewhere between Ford and Lang is Billy Wilder. Each of these three directors had a fifty-year career, and each had a distinctive voice. In the case of Billy Wilder, his voice fluctuates between two extremes—romanticism and cynicism. The best expressions of Wilder's romanticism are present in his first and one of his last films: *Five Graves to Cairo* (1943) and *The Private Life of Sherlock Holmes* (1970). *Five Graves to Cairo* is set in 1942 in North Africa. A British tank commander, Corporal John Bramble, is lost during the large-scale British retreat. He hides in a hotel to elude Rommel's advancing troops. By remarkable coincidence, Rommel himself makes the hotel his headquarters, and there the British tank commander, now a waiter, learns the secret of Rommel's success—how he has hidden depots of fuel and ammunition at archeological sites all the way to Cairo. By feigning to be the German informer at the hotel (the real waiter), Corporal Bramble has an escape route. Rommel will send him to Cairo.

In the relationships between Corporal Bramble and the French waitress, Mouche, in the hotel, between Mouche and a lieutenant on Rommel's staff, and between Rommel and the other characters in the story, Wilder creates a deeply romantic film about commitment and loyalty, personal and national. There is none of the darkness one associates with Billy Wilder. The same can be said for *Some Like It Hot* (1959) and for *The Private Life of Sherlock Holmes* (1970). In this version of the Holmes story, Holmes is melancholic about the love of his life, and it is this love that leads him in a gentle way into depression and drug-taking.

The apogee of Wilder's romanticism is his film *Avanti* (1977), a story about a stiff American businessman, Wendell Armbruster, who comes to Italy to pick up his father's body. It seems the industrialist died at a resort to which he had returned year after year. When Wendell arrives he discovers a secret—his father had a mistress; that was the reason for his trips. They died together in an automobile accident. Also present is the mistress' daughter, Pamela Piggott, who is there to pick up her mother's body. Naturally, Wendell falls in love with Pamela. What to say to the thousands of employees about his father, and what to say to his own wife? These are the challenges to the main character.

The darker, more cynical side of Billy Wilder's work is well known. This is found in his stories of moral turpitude to advance one's desire for a woman, as in *Double Indemnity* (1944), and one's desire for a career, as in *Ace in the Hole* (1951) and *Sunset Boulevard* (1950). In each case, the main character pays with his life for that desire. But en route, that desire takes the characters through lying, manipulation, even murder, to achieve their goals.

Ace in the Hole captures the pervasive cynicism of each of these screen stories. A New York journalist, Charles Tatum, has to go to the Southwest to get a job after questionable behavior with his former employer. He works for a small New Mexico paper, but he hasn't given up his ambition of being big again. One day he trips over a story about a local man stuck in a shaft in which he had been looking for Indian artifacts in a burial site. Tatum wants to develop and exploit this situation as a human interest story. He organizes with the police to get the man out more slowly. The story grows and in fact goes national. The problem, however, is that his judgment is skewed by his own desire and the man dies before he can be rescued. The American dream of success has turned into the American nightmare, and Tatum suffers an appropriate fate. He is killed.

Ace in the Hole is representative of Wilder's dark stories, but he has also been responsible for screen stories that exhibit both the darkness and the romanticism, primarily his early film *The Major and the Minor* (1942) and the film he's best known for, *The Apartment* (1960). Both dimensions of voice are exhibited in the visual and verbal detailing of the screen stories, the nature of the character, the dramatic arc of the character, and the type of incidents that make up that arc.

THE CASE OF THE FILMS OF STONE, LEE, MAMET, BERTOLUCCI, AND EGOYAN

Turning to a more current profile of voice, we begin to see patterns of a far greater assertion of voice. Few writer-directors have opted for as visceral a voice as Oliver Stone. In his Vietnam War film trilogy—*Platoon* (1986), *Born on the Fourth of July* (1989), and *Heaven and Earth* (1993)—Stone has been singular in the notion that ideals were lost, whether through the betrayal of colleagues (*Platoon*) or political knowledge (*Born on the Fourth of July*). He has broadened this idea through his examination of power and politics in *JFK* (1991) and *Nixon* (1996). Personal tragedy and national tragedy undermine personal idealism and the belief in one's "country." That loss of belief gets carried over into a critique of the media that support or exploit the power structure—journalism in *Salvador* (1986) and television in *Natural Born Killers* (1995). And this dark, disapproving vision culminates in the idea that the system will destroy you whether you are a rock star (*The Doors* [1991]) or a petty criminal (*U-Turn* [1998]). The incident will be treated aggressively; the character will be treated as operating with knowledge (as opposed to being an innocent); the dramatic arc will be tragic, moving inevitably toward destruction—all contributing to a sense of inevitability and doom: these are the ingredients that create the assertive voice of Oliver Stone.

In the case of Spike Lee, we also have a writer-director who has a strong voice, but in the case of Lee, his goal differs considerably. Spike Lee made his reputation with a number of melodramas: *She's Gotta Have It* (1986), *Do the Right Thing* (1989), and *Jungle Fever* (1991). More recently he has shifted to genre films: *Clockers* (1995), *He Got Game* (1997), and *Summer of Sam* (1999). Throughout his work, Spike Lee has an overriding and powerful goal—to exhort and educate his community, the African-American community, to have stronger family ties (*Crooklyn* [1996], *Clockers*), to be fathers that care for their sons (*He Got Game*), and to understand that community prejudice is as corrosive and violent as personal prejudice (*Do the Right Thing, Jungle Fever*). The treatment of character, visual detail, dialogue, dramatic arc, all serve this single purpose; education. And so the issue of voice for Spike Lee is to above all speak to his own community, to incite his own community to become educated and informed and to act for the benefit of other members of the community—their brothers, their children, and themselves. This is the purpose that overrides all else in Spike Lee's work; this is the voice in his work.

Another assertive voice is the writer-director David Mamet. In a series of very different films—*Things Change* (1988), *Homicide* (1991), *The Spanish Prisoner* (1998), *The Winslow Boy* (1999)—Mamet is concerned with more personal issues. They include the issue of maleness: what is the nature of give and take between males, particularly in America (his play *Glengarry Glen Ross*), and what is the nature of adolescent-adult maleness (*Sexual Perversity in Chicago* [1984]) and of father-son maleness (*The Winslow Boy*). In the films that Mamet has written and directed, the main character struggles with the various dimensions of his identity as a man (best presented in *Homicide*). In his screenplays, he has articulated the moral struggle for integrity together with a goal—eliminating the Capone mob in *The Untouchables* (1987) and regaining personal dignity through a professional case, a law suit against medical malpractice in *The Verdict* (1982)—and in his plays that struggle carries a darker price when embracing one's goal (*Glengarry Glen Ross, Speed the Plow*).

In this body of work, Mamet illustrates the layers of creative tension between those elements that contribute to the male identity, but essentially, he helps us feel good about embracing all of the contradictions in feeling and behavior. In this sense, he differs radically in his voice from an Oliver Stone or a Fritz Lang. Although he is very much the modern writer, he is also saying that we define ourselves by action, not words. In *The Winslow Boy*, a period British play, a father sacrifices everything to prove his son's innocence in the matter of a petty theft he is accused of at boarding school. This sacrifice is very compatible with the actions taken by Elliot Ness in *The Untouchables* and by Frank Galvin in *The Verdict*. These men risk everything because they believe and need to believe in a cause, in a case, in a son. Without that belief, they are diminished and life is no longer livable.

Two non-American examples will flesh out this contextual consideration of current voice, the work of Bernardo Bertolucci and of Atom Egoyan. Bernardo Bertolucci came to prominence with a series of films in the 1960s that were poetic, literary, and above all obsessed with verboten behavior, particularly love relationships. This tendency never left him. When one looks at *The Conformist* (1970), *Last Tango in Paris* (1972), *Luna* (1979), *The Sheltering Sky* (1990), and *Beseiged* (1999), one is struck by the improbability of the couplings involved. Older men with younger women, mothers with sons, political adversaries, class adversaries, racial intermixing out of keeping with the class of one of the characters—all of these have populated Bertolucci's work, as if the unconscious controlled the conscious choice of the main characters.

The other theme that runs through Bertolucci's work is the orthodoxy and betrayal of political belief. Politics never equals personal desire but it often destroys desire. *1900* (1976), *The Tragedy of a Ridiculous Man* (1981), *The Conformist*, *Before the Revolution* (1964), all of these are screen stories of political orthodoxy and personal tragedy. In *The Conformist*, a man in Mussolini's Italy must conform because his upper class parents were non-conformists. To gain membership in the Fascist party, he has to betray a former professor, now escaped to Paris. The assignment is to facilitate the assassination of the professor. The problem is he has fallen in love with the professor's wife. She too is sacrificed to his need to belong in this time and place, to the Fascist party.

Love and politics are the throughlines in Bertolucci's work. His voice encompasses the power of desire (the unconscious world) and the disappointment of politics (the conscious world). No film displays the duality of these two themes as clearly as Bertolucci's *The Last Emporer* (1987). The earthiness of the visual details and the conscious destructiveness of the political choices coexist in the same character and in his narrative. The life force of sexuality and the death instinct inherent in politics, this dialectic constitutes the voice of Bernardo Bertolucci.

Atom Egoyan's voice is more elusive, less conscious, but no less powerful. An Armenian immigrant to Canada, a young artist in the age of technology, Egoyan is interested in the converging lines, the discontinuity in identity resulting from immigration, and the convergence between intellect and feeling in an age of technology. The result is a profound sense of anxiety in his work. Whether it is *Family Viewing* (1987), *Exotica* (1997), *The Sweet Hereafter* (1998), or *The Adjuster* (1991), Egoyan's characters are caught in a crises of meaning and self-worth. Whether they are the result of their own doing or the result of social forces beyond their control, the crises of these characters become metaphors for postmodern doubt and the perpetual searching for relief—but finding none. Sensual experience is momentary and to be relished in a world where tragedy and loss are the norm. This is a very dark voice, but not as dark as the voice of Fritz Lang. In a sense it is an exploratory voice looking for coping strategies. In this sense, the work has overtones of Bergman and Tarkovsky. Visual detail, dialogue, and the dramatic arc have to present a discontinuous sensibility. Linear storytelling is simply too stable for this voice. Consequently, Egoyan has turned to nonlinear structure to portray his ideas and to articulate his voice, as I will discuss in greater detail in Chapter 9, "New Models."

GENRES THAT ELEVATE VOICE

Most genres can mask voice in the schematics of screen story. Melodrama, for example, invites us to identify with the main characters and their goals. If we do identify with the main character, voice, although present, is subtle, masked by that identification. It is easier to identify with the writer-director when the main character is a victim. This does not entirely distance us, but when coupled with a literary style, as in film noir, it begins the process of posing the question, do I want to identify with this character? And when we ask that question, we begin to see voice more clearly.

There are however, particular genres where the construction is such that it is voice that we clearly hear and see. This requires the process of distancing us from the main character to go much further. It may mean multiple main characters or no main character. It will mean deploying narrative techniques that highlight voice and deepen the distancing effect—the use of irony, for example. Whatever the techniques deployed, the upshot is a clear relationship between audience and writer-director. Character and structure will become part of the distancing technique rather than the means of identification. It is to three of these genres that emphasize voice that we now turn.

The Case of Satire

Satire as a genre has particular characteristics that differentiate it from other genres. Specifically, satire has no main character. Replacing the main character is a premise that attacks and criticizes a significant organization, an ideology, or a set of values. In a sense, the voice of the writer-director becomes the substitute for the main character in other genres, such as melodrama or the thriller. If the story follows a character, that character is the vehicle for the narrative rather than a main character with whom to identify.

In Sydney Lumet's *Network* (1976), the target of the satire is the power of television. The conscience-ridden producer, Max Schumacher (William Holden), is the character we follow through the story. In Arthur Hiller's *Hospital*, it is writer Paddy Chayevsky's outrage about the dangerous state of the medical care system that is the premise of the narrative and it is the chief of medicine, Dr. Herb Bock (George C. Scott), who is the vehicle for the narrative. In Stanley Kubrick's *Dr. Strangelove* there is no main character, only an incident that leads to nuclear holocaust. The premise is that human beings are fallible and will make mistakes that in the military will lead to the destruction of the world as we know it. Lindsay Anderson's *O Lucky Man* (1972) is a critique of capitalism; Robert Altman's *Short Cuts* (1993) is a satire on the consequences of ultra-urbanization. His film *The Player* (1992) is a satire on Hollywood and its values.

Satire needs a big target to be effective. But having chosen that target, it has other notable qualities. Satire has great latitude in tone. It can shift tone, and that tone can range from realism to the absurd to the fantastic. This shifting is part of the process of distancing us from the characters. Satire is also plot-intensive. A great deal happens in satire. Humor is present in abundance in the satire. Recall the executions on air to boost ratings in *Network* and the final ride of the bomb to its target in *Dr. Strangelove*.

Turning now to two examples of satire, we look first at Michael Ritchie's *Smile* (1974). Ritchie's film is focused on a beauty contest that takes place in California. The beauty contest for adolescents, the Young Miss America pageant, takes place over one week. There is no single main character. The premise is that great hypocrisy abounds in these contests. Although they talk about encouraging community and good values, they are actually about competition and commerce. The narrative focal point is on the duality of behavior in virtually all the characters, participants, judges, and members of the Santa Rosa community. Humor, often cruel humor, is aimed at the characters. One example will illustrate the point. The head of the judging panel is Big Bob (Bruce Dern), a man who considers himself a pillar of the community. When his son is caught taking Polaroids of the participants in their changing room, Big Bob and Little Bob must go to a psychiatrist for counseling. Big Bob's aggression and his lack of understanding about his responsibility for his son's behavior is covered up by Big Bob's overstated commitment to the appearance of good manners—the importance of the situation is to be polite rather than to look at and alter inappropriate behavior.

No target goes untouched in this satire. In the final scene the real victims, the contestants who are being sexually exploited, become, in the next scene, the target of Ritchie's commentary on these beauty contests. Two of the contestants sabotage the public presentation of the Mexican-American contestant. The real reason they cruelly destroy her act is that they are so competitive. They fear that the guacamole dip she keeps foisting on the judges will be effective. If they ruin her performance, there will be less competition for them. No target goes unspared in Ritchie's film.

Warren Beatty's *Bulworth* (1998) is the story of a conservative senator running for reelection. He decides he can't win anyway, so he might as well try to change. He is attracted to a young African-American woman and that desire transforms him into a man who begins to speak his mind about political, social, and economic issues. He changes from a far-right, anti-Semitic racist to an extreme rap-jiving, left-speaking radical politico. In terms of moving from a man of the establishment to a man against the establishment he has become dangerous. And so in the end he is killed.

Bulworth in its extremes illustrates how tonal shifts work in the satire. When we look at the narrative progression in a rational way, we see how illogical and unbelievable that progression is. But in satire, the issue of voice is actually aided by this kind of narrative transgression. Tonal shifts and sudden transformations, these are the very devices that move us away from a credible identification with character and toward a powerful sense of the voice of the writer-director.

To repeat, in satire the target has to be significant enough for us to engage readily with the screen story. Both *Smile* and *Bulworth* are critical of American economic, social, and political values. We could call them both criticisms of American values, with the beauty contest and the political contest as the institutions that provide the dramatic arcs of the two screen stories.

The Case of Hyperdrama

Hyperdrama is a moral fable for adults. The goal of the writer-director is the moral of the tale. Character and plot serve the moral (the voice of the author). This means that we need to be distanced from character and plot. Whereas there is no main character in satire, there is a main character in hyperdrama. How that distancing takes place is through tonal shifts, as in satire, and in the nature of the character presented in the hyperdrama.

The character can be a guide to the narrative, as he is in Frank Capra's *It's a Wonderful Life* (1946), the story of an ordinary man who, when facing a crisis, contemplates suicide. An angel comes down from heaven to show him what life would have been like without him, that is, had he never been born. The purpose is to show this man, George Bailey, that even though his has been a life with limits and personal sacrifice, it has been a worthwhile life.

Another approach to character is to make the character pivotal to the narrative but disappointing in his or her nature. John Boorman's retelling of the Arthur-Camelot legend, *Excalibur* (1981), is a study in an all-too-human but not necessarily sympathetic character.

A third approach to character in the hyperdrama is to make the character so excessive and inconsistent that again we are distanced from him or her. This is the approach taken by Emir Kusterica in his film *Underground* (1995). An imaginative telling of the history of Yugoslavia from 1944 to 1994, it is a tale of personal aggression, betrayal, and a self-imposed dementia. The main character has charisma and tremendous energy, but his actions illustrate a self-destructive impulse that goes further and further. This narrative direction distances us from a character we are initially drawn to.

Another atypical narrative device that distances us from character and plot is the tonal shifts in hyperdrama. Whether it is the over-the-top narrative elements of Stanley Kubrick's *A Clockwork Orange* (1971), which shifts from the excessive, stylized violence of the first half of the film to the realistic melodrama approach taken to the conditioning of Alex in the second half, it is the degree of the shift that pushes us toward what Kubrick is trying to say in his fable—that government control over the individual requires a big stick. The orchestration of violence in the society creates a condition of receptivity to the power of government.

In Lars Von Trier's *Breaking the Waves* (1996), it is the excessive tone of realism that permeates the major part of the narrative until it gives way to the fantastic last section of the screen story. The transition from ascetic realism to an almost spiritual fantasy results in our questioning what the story seemed to be about. An unusual couple marries; Bess is mentally limited, Jan is an emotionally high-spirited foreigner. An oil rig accident quickly cripples Jan, and he puts her love through a series of tests that in the end costs her her life. But in her sacrifice, in the aura of such love, he is resurrected: the cripple is no longer crippled. This narrative transition, this tonal shift, implies something new about the story—that love can overcome even physical limitations, if it is powerful enough.

The final narrative quality that is notable and necessary in hyperdrama is that as a genre it is not only plot-intensive, it is plot-excessive. Hyperdrama has far more plot than the traditional narrative. Recall the amount of plot in Robert Zemeckis' *Forrest Gump* (1992)—forty years in a man's life. The moral of the fable is that even a limited man like Forrest Gump can have enormous impact upon those whom he encounters, personally and casually. This, of course, is an absurd idea from a rational point of view, but hyperdrama is not rational, and the moral, because of the level of the plot (and the tone) is powerful.

Another film that exhibits this plot characteristic is Victor Fleming's *The Wizard of Oz* (1939). A great deal happens to Dorothy on her journey. The purpose here is to echo the idea that imagination is a positive escape from loneliness, a notion initially directed toward children but no less relevant for adults.

To recap all of these characteristics, I turn to the example of Volker Schlondorff's *The Tin Drum* (1979), a screen story based on the Günter Grass novel of the same name. Here the moral is that Nazism (politics) is unhealthy for growing children. Oscar, the main character, is born in Danzig, a town that has shifted in national affiliation from German to Polish and back to German and on and on. The time is the early 1920s and Oscar's mother has a German husband and a Polish lover. Who Oscar's father is remains an open question. But because of what he sees and hears, Oscar, an eccentric five-year-old, decides to stop growing. He throws himself down a set of stairs and he stops. Twenty years later, at the very end of World War II, he decides to resume growing. His brother throws a stone that injures his head and Oscar rapidly regains a more normal size.

Such a tale brings with it attendant narrative exaggerations: Oscar can yell at such a high pitch that glass shatters; his mother commits suicide by overeating eels; his father chokes to death when he swallows his Nazi party pin. These events, all of which are part of the plot, are absurdist on one level, but cumulatively contribute to the moral of the story—that Nazism isn't healthy for its people, particularly children.

Although these events contribute to the tone, the other aspect of the tone is an earthiness, a life force in the midst of all this death. Here the visual details— the birth of Oscar's mother, the fate of his grandfather, the first Nazi rally he observes—all contribute to an almost ritual sense of people and events. It's all part of a grand design, and Oscar is our guide and our interpreter. Because our interpretation remains so distant from people and events, we do as well. Consequently, it is through the voice of Schlondorff interpreting the Günter Grass novel that we see and hear.

The Case of Docudrama

Docudrama, unlike the examples of hyperdrama and satire, does not rely on shifts in tone to help distance us from character and plot. In fact, docudrama has a realistic tone and adheres to that tone in a very orthodox fashion. Indeed, realism, credibility, and the notion that this narrative actually happened and that the characters in it are real, goes to the core of docudrama.

The other notable quality that in which docudrama differs from hyperdrama and satire is that the dramatic arc resembles a case that is being presented to us, the audience. The dramatic arc in both hyperdrama and satire resembles a journey. In terms of character, docudrama, like the other two genres, uses character to deliver the moral or the message. In this sense, the main character may be an observer or the victim of the plot. And like satire, docudrama can proceed without a main character if that is a desired choice.

Docudrama is a genre powerfully associated with British filmmakers such as Peter Watkins and Ken Loach. But as a story form, it has been emulated wherever there is a strong documentary tradition. Because documentary as a form quite often has educational, social, and political goals, here is the heart of the issue of voice in the docudrama. The purpose of voice is, with a sense of authenticity, to alter the audience's view on an issue. In Ken Loach's *Land and Freedom* (1995), his goal was to demythologize the Left's participation in the Spanish Civil War. In *Edvard Munch* (1974), Peter Watkins wanted to point out how conformity, societal conformity in particular, is the enemy of art. And in his film *Culloden* (1964), Watkins wanted to attack British imperialism. The film focuses on the last battle fought on British soil: the quashing of the eighteenth-century Scottish rebellion.

Whether the issue is poverty or royalty or alcoholism or mental illness, the docudrama takes a position on the issue and makes its case using character and plot, as well as a veracity that derives from a preservation that stresses actual people and actual events.

An early and powerful example of docudrama is Ken Loach's *Family Life* (1972), a film to which we now turn. *Family Life* is the story of Janice Blaidon, a young woman who lives with her parents. It's a story of her descent into mental illness. We follow her from being troubled at the outset to the resolution, when she has become, now mute, a case study in schizophrenia in a medical classroom and probably hospitalized for life. How did this happen? Should it have happened? Loach thinks not, and he uses the narrative to take a position that Janice is destroyed by controlling parents, her own too-needy nature, and a medical system that is insensitive to the tension between generational autonomy and generational continuity.

In *Family Life*, Janice is certainly presented as a victim. Loach's case is made principally by showing two conflictual areas—home and hospital. At home, Janice's parents force her to have an abortion against her will and have her hospitalized against her will. When her older sister, Barbara, tries to help Janice by offering to have her live with her, the parents aggressively attack the ungrateful sister, her husband, her values, and isolate Janice. They also forbid her from seeing or being with her boyfriend. Home is the portrait of a hell that imposes illness on Janice, the only defense she has against powerful parents.

In the hospital, Janice is initially treated by an "unconventional" psychiatrist under whose care she begins to improve, but when he is replaced by a more traditional "shock and pill" man, she is more isolated than ever and she deteriorates. The last straw is that parents and hospital conspire to have Janice committed. At last she is sacrificed to the powerful, controlling, insensitive power structure, represented by her parents and by the hospital staff.

Loach makes his case emotionally and powerfully. If society doesn't change its attitude about childrearing, about psychiatry, and tolerate the next generation and its need to be different from the prior generation, society will be in deep trouble. This is the voice of Ken Loach. Character and plot, incident and a particular case, all of which are put together with an air of authenticity, these are the strengths of docudrama as a vehicle for voice.

PART II

PARTICULARS ABOUT SCRIPTWRITING

THE HOLLYWOOD MODEL

In this chapter we will focus on the Hollywood model of screen story. Our purpose is to understand the various options that are available to the writer. On a deeper level, we also want to understand why the Hollywood screen story has become so dominant as a form worldwide.

Hollywood has been global from its beginnings. One reason for this is that from its outset, the Hollywood film industry has been a private as opposed to a public industry.[1] A second reason is that the Hollywood film saw itself as one of the popular arts and aligned itself with the popular arts—theater, burlesque, comic books, popular radio plays and players, and later television. Popular novels were the basis for many films. Margaret Mitchell's *Gone with the Wind* (1939), Mario Puzo's *The Godfather* (1972), and Peter Benchley's *Jaws* (1975) are but a few examples. Popular playwrights such as George S. Kauffman (*You Can't Take It with You*), Samuel Raphaelson (*The Jazz Singer*), and Clifford Odets (*The Golden Boy*) became the screenwriters of choice in the 1930s and 1940s, as did journalist Ben Hecht.

This alignment with the popular arts had ramifications for the prevailing approach to the screen story.[2] Before we elaborate on that approach to screen story, it would be useful to summarize the characteristics that are unique to the Hollywood model. To a degree, these exist in European film and even in modest proportion in the independent film, but these characteristics are not used collectively with a view to maximizing the appeal of the Hollywood film to the widest possible audience outside of the United States.

The Hollywood approach could be summarized as follows:

1. A can-do main character, in spite of the limitations of the character or of the situation on the character.
2. The use of plot to dynamically challenge the character and his goal. This propensity for plot is a natural for a visual medium where action rather than reflection is dynamic and appealing.
3. The attraction to genres of action, and to their exploitation in a manner that celebrates the triumph of character over circumstance.
4. If there is a voice in the Hollywood film, it is the voice that celebrates possibility over adversity.
5. The maximization of conflictual elements that make the main character a hero; the role of the antagonist is critical here.

6. The flexibility to absorb alternative views and stories, particularly from creative European filmmakers.[3]

THE CAN-DO CHARACTER

When I speak of the can-do character, I don't mean the character who gets what he or she wants. That would be too limiting a view of the Hollywood film. What I mean is, a character who believes that she can achieve her goal, believes she will survive a life challenge, whose sense of desire outweighs her sense of fear. This sort of character will struggle all the more to achieve his or her goal, principally because he or she believes it is achievable.

Whether this position is realistic or delusional, we will find out in the course of the screen story. A side benefit of this kind of attitude in a character is that the character is naturally dramatic, for as certain as they are in their desire, they prove to be just as certain to meet opposition to their goal. That opposition, together with the pressure of plot, will amplify the dramatic arc of the character. Whether the wind will favor the character or blow against him, the trip will be vigorous and energetic because of the existence of that wind amplifying the dramatic arc.

Think about the Holocaust films and their main characters. Here is a situation that in life made victims of so many. In the independent film, we have the reflective, angry Sol Nazerman in Sydney Lumet's *The Pawnbroker* (1965). He spends the entire narrative with the goal of denying his past traumatic experience. In the German film, Frank Beyer's *Jacob the Liar* (1974), the main character weaves a fantasy to make the pain of death's imminence more bearable for his fellow inmates and himself. But the Hollywood Holocaust character is different from these two characters. Tino, in Robert Young's *Triumph of the Spirit* (1989), is deported to Auschwitz from Greece at the beginning of the film, and at the end he walks out, free. Tino's goal is to live, and he has a useful skill to achieve this end. He was the Greek boxing champion, and he is invited to fight for the entertainment of the Germans. He does, and thus he lives. What are the odds of coming out of Auschwitz alive? Tino wants to live. He loses his brother and his father in the struggle to live. If he loses a fight in the ring, he will be killed. Tino, both in his will and in the challenges he faces, represents the "Hollywood" character.

Turning to another example, let's look at the main character in Tony Goldwyn's *A Walk on the Moon* (1999). Pearl is a married woman in her early thirties. She is going with her family on a summer vacation outside New York City. The time is the 1960s. She has two children, a hard-working husband, and a hard-worrying mother-in-law. She feels that by marrying young she has missed out on her dreams. Her goal is to rekindle those dreams. In the summer cottage community, she meets a man selling clothing out of a truck. She thinks he may be the solution to her desires, and she begins an affair with him. Complicating the story for her is the budding sexuality of her daughter—and, of course, the profound hurt her affair causes to her relationship with her husband. Pearl powerfully and passionately pursues her goal. In the end, she chooses to return to her husband,

and we are not sure if they will together pursue their dreams, or whether Pearl will continue to feel unfulfilled in the marriage. What is significant about this character for our discussion is that she believes she can achieve her dream. This ties her to other Hollywood characters who struggle for their dream. Michael Dorsey dreams of being a successful actor in *Tootsie* (1982). And he becomes a successful actor. Aaron Kurlander, in Steven Soderbergh's *King of the Hill* (1992), believes his confidence in himself will get him out of St. Louis in 1933. His family's economic plight is dire—his brother is sent away, his mother is ill and hospitalized, his father must go away for a job, and they may, at any moment, be thrown out of the hotel where they are living. Yet Aaron believes he can and will master the situation. This is the nature of the can-do character.

THE USE OF PLOT

The Hollywood film is dominated by plot. To reframe this dramatic statement, think of structure again, with its layers of plot and character. What will become abundantly clear after you read the next few chapters is that the writer-director has choices, and that in the context of the independent film and the majority of national European and Asian films, the character dominates. Even in genres known for their plot orientation, such as the French police story *Le Boucher* (1969) by Claude Chabrol, the choice in structure is the dominance of the character layer. Exactly the opposite is the case in the Hollywood film. As I mentioned in Chapter 4, "Genre," the character layer dominates the melodrama, and yet the melodrama *The Insider* is dominated by plot. I don't think I can overstate the case that this is one of the most important reasons for Hollywood's success!

So how does plot work in the Hollywood film? I will frame the explanation in terms of its deployment to challenge the main character and his or her goal.

In plot-dominated genres such as the action-adventure, this dynamic is most transparent. John McClane's goal in *Die Hard* (1988) is to visit his wife and kids for Christmas. He is a New York policeman, and she has taken a high executive position with a Japanese corporation at their American headquarters in Los Angeles. John goes to see his wife, Holly, at her office, and this is where the plot kicks in. A group of international terrorists in essence "kidnap" the building and its occupants. They are proficient and merciless—and they have John McClane's wife. The only way to achieve his goal is to stop the terrorists.

In the less plot-dominated genre of film noir, plot works in exactly the same way but it's less obvious and takes up a smaller proportion of the screen story. In Jules Dassin's *Night and the City* (1950), Harry Fabian is a small-time swindler in London. He is a man of enormous charm and energy, and his goal is to make a success of himself. This means owning his own club. He wants to be a successful businessman. But he has no assets and no credit. So he steals or lies or cheats to get to his goal. The plot is his effort to set up business with Gregorius, a formerly famous Greek wrestler. The problem is that Cristo, who runs wrestling and other seamy businesses in London, is Gregorius's son. He lies and manipulates to get Gregorius and the Strangler to wrestle. But when Gregorius's young protégé breaks his wrist, Gregorius steps in, fights the Strangler, and wins—then dies. Now Harry is a dead man. Cristo puts out the word: a reward to whoever kills the main character, Harry Fabian. Fabian in the end is killed by the Strangler.

The character layer is dominated by two relationships Harry has with women, and he lies to them both. He does love his girlfriend Mary, but his habitual self-deception and his desire get the best of him, and he self-destructs.

Harry has all the qualities of the film noir main character: he is desperate; he is looking for a relationship with a woman to save him—and get him the money he needs; and he will self-destruct and be a victim of his own desire. That desire is so overwhelming that his judgment is clouded if not delusional.

Here the plot makes Harry's goal even more dangerous. If he fails, Gregorius' son will kill him. In a sense, the plot not only prevents him from achieving his goal, the plot also destroys him.

In David Miller's *Sudden Fear* (1952), an older woman, Myra Hudson, who is a playwright, falls in love with a younger man, Lester Blaine, an actor. The critical moment in the story is a rehearsal where she fires Lester from the cast of her current play. The premise of the film is the classic film noir, where Myra (the playwright) is desperate (given her age) and looks to a relationship (with the younger actor) to save her. The plot is that he marries her for her money, then after she makes him her beneficiary, he will kill her—and make it look like an accident, of course.

Here, too, the plot deeply challenges Myra's goal: to be successful in a relationship, a relationship that will save her. The dramatic effect of the plot is also amplified via triangulation in the character layer. Her relationship with her lawyer, Steve Kearney, is an alternative for her. He is her age and from her socioeconomic class, and he clearly cares about her. The relationship with her new husband clearly conflicts with his goal, which is to kill her and to take over her wealth. Whether the reason for Lester's antipathy is his duplicitous nature, or revenge for the narcissistic wound (the firing) that opens the film, or both, is unclear. But Lester's position in the character layer and in the plot creates an additional tension that energizes this screen story.

THE ATTRACTION TO GENRES OF ACTION

The fact that the musical, the western and the gangster films began and flourished as Hollywood genres is indicative of a propensity for plot-oriented genres of action. Of course, putting on a show, capturing the cattle rustlers, or creating a flourishing career as a gangster all require a great deal of action. What is critical is to understand these are not narrative ends in themselves but rather the means to achieve a goal—a desired relationship or career or both in the musical; a corrective action to achieve moral equilibrium in the western; and the fulfillment of the immigrant's dream, to be an american success story, in the gangster film.

The fact that these genres flourished and grew in Hollywood is important. But additionally these are the genres that the rest of the world identified as American—what was right and wrong with America. Of course, other genres flourished but it must be mentioned that many of them were imported via the film-makers who gravitated toward them. Fred Murnau, the creator of *Nosferatu* (1922) in Germany, and James Whale of the UK were powerful influences on the horror film in Hollywood. Fritz Lang, Robert Siodmak, and Edgar Ulmer of Germany brought to Hollywood the sensibility of film noir. And Ernst Lubitsch of Germany was a great contributor to the success of the romantic comedies of the 1930s in Hollywood. All of these filmmakers appreciated the importance of plot (action) even if they were working in character-driven genres such as film noir and romantic comedy.

No discussion of Hollywood and action-oriented genres would be complete without acknowledgment of the Hollywood elaboration of the genre Alfred Hitchcock, in essence, created in the UK—the thriller. Beginning with *Rebecca* (1940), and ending with *Family Plot* (1976) almost forty years later, no filmmaker has been more identified with the audience or more influential on filmmakers, such as Steven Spielberg, than has Alfred Hitchcock. The thriller, in essence a prolonged chase, has been quintessential Hollywood because it's plot-driven and it's a chase that ends with the main character surviving and a hero to boot for having done so. The dramatic arc of the thriller is fully compatible with the can-do character and with the propensity for plot-driven films. Although an import from the UK, the thriller has become the modern equivalent of the Western with the primacy of the ordinary person as opposed to "the primitive moralist" of the classic western. That person is caught up in a struggle of survival, a dramatic duel to the death, and the character's survival, a modern hero is born. This is the reason the thrillers made from Tom Clancy books such as *Patriot Games* (1992) and *A Clear and Present Danger* (1994) and the John Grisham novels such as *The Firm* (1993) and *The Pelican Brief* (1994) have been as successful as they have been. Just as the western did, they affirm a character and an action-oriented experience that goes to the heart of the Hollywood model.

THE VOICE OF POSSIBILITY OVER ADVERSITY

At its extreme, the Hollywood film likes to present stories of transformation. An angry young woman who has a gift for the ministry seeks vengeance after her preacher father dies. She takes over his calling but more cynically. She is tremendously successful, far beyond her father, but it's all false, that is, until she meets a blind man. In falling in love with this person, she finds faith, cleanses herself as she confesses to her followers. In doing so, she is transformed. This is Frank Capra's *Miracle Woman* (1931) and transformation is the dramatic arc.

But transformation is not always dramatically believable. What audiences relate to is the intention to change, the move toward transformation, what I call the possibility (of transformation) as opposed to the victimization of the character. A powerful dimension of the Hollywood film is this move toward the possibility, toward the light as opposed to the darkness.

Sydney Falco in Alexander Mackendrick's *The Sweet Smell of Success* (1956) is a character who desperately seeks success. He is a press agent in New York City and in order to gain access to the most important column in the New York papers, the column of J.J. Hunsecker; he will do anything short of murder. He betrays friends, he uses vulnerable people, all in the name of his interests. Falco is a despicable character. But the dramatic arc of the story takes him almost to the point of no return; but in the end, he finds a small corner of his humanity and tries to do the right thing. He acts to redeem himself. This action implies the possibility that Sydney Falco will become a different kind of person.

Another example is the main character in Tony Kaye's *American History X* (1998), a narrative about a neo-Nazi, Derek, who recants and tries to save his younger brother, Danny, from becoming what he became—a mindless instrument of a totalitarian ideology and a killer. The film opens with Derek murdering two young Blacks who are breaking into his car and house. He does so with a chilling hatred. Tattooed with a swastika, he is the ultimate neo-Nazi who sees himself as a superman, a superior being, with ultimate rights over others (life and death). For his action he is idealized by fellow neo-Nazis and by his younger brother. And for his action he is imprisoned and it is in prison that he changes. He sees he has more in common with a black man than with the white inmates. When Derek is released from prison his mission is to save Danny from becoming what he became. But it's too late. The resolution of the narrative is the death of Danny at the hands of young blacks. The fact that the killing takes place in his high school adds a chill to the notion that there is nowhere one can hide from the consequences of hatred.

What is important about the actions of the main character and his dramatic arc is that he moves from being a brutal killer to a man who cares about his family, a man whose goal is to save his family, especially its most-endangered member, his brother. The desire to save Danny echoes the impulse of the Hollywood film—to give voice to the possibility of transformation in the face of great adversity. In this case the character fails in his goal but we can relate to the urgency of his goal and to what it implies about the character and the character's newfound ideology (family above all).

THE TRANSFORMATION OF THE MAIN CHARACTER INTO A HERO

It is obvious in a police story such as Paul Verhoeven's *Robocop* (1987) that the main character, Robocop, is a hero. He essentially faces a level of criminality in Detroit akin to total anarchy, and he faces an antagonist, the mastermind behind the purpose of all this criminality, profit and power, who is daunting. Both of these narrative qualities make Robocop a hero. But given the mix of police story and science fiction that layer this screen story, Robocop's heroism could be called genre-expected.

This impulse to see the main character as a hero runs across genres and even the random selection of a melodrama such as Delbert Mann's *Marty* (1956) presents the barriers to choosing a mate and the courage to commit to that choice, as nothing less than heroic. The dramatic arc and the opposition together with the critical moment of *Marty* and Marty's character (a poor self-image) create the transformation of Marty into a hero.

To explore this further we turn to two examples of realist genres where the character's actions and nature mitigate against a heroic outcome. And yet, that outcome, is precisely what these two films move toward.

Mike Nichols' *Wolf* (1994) is a screen story about an older professional man being fired from his job. In the melodrama the powerless person whether young, a woman, a member of a minority or an old person, is presented as a powerless main character. And in the melodrama such a person sets out to gain power from the power structure. We saw this trajectory as the dramatic arc of *Erin Brockovich* (2000), an unemployed mother of two, and we saw this motion as the dramatic arc of *Good Will Hunting* (1998), a working-class young man working in an elite Boston university. In *Wolf*, the main character is Will Randall, an editor at a prestigious New York publishing house. When his company is taken over, he is fired.

There are not too many choices for a middle-aged man who has been fired. The dramatic arc will follow the progress of his career from the start point of the firing. What amplifies this dramatic arc is the plot. At the critical moment of the narrative (the firing is the catalytic event), Will is bitten by a wolf, in essence, making him a wolf. This transformation actually empowers him. He becomes "sexier," his senses (hearing and seeing) become acute. In essence, he becomes stronger. Simultaneously he discovers that the man who will replace him (in the job and with his wife) is his protégé, the head of marketing. This character, Stuart, becomes the antagonist. Because Stuart is younger (more energetic, more virile) he is an imposing antagonist. How can a middle-aged man overcome the efforts of a younger man to displace him? Of course, this issue is a very real one today and it makes the melodrama very timely. The answer in this case comes from the plot. When Will becomes a wolf, he is transformed, he can combat the efforts of the industrialist and of Stuart and he can and does overcome them. He becomes a hero.

In John Frankenheimer's *The Manchurian Candidate* (1962), the main character, Raymond Shaw, is even less likely a hero. Raymond is a man who is captured by the Chinese in Korea and transformed via brainwashing into an assassin. He is also a very unpleasant character. The plot of *The Manchurian Candidate* is the creation of an assassin who will be beyond suspicion in terms of his access to powerful people. He has been trained to kill a powerful candidate at the nominating convention. The assassination will allow the vice-presidential candidate to ascend to the presidential candidacy. The vice-presidential candidate's wife, Raymond's mother, works for the Chinese Communists. So we have a reluctant hero as a main character and a plot that is elaborate. What makes Raymond a hero is the antagonist, his mother, Mrs. Iselin. It is the overpowering Mrs. Iselin who has control over her son and her husband, the vice-presidential candidate, Senator Iselin. She ruins the one positive relationship in his life, Jocie Jordon, the daughter of a political rival. She forces him into the Army, where he can be kidnapped by the North Koreans and the Chinese. She is a powerful antagonist and in the end, his resistance to her (he shoots the vice-presidential candidate and his own mother, rather than the presidential candidate) is an act of courage. And his suicide is not an act of desperation but rather the heroic action of a man who has been victimized endlessly in the narrative. In the end, Raymond Shaw is made a hero by virtue of his actions and by the power of his antagonist, his mother.

THE ROLE OF DISSENT IN THE HOLLYWOOD FILM

The Hollywood film has absorbed creative voices from around the world and very often those have been the voices of dissent. Dissent is as important to the nature of Hollywood film as is the role of the hero. And if it's possible to combine the issue of dissent with the dramatic arc of the hero (the dissenter as hero), the narrative optimizes both of these impulses in the Hollywood film. Before I illustrate this process, it's worth turning the table for a moment and imagining the appeal of dissent and heroism as it appears to those outside the United States, in Europe and in Asia. Without making stereotypical statements or sweeping statements about other societies, it's fair to say that most societies have a vastly different history from that of the United States. And whether this has translated into a highly stratified society, a rigid society, an unstable society or an immature society in terms of social or political tradition, one can imagine that dissent particularly framed in heroic terms, could be interpreted in a wide variety of ways. It certainly signals for an international audience a notion about the United States, a notion that could be threatening or it could be appealing. Certainly it could contribute to the appeal of the Hollywood film. I believe it does contribute to the success of the Hollywood film.

Part of the presentation of dissent in the Hollywood film is to look at the representation of the dispossessed, the Joads in John Ford's *The Grapes of Wrath* (1940), of individualists who stand for unpopular causes, Abe Lincoln in John Ford's *Young Mr. Lincoln* (1939), of foreigners in Michael Cimino's *Heaven's Gate* (1980), of non-conformists and artists in Fred Zinnemann's *Julia* (1977), of political radicals in Warren Beatty's *Reds* (1981). In every case these "dissenters" become heroes, whose dramatic arc proceeds in opposition to the prevailing norms of their community or society. In a sense this impulse is behind the "anti-hero" character portrayed by Humphrey Bogart in *Casablanca* (1942), by Paul Newman in *Hud* (1963), by Steve McQueen in *The Getaway* (1972), and the character immortalized by Marlon Brando in *The Wild One* (1953). And it is this persona as a narrative character that has fueled the careers of Schwartzenegger, Stallone, and other action heroes. Above all, they are characters aligned with dissent and their dramatic arc transforms them into reluctant heroes.

To look at this impulse more specifically, I turn to two examples closely linked to social issues, which remain visceral in American society to this day. The first example is Andrei Konchalovsky's *Runaway Train* (1985). The issue involves incarceration of society's most dangerous criminals. This film is set in the desolation of Alaska where criminals can be housed far from society. It's also about the most rebellious of these prisoners, Manny (Jon Voight). He has been in solitary on-and-off, the warden's punishment for his ongoing impulse to be free—he keeps breaking out of prison and is consequently something of a mythic figure for his fellow

prisoners. We join the story at the moment of his release from solitary. He immediately plans his escape. Although the warden presents as a tough antagonist,
Manny insists on challenging all the odds—weather, the vigilance and persis-
tence of the antagonist, to go, whatever the cost. After the catalytic event, the escape, the balance of the story is the escape. He escapes with a young prisoner,
Buck (Eric Roberts), and at the turning point they find a train. Unfortunately the
engineer of the train has a heart attack and unbeknownst to them they are on a
train that dangerously accelerates. To avoid a disaster, train authorities will route
the train to derailment and destruction. Can the prisoners uncouple the cars from
the engine? Can they evade the warden who is dropped onto the train via a helicopter? Can they evade destruction and a return to prison? The narrative poses
these questions and embraces only one answer—that personal freedom, no matter who you are, is the most important element in life. It's the only thing worth living for and it's worth dying for. This is the essence of this narrative and in the end
in his dissent and in his willingness to die for his beliefs, Manny becomes a hero.

A second example is Steven Spielberg's *Amistad* (1998). The film is based on a
slave revolt that took place on an American ship transporting slaves into slavery
in America. The revolt, which begins the film is the plot of the film. The consequent trial and its outcome is the balance of the plot. The main character, Roger
Baldwin, is the lawyer who takes up this unpopular case, to defend Cinque, the
leader of the revolt before a white American jury. The character layer explores his
relationship with Cinque and his relationship with the pillars of the community.
In terms of underlying values and premise, the themes explored are freedom and
slavery in a literal and metaphorical sense.

In order to undertake this case, Baldwin must dissent from the prevailing values, that slavery of blacks is a fundamental right and necessity for the economic
well-being of the nation. To defend a slave is to attack the values of the nation.
But in doing so, the dramatic arc moves him toward heroic opposition to the
power structure. And in the end, with help from John Quincy Adams, he prevails
and wins freedom for Cinque, the slave.

As in the case of *Runaway Train*, *Amistad* deals with a powerful idea—here
slavery and its legacy, remains as alive an issue today. It is because it is as visceral
an issue as it is, that the main character can be viewed as a dissenter, a man struggling against the prevailing views, a factor that also contributes, together with
the narrative devices of plot and antagonist, to the creation of a dramatic arc that
makes a hero out of the main character.

Having given some detail to the characteristics of the Hollywood film, we now
turn to two examples to see how they work together.

THE CASE OF HOWARD HAWKS' *BALL OF FIRE* (1941)

Bertram Potts (Gary Cooper) leads seven other scholars in the creation of the definitive encyclopedia. His goal is to be as fullsome as he possibly can. When he
discovers his article on "slang," all 800 references are twenty years out of date, he
decides to go out into the streets of New York to research current slang. This takes

him to view and learn from Sugarpuss O'Shea (Barbara Stanwyck), a performer whose speech is peppered with contemporary slang. She is, in short, a researcher's dream. Since she has to be hidden so that she can't testify against her mobster lover, she hides out with Potts and his "seven dwarfs." She and Potts fall in love. The mobster, seeing her as a threat, decides to marry her (a wife can't testify against her husband) or kill her. How Potts feels about this, what he will do to rescue this damsel in distress, is Act III in the narrative.

There is little question that Potts is a can-do character. He is goal-directed and passionate about the encyclopedia and he is goal-directed and passionate about the relationship with Sugarpuss, and once she is at risk from the mob, he transfers all that passion to her rescue.

Moving on to the use of plot in *Ball of Fire*, although this is a situation comedy (character-driven), there is lots of plot (courtesy of writers Charles Brackett and Billy Wilder). The plot—hiding Sugarpuss from the subpoena-servers and later, the effort to suppress her potentially incriminating testimony, is the plot. This plot stands directly in opposition to Potts and his goal of securing a relationship with her. This dynamic amplifies the conflictual elements operating in the narrative.

Turning to the third dimension of the Hollywood film, the question is whether action genres and their applicability are relevant to this particular narrative. *Ball of Fire*, although framed as a situation comedy with a romantic relationship at it core, is overlaid with a plot that is action from its introduction. At the point of the catalytic event, Potts meeting Sugarpuss, the plot to get rid of her as a potential witness, is simultaneously introduced. And the relationship story never really unlinks from the progress of the plot. In fact, it is the plot that pushes the main character to act. In this sense, the use of an action-oriented genre introduced into a situation comedy can be seen as a benchmark of the writer Billy Wilder. The pretense of being twelve years old (a deception) to be able to afford a train trip in *The Major and the Minor* (1942), running away from the mob after witnessing the St. Valentine's Day Massacre in *Some Like It Hot* (1959), the apartment loan for trysts in *The Apartment* (1960), the insurance swindle in *The Fortune Cookie* (1966), all illustrate how Wilder borrows plot from action-oriented genres in order to generate a different level of energy in his situation comedies.

In terms of voice, *Ball of Fire* is certainly a tale of the possibilities, that a man who comes from one class, educated, remote from the ways of the world, can find a street-wise, working woman appealing, and moving beyond curiosity and education, he finds her the object of his desire. The classlessness of the narrative together with the desirability of mixing his knowledge with her pragmatism implies a society where this kind of open mobility is a possibility in spite of the lack of common experience, which could be perceived of as a barrier to such a relationship.

In terms of the transformation of Potts into a hero, this is precisely what his goal-directedness and the plot inspire to create. Although Joe Lilac is a threatening antagonist, it is the fire power of his associates that makes Potts' plan to capture Joe Lilac and rescue Sugarpuss a heroic act. In the end, Potts gets the girl but from our vantage point his becoming a hero conforms to the Hollywood formula for success.

The issue of dissent in the film is a subtle one, although a presence. Potts is an intellectual in a pragmatic, passionate world. At the beginning, he is presented as an outsider to this world and as such, he is a marginal character in that world. As an academic, he does represent a minority that the majority has often found questionable in its value. The intellectual outsider is as marginalized as the criminal, the immigrant, the mentally ill. Indeed anyone who doesn't fit into the majority profile can and has been so positioned in the Hollywood film.

THE CASE OF *SAVING PRIVATE RYAN* (1998)

Steven Spielberg's *Saving Private Ryan*, set against the D-Day Invasion, June 1944, focuses on Captain Miller (Tom Hanks) and his troops. We join the screen story at the critical moment of the D-Day invasion, June 6. The catalytic event is the assignment to find and bring out Private Ryan, a man who has lost three brothers in the war. He is the sole survivor. The rescue of Private Ryan, the mission and its outcome, is the balance of the screen story. As I mention earlier, the premise for Captain Miller is more precise than the conventional goal of a main character in the war, which is to survive. Here the question is turned on its hero—what is worth dying for? In his efforts to save the life of his own men and the life of Private Ryan, as well as his own, this is the question that forms the premise of *Saving Private Ryan*.

The first issue for us is the nature of this main character. Captain Miller is definitely a can-do character. At the very beginning, he is concerned for his men and he is concerned about fulfilling their mission, securing and holding a position on Omaha Beach. The presentation of a variety of behaviors from anxiety to fear to confusion contrasts with the goal-directedness of Captain Miller. Although there will be issue of doubt raised, Captain Miller, his willingness to carry out his mission, to make decisions, and to move toward his goal, is very much the can-do character that epitomizes the main character in the Hollywood film.

The plot, essentially the progress of the war mitigates against the goal in the war film, to survive, and in Captain Miller's goal, to save the lives of his men. Because the mission to save Private Ryan essentially takes Miller and his men deeply into German-held territory, the pressure against achieving his goal is considerable. The fact that the war film is a plot-oriented genre makes this kind of exposition expected. The degree of threat and the plot have to proceed however within the expected tone, realism, and it does.

Nevertheless because the war film is a genre in which we anticipate a great deal of action, albeit realistic, allows the narrative to focus on one of the important ingredients of the Hollywood film, the bias toward action to energize the narrative.

In terms of voice, Steven Spielberg has depicted this story of sacrifice as a story of choice. In the end, Captain Miller chooses to stay to help Private Ryan defend the town, to be with his friends and his fellow soldiers. In doing so, Captain Miller chooses to give up his own life to save Private Ryan. The fact that these are choices speaks to the notion that his is a world where survival was possible but in the face of adversity, he chooses sacrifice. The ending suggests that the main character has accomplished his mission (but lost his life). It affirms the possibility of survival in the real life of Private Ryan, who we see revisit the Normandy gravesite where Captain Miller and so many of his colleagues are buried. This is a moment which could be framed in many ways but in the Hollywood tradition, its framing is one of a positive loss.

Captain Miller, a reluctant hero, is nevertheless a hero. His nature, his actions, together with the scale of the opposition within the plot, make him a hero. A particularly important character in this transformation is the German prisoner who Miller frees. We have already seen German prisoners shot by Americans, so Miller's gesture takes on some significance—that he is humane. However, when this same prisoner kills the Jewish member of Miller's squad, a killing that proceeds with great cruelty, that character is transformed into a powerful antagonist. In both narrative actions, saving the German prisoner and the killing of the Jewish GI by the German, we have a conflictual set of values that makes a monster of the antagonist and a humanist and hero in the case of the protagonist.

Dissent is given an important role in Captain Miller's character. He is a most reluctant hero. He is not a killer. Indeed, two-thirds of the way through the narrative, we find out he is a teacher and that he is a man who doesn't necessarily believe in the values war implies. In this sense, he reminds us of the reluctant main character in Kubrick's *Paths of Glory* (1958) and in Robert Aldrich's *Attack* (1957). Both men value life far more than they value death. Both men are officers who care for their men with a human sense out of keeping with the setting of the war film. In this sense, Captain Miller, in his reluctance and in his humanity, is the opposite of a character such as General Patton as presented in Schaffer's film, *Patton* (1969). At its most characteristic, we can call Miller a reluctant hero.

Both *Ball of Fire* and *Saving Private Ryan* exemplify those qualities that are singular in the Hollywood film. In good measure they are responsible in a narrative sense for the great success of the Hollywood film. But there are other kinds of stories and to begin to understand those other choices, we now move on to the Independent Film.

NOTES

1. In every film industry in the world, except the United States, the film and television industries are directly and indirectly supported by national governments.
2. There were also other ramifications: the development of an industrial organization to maximize profit—a factory system of production to benefit from scale; a tendency towards vertical integration, including ownership of distribution and exhibition arms; and the most critical, the development of a star system to enhance the appeal of the product, the films themselves.
3. Ernst Lubitsch, William Wyler, Fritz Lang, Douglas Sirk—all of these directors immigrated to Hollywood from Germany. Fred Zinneman came from Austria. Alfred Hitchcock came from England. Billy Wilder, Julien Duvivier, and Max Ophuls came from France. Wilder, originally Austrian, and Ophuls, originally German, made films in France before immigrating to Hollywood.

7

THE INDEPENDENT
MODEL

If the primary influence on the Hollywood film is its relationship to the popular or entertainment-oriented arts, the primary influence on the independent film is its relationship to the fine arts: photography, painting, the literary novel, the short story, and the poem. In its evolution, the independent film has also been influenced by the documentary film and the experimental film. Its history proceeded in tandem with these two other metagenres. And like those genres, its goals were not to entertain, as was the case with the Hollywood film, but rather to educate like the documentary, or to explore an artistic personal issue as was the case of the experimental film.

Another point that needs to be made is that Hollywood has had its own independents: producers such as Samuel Goldwyn, who produced high-class entertainments; David O. Selznick, who out-MGM'ed his father-in-law Louis B. Mayer with the scale of his independent productions; and Stanley Kramer, who produced social issue features. But those producers worked inside the system, even though they were not part of the major studios (although they distributed their films through the distribution arm of MGM or Columbia or United Artists). The producer-directors I will discuss in this chapter are the real outsiders, those who make up the independent movement that was kick-started by John Cassavetes in the late 1950s. (There had been predecessors before that, including Howard Hughes, Orson Welles, and a number of the blacklisted writers, directors, and producers.) Just as filmmakers such as Welles and directors such as Joseph Losey and Jules Dassin viewed themselves as aligned with the goals of the European art film, so too the independents of today view themselves as a creative alternative to the Hollywood film. Whereas the independents such as John Cassavetes were viewed as marginal and for the most part inhabited the margin throughout their careers, the current career path for the independent filmmaker is quite different. John Sayles moves easily between the independent self-financed film and the Hollywood film. Martin Scorsese's independent film *Mean Streets* (1974) was a real breakthrough. Since then, studios have clamored to produce his work.[1] An independent film such as David Russell's *Spanking the Monkey* (1995) led, two films later, to the large-scale Warner Brothers production, *Three Kings* (1999). The careers of Ang Lee, Martha Coolidge, and Ed Burns have followed this trajectory.

In this sense, the independent film has become a talent pool for the Hollywood film. This is confirmed by the corporate relationship of New Line, Miramax, and Good Machine, production companies associated with the growth of independent film, to Hollywood's industrial organization.

Just as there are distinguishing characteristics to the Hollywood film, there are also particular qualities of character, structure, genre, and voice that distinguish the independent film. We turn now to those characteristics.

1. *Character.* In many ways the independent film is obsessed with character, but what must be said is that the approach to character could not differ more from the Hollywood film. If the Hollywood film's character is goal-directed and energetic in the pursuit of that goal, the main character in the independent film is a character who probably has no goal. Indeed, the main character in the independent film could best be characterized as an ambivalent character, ambiguous in his or her nature and marginal in his or her positioning relative to the community. Instead of moving through a dramatic arc with a goal-directed character, here we observe the main character. It isn't the intention of the writer-director to identify with the character; it will be all we can do to watch and to try to understand the character.

2. *Plot.* With regard to plot, an important feature of the Hollywood film, there is rarely a plot in the independent film. Structurally, the narrative is character-driven. Because the character is not goal-directed, the three-act structure often does not apply. Without a goal, resolution makes no sense, and so often a two-act structure is a more appropriate structural frame for the independent film.

3. *Genre.* In terms of genre, the most appropriate story form is the melodrama, since independent films so often have a realist base. Where the relationships are more stylized, the experimental narrative becomes the story form of choice for the independent film.[2]

4. *Voice.* The issue of voice is central in the independent film. The ideas of the writer-director, whether they are conveyed through the character or the structure, are more important than the character or the events of the screen story.

5. *Relationship with Society.* An issue of the day, an intellectual current, a sociopolitical position—all of these are far more prevalent in the independent film than is the case in the Hollywood film.

6. *The Unconventional Point of View.* If the Hollywood film is about relating to an audience through a set of narrative conventions, the independent film often defines itself by challenging or breaking those very conventions. The more unorthodox the approach, the greater the sense of independence. Breaking the rules is one of the rules of making an independent film.

THE CENTRALITY OF CHARACTER: THE CASE OF
JOHN CASSAVETES—*HUSBANDS* AND *OPENING NIGHT*

John Cassavetes had already produced a number of independent films, including *Shadows* (1958) and *Faces* (1967), when he had the opportunity to make a studio-financed film called *Husbands* (1970). Although financed by Columbia, *Husbands* is actually the quintessential independent film, even though its actors Peter Falk, Ben Gazzara, and Cassavetes himself, worked extensively in the mainstream industry as actors.

Husbands is quintessential independent film storytelling in the sense that it has almost no plot and that it is primarily character-driven. It is typical as well in dealing with three characters, one of whom drives the first half of the story, and another who becomes the focus of the second half of the story.

Three men—Harry (Ben Gazzara), Archie (Peter Falk), and Gus (John Cassavetes)—friends and neighbors in the suburbs of New York, react to a critical event. A close friend dies. The balance of the film is their attempt to cope with the loss. They get drunk, they party, they avoid home and work, and halfway through the narrative Harry, whose marriage is falling apart, decides to run off to London. The others join him but do so for only a day or two. They return home while Harry remains in London.

This narrative summary does nothing to capture the camaraderie, the immaturity, the fear, the humor, or the cruelty of their relationships, or of the individual manner of each man to attempt to deal with his mortality. Feeling and avoiding feeling is the throughline of their response to loss. Women clearly threaten their bond, and so wives and lovers are played with, feared, and demonized. These are men as little boys. This view is periodically broken by seeing two of the men at work. Gus is a dentist, and Harry is a creative director in advertising. In both cases, their work does not stop their slide into emotional panic.

Cassavetes calls the film "A comedy about life, death, and freedom." This is a very painful comedy. In its obsession with character, *Husbands* illustrates one aspect of the independent film. We are watching behavior, observing rather than being invited to identify with any of these men. For a long time we don't even understand them. We are kept outside, at arm's length, as they keep feeling pain.

In terms of structure, we do join the story at a critical moment: the death of a friend. But after that point, we only have sequences—the wake, the funeral, its aftermath, work, the decision to go to London, and return. And we do have a main character, Harry, whose marriage and life are clearly in crisis. But none of the ancillary relationships, with friends, family, fellow workers, or the women they pick up in London, bring the story to resolution for Harry either. Without a goal, resolution is not possible—unless we consider not accepting mortality to be the goal. And so we spend time with Harry, Archie, and Gus. But we don't really understand them. Just as Cassavetes calls them husbands, a role rather than an identity, they don't become more than that because they undergo no transformation here.

Cassavetes is as interested in the behavior of women under stress as he is in the behavior of men. In *Opening Night* (1977) the stressor is the pressure of performance. A woman closer to the end of her career than the beginning is hired for a role. Myrtle Gordon (Gena Rowlands) has had an esteemed career. But just as the death of a friend shakes up the sense of mortality in the three men in *Husbands*, the new role triggers the actress' anxiety about her mortality as an actor. The narrative takes us up to opening night, and the question is whether Myrtle will be able to go on. Just as Gus in *Husbands* returns to be "a husband" at the conclusion of *Husbands,* the main character is very much "the actress" at the end of *Opening Night.* It's as if the dramatic arc or each of these films is the struggle between life and death in each of these characters, and in the end the character returns to the habitual impulse of what she knows—to act. Her life remains a mess, but she does make it through this crisis of confidence. Habitual implies not triumph (as in the Hollywood film) but rather coping with the crisis. More accurately, the character finds herself clinging to life.

What marks these films as so very different from the Hollywood film is that these characters readily make fools of themselves. They expose themselves to us—it's as if the film is one long private embarrassing moment. There is enormous pain in these films, which is again very different from the Hollywood film. In a sense, they are emotional "documentaries" about the lives of the characters.

I should add that *Opening Night* has a modest plot—the putting on of the play. For comparison, Woody Allen's *Bullets Over Broadway* (1994) provides a good example of a Hollywood film dealing with a similar topic; Allen's film has a much bigger plot, and his characters are positioned differently—they have goals.

POLITICS AND THE INDEPENDENT FILM I:
THE CASE OF *THE BALLAD OF LITTLE JO*

Maggie Greenwald's *The Ballad of Little Jo* (1992) is based on a true story of a woman who pretended to be a man in order to live in a man's world—the West. Jo is a classic melodrama main character, and at its core, *The Ballad of Little Jo* is a classic melodrama. It is also a feminist treatment of the West, and from a feminist perspective, the West is a threatening environment for women. The first issue for Greenwald is to sidestep the plot—the western dimensions of the narrative. The western classically has to do with civilization (e.g., bankers and railway men) who are materially encroaching on the rights of the primitive—the western hero. This struggle is present in *The Ballad of Little Jo* for example, in the form of land-hungry cattle company from the East. There is violence—the killings of immigrants who try to settle on the land coveted by the cattle company. Jo is threatened by the cattle company. But instead of a ritualized showdown with the cattle company, the gunfight, Greenwald presents such struggles not as battles of titans but rather as skirmishes, and the main character, having defended herself, is bothered no longer.

The western plot, then, is not treated as it would be in Hollywood film. Here plot is a matter of fact rather than ritual action. Nothing should distract us from the primary struggle—a woman pretending to be a man in order to survive in a man's world. Far more critical are the issues of her own femininity and her sexuality, which are questioned and challenged by her employer, Frank Badger, who has employed her as a sheep herder; by Percy, whom she rents a room from; and by the Chinese cook she rescues from hanging. These relationships, by their nature, are far more accepting given that she is perceived to be a man by Badger and recognized as a woman by the Chinese cook, in contrast with the relationship with her father and her lover back East. In the East, they viewed her as a woman in the most rigid sense, too rigid for her expansive spirit. She needed the West, a frontier, to flourish as a person. The implication is that women cannot be constrained by roles; they need a "frontier" to actualize themselves. This is the feminist voice of Greenwald, who uses the narrative to convey the passion of her ideas.

POLITICS AND THE INDEPENDENT FILM II:
THE CASE OF *SLAM*

Slam (1998) by Marc Levin tells the story of a young black man, Ray Joshua. As in *The Ballad of Little Jo*, *Slam* has a plot—a young man goes to jail when the dealer he buys marijuana from is shot in his presence. He is almost immediately arrested for possession. As he puts it later to a lawyer, he's not a dealer, he's just been trying to survive in Washington, D.C. The plot of the gangster film has a rise and fall shape. Levin positions Ray to be a victim of his circumstances. This is the politics of being young and black in D.C. His positioning, then, is as a victim of society. The gangster genre leads us to anticipate a tale of the creation of a gangster via the jail experience. But this isn't what we get. Ray is neither violent nor angry; he is a man with a different goal. He is an aspiring rapper, and so *Slam* becomes a study in an alternative character who counters our expectations. Ray's energy and feeling is channeled into his poetry.

As in the case of *The Ballad of Little Jo*, the political position of the oppressed person is transformed from the mainstream model to another model. In a sense, both relationships and an inner self save Ray. *Slam* is the celebration of a character who is saved by his art. Consequently, Ray's behavior toward others, his peers as well as the art teacher with whom he becomes involved, is channeled into his poetry. Instead of impulsivity Ray projects calm; instead of volatility, Ray radiates inner peace; and instead of hate, Ray is a man capable of love. This is the political dimension of the narrative. And as in the case of *The Ballad of Little Jo*, *Slam* uses character and behavior to explore a narrative purpose that is socio-political in the contemporary sense. Both *The Ballad of Little Jo* and *Slam* transform a contemporary marginal character into an alternative—an actualized person; actualized on their own terms rather than those terms that prevail in the contemporary society.

POLITICS AND THE INDEPENDENT FILM III:
THE CASE OF *BOYS DON'T CRY*

Kimberly Peirce's *Boys Don't Cry* (1998) is also based on an actual story. A twenty-year-old girl, Teena Brandon, changed her name to Brandon Teena, dressed and passed as a male, developed a relationship with a woman, and became close to her family. But when the girl's brother found out the truth, he raped Brandon Teena and, together with a friend, killed her.

Of the three stories discussed here, *Boys Don't Cry* has the greatest amount of plot—the deception and its consequences—the rape and murder of Brandon Teena. As in classic melodrama, the plot works against the character's goal: to pass. In this sense, the structure of *Boys Don't Cry* is closest to the Hollywood film. However, the goal of the writer and director is to study the question of sexual identity—both its emotional and its physical sides. Brandon Teena is not a character whose deceptive act justifies her murder, and here lies the political layer of the film. Just as the destruction of the protagonist is at the heart of the political layer of John Sayles' *Matewan* (1987), the death of Brandon Teena pushes the audience to deliberate on gender, homophobia, and family violence. The fact that Brandon Teena could be accused at most of lying about who she is, goes to the heart of the power of the screen story. Her naïve nature, particularly in light of the character of the two young men who become her killers, explores and reveals the issue of the power struggle between men and women—in relationships, in communities, and in society. In the fate of Brandon Teena is Peirce's political message, and in a sense it's as powerful as the message of the oppressed character of Ray in *Slam* and of Jo (Josephine) in *The Ballad of Little Jo*, that characters deserve the possibility to actualize themselves, whether they are men or women, black or white, heterosexual or homosexual.

THE EXPERIMENTAL NARRATIVE I:
THE CASE OF *THE DRAUGHTSMAN'S CONTRACT*

The experimental narrative as a genre occupies an important position in independent film. Writer-directors such as Luis Buñuel, Robert Bresson, Miklos Jansco, Sally Potter, Terence Davies, and Atom Egoyan have each embraced the genre in order to give voice to their screen stories. The experimental narrative has particular characteristics. Character is not very important. In terms of structure, a nonlinear structure is often attractive, to obscure either plot or the character layer or both. The genre does have a unique ritualistic quality. Repetitions of scenes or actions not only formalize the narrative, they also give clues to its meaning. There is a strong linkage of the genre to other arts—painting, photography, and architecture—and there is an intellectual conceit that drives the linkage between the structure and meaning. Finally, the voice of the writer-director is central. The ritualized tone of the narrative distances us from character and structure but clearly directs us to the voice of the writer-director.

Peter Greenaway's *The Draughtsman's Contract* (1982), which is set in late-seventeenth-century England, can be viewed in a number of ways: as a comedy of manners criticizing upper-class hypocrisy; as a story about art and artists; and as a murder mystery. An artist, Mr. Neville, is contracted by Mrs. Herbert, the wife of a rich but indifferent husband, to sketch twelve landscapes of an estate. The payment will be money, board, and pleasuring Mrs. Herbert while her husband is away. Halfway through the sketches, the mistress's daughter, Mrs. Talmann, offers an interpretation of the sketches: they are clues to a murder, of the lord of the manor, her father, as well as to her own contract—her pleasuring. First, the mother and now Mr. Neville is obliged to oblige the daughter. The balance of the sketches focuses on the evidence of Mrs. Herbert's own adultery. At the end of the contract, the lord of the manor is found dead in the moat around the manor. Quickly the agendas of all the participants are laid bare: a suitor of Mrs. Herbert, the man who is the notary who recorded the contracts, Mr. Noyes, promotes the sale of the damning sketches; Mrs. Herbert celebrates her freedom; Mrs. Talmann acknowledges sexually using the artist to create an heir to the estate; and all the players point toward the artist as the expendable witness and the perfect scapegoat. They kill him and burn the evidence, his sketches.

This summary can't do justice to the core of the narrative or the powerful voice of Greenaway. The artist as presented by Greenaway is a commodity, a commodity that is about producing pleasure—visual pleasure, aural and oral pleasure, and sexual pleasure. He's like a machine that produces artifacts, sketches, but he also lives for the self. Not that the other characters are not self-directed, but they can't be obvious about their desires; they have to be concerned with appearances, their standing. They have something to hide; in Greenaway's view, the baseness that lies beneath their civil surfaces. Because the painter paints what he sees, surfaces, these people feel exposed by him. Thus he is a dangerous man, at least to them, and they must destroy both the evidence, the sketches, and the acute observer, the artist.

The main character as presented by Greenaway is not very sympathetic. Mr. Neville is rude, arrogant, and blunt. His passion seems physical and not terribly appealing. We do see the vulnerability of Mrs. Herbert, but we don't really understand her. Is she simply a rich woman who hates her husband all the more because she has no legal rights, such as inheritance, in the British system? We are not given a clear sense of her. Mrs. Talmann, however, is clearly more scheming to produce an heir when Mr. Talmann cannot make her pregnant. We do get a sense from both women that they resent the proprietary limits of their gender. The consequent manipulation of others with their sexuality, their bodies becomes all the more understandable under these circumstances. Control of their bodies is the only control they have in their lives, even though the estate came to the lord of the manor through the woman's side of the family. In this sense the artist and the women are victims of the existing power structure—the male title to property and inheritance. But if this were all there was to Greenaway's voice the narrative would not be as powerful as it is.

Greenaway is very interested in human action and the environment that motivates action. He sexualizes the interactions between characters, and makes sexuality and violence the undercurrents of his narrative. The creation of a tone that intensifies the meaning of the narrative is his real goal—creating the voice of Greenaway. Just as Buñuel infuses his work with subtextual "unconscious" feelings about sexuality and violence, so too does Greenaway. This is the emotional intent behind the highly intellectualized narrative Greenaway constructs.

THE EXPERIMENTAL NARRATIVE II: THE CASE OF
THE COOK, THE THIEF, HIS WIFE AND HER LOVER

Greenaway carries on this exploration of sexuality and violence in his production *The Cook, the Thief, His Wife and Her Lover* (1990). The title describes the four principal characters in the narrative. The setting is a restaurant that is presented as a temple to cooking and eating. The kitchen is a world unto itself—sensual and violent. The cook, Richard, is all seeing and knowing in his world. The owner of the restaurant is Albert, the thief, who eats there regularly with his wife, Georgina. Georgina is frustrated and abused in this marriage. She sees another customer Michael, who appeals to her, and they begin an affair first in the bathroom of the restaurant, then later, to evade her husband, they move to a sheltered area in the kitchen. The majority of the narrative takes place in the restaurant. The turning point is the discovery by Albert that his wife is carrying on an affair. Although Richard helps the lovers escape, Albert finds Michael and kills him brutally. To avenge the loss, Georgina proposes that Michael be cooked by Richard and served to Albert. She forces Albert to be a cannibal and eat Michael—then she kills the cannibal.

As in *The Draughtsman's Contract*, a narrative summary does not do justice to the experience of the screen story. Greenaway ritualizes eating, sex, and even killing; each sensual desire is given its own architecture. But in the end it all comes down to eating. It's as if the eating of a meal is akin to a life cycle. It is also a ritual. Greenaway uses eating as a metaphor for the full range of human activity. The fact that Michael's body is found with his orifices stuffed with books relates to violence and violation, but also to his profession as a bookseller and to his passion for books. We always see him reading (and eating) in the restaurant.

This prism, eating, is the currency for Albert's violence as well, and also for Richard's good will toward Georgina. In a sense, Greenaway has constructed the narrative, whatever occurs, as a series of meals. He structurally presents the narrative with scene/title cards that list the day of the action as a menu for the day. So food becomes as important as character and structure in conveying the voice of the writer-director. Whether he is celebrating the decadence of the material world or condemning that decadence—or both—Greenaway is not inviting us into a relationship with these four characters. They are as metaphorical as were the characters in *The Draughtsman's Contract*. They are used to articulate Greenaway's notions about the sensual world and the material world. They coexist in conflict with one another, and the result of that conflict is a celebration of the primacy of the sensual over the cerebral.

BREAKING THE RULES

A reaction against convention is a primary characteristic of the independent film. If we use the principal qualities of the Hollywood film as a baseline, we can see precisely how those rules are broken in the independent film. In terms of character, this means creating characters who are the opposite of the goal-directed character. It may also mean the absence of a clear single main character. In terms of structure, the choices are several. Instead of using the traditional three-act structure, the independent filmmaker may choose to drop the act of resolution. He or she may also choose to sidestep plot, or to use it differently than it is used in the Hollywood film, such as the way the character layer is used. In a Hollywood film, two opposing relationships would be explored. A less conventional approach is to explore a single relationship or a series of relationships.

In terms of genre, a particular motif may be challenged, or genres may be mixed in order to challenge expectations and to alter the sense of the story. Breaking the rules means going against mainstream expectations. We now turn to three examples of how filmmakers have gone against mainstream expectations.

BREAKING THE RULES I:
THE CASE OF *SHE'S GOTTA HAVE IT*

Spike Lee's *She's Gotta Have It* (1987) is a melodrama in which a woman, Nola Darling, considers her relationship choices. She is vivacious and involved with three lovers. Which will she choose, or to reframe the question, will she choose at all? Lee presents Nola as the principal narrator of her narrative. But the presentation is not as a reliable narrator. Were she reliable, the tone of the narrative would be realistic and emotional, and it would encourage our identification with Nola. This is not what happens. In the end we expect Nola to make her choice, but instead she declares herself open to carrying on without a commitment or a choice. The open-ended declaration leaves us in a unresolved position. Is Nola being provocative and simply challenging our expectations, or is she acting as a man would if she were a man? Whatever the explanation, she is acting in an unpredictable and unforeseen manner. The open ending leaves us unresolved and unsettled. This twist is the first break with the rules. The ending is ironic and distancing as opposed to closed. The ending also shows how Spike Lee has chosen a two-act structure for *She's Gotta Have It*. There is no resolution and so we are left awaiting closure.

I would also suggest that Spike Lee's decision to make Nola an unreliable narrator also contributes to the unsettled quality we are left with in our relationship with Nola. Up until the point of the ending, what we are anticipating is a relationship story of a young person, in this case a woman who is considering the question, which of these three men should I choose? The direction of inquiry, incident, and voice implies that in the end the character will make the choice. The fact that she not only doesn't choose, but also declares her indifference to the whole issue of choosing, throws into question the attitudes and information she has shared with us up to this point. In part this can be explained by saying she changed her mind, or she's young, or she is hurt by the fact that the relationship with one of the lovers, Jamie, didn't work, and she's reacting to that hurt. We don't know. Or the narrative may be implying that Nola simply loves the romantic pursuit, as opposed to the actuality of a relationship, and that she has been disingenuous with us—as she has been with the lovers. Again, we are left in doubt about Nola's intentions.

The two-act structure and the lack of resolution, which together with the unreliable narrator distance us from the character of Nola, makes *She's Gotta Have It* a melodrama with an ironic tone. All four of these narrative strategies challenge our genre expectations and alter our experience of the narrative.

BREAKING THE RULES II:
THE CASE OF *MEAN STREETS*

If *She's Gotta Have It* is a two-act melodrama, *Mean Streets* (1973) is a one-act melodrama. As in *She's Gotta Have It*, there is a simple situation that is the focus of the screen story in *Mean Streets*. A group of four petty criminals who are young are dealing with life issues—friendship, loyalty, self-image, and the powerful influence of each other in each of their lives. None is adult, but the impulse to act as if they are adult is powerful. The critical moment when we join the story is the nonpayment of a debt by one of them, Johnny Boy, to another, Michael. The go-between is Charlie, whose overdeveloped sense of responsibility puts him in the middle. The story ends when Charlie is shot by Michael. He has been trying to help Johnny Boy flee. Scorsese focuses on the behavior of these four young men, on the environment they inhabit, and on their inability to reconcile loyalty and responsibility on one side and the need to prove oneself on the other. The result is the inability to survive on these mean streets.

Scorsese breaks the rules of the mainstream film by focusing not on one character but rather four characters. He also subverts the issue of a goal by making it a very short-term goal. These characters want to get through the next moment, to survive, rather than to challenge the power structure—the goal we expect in melodrama. Although *Mean Streets* is not presented as film noir, these characters are given the goal of the noir character: to be saved by entering a relationship. These characters are already in relationships. Only Charlie develops a new relationship, with Teresa, and it is clear that he cannot be saved by this relationship. So none of these characters, with the exception of Michael (who wants to move up in the mob), has a goal as clear as that of a classic melodrama's main character.

The most challenging break with the rules, however, is the one-act structure of *Mean Streets*. Without any turning points we are left with an intense, relentless experience of four characters in a desperate, dangerous situation. Their natures do not help them emerge from the situation; rather, their characters make the outcome of murder a stronger possibility. Each character seems trapped in a predetermined destiny. The narrative plays out this predetermined destiny precluding the conventional choice a character must make in the three-act structured screen story.

BREAKING THE RULES III:
THE CASE OF *THE NASTY GIRL*

Michael Verhoeven's *The Nasty Girl* (1985) challenges the rules on multiple levels of character, structure, and form. *The Nasty Girl* is the story of a young woman who, in her attempt to prove her goodwill toward her hometown, decides to enter a writing contest. Her subject will be "How My Hometown Exhibited Model Behavior during the Third Reich." She enters believing that such behavior was exemplified by a martyred priest who stood up against the Nazis. What she discovers is that the town not only cooperated with the Nazis, but that its leading theologians were anti-Semitic, and that the leading industrialists were also pro-Nazi.

This narrative could have been presented as a documentary (it is based on a true story) or as a melodrama, but Verhoeven instead chooses to present the story as a hyperdrama, a moral tale about disillusionment with the adult version of reality. Consequently Sonya, the main character, becomes the narrator. We meet her as an adult who then tells us her life story. The narration is filled with irony. She narrates from an adult present, but she uses her innocent eyes to do so. Consequently, she is not an unreliable narrator so much as she is the innocent guide to a narrative about her own loss of innocence.

Verhoeven begins to challenge the rules in his tonal shifts. He uses irony increasingly as we move through the narrative. He also includes documentary or realistic scenes that are followed by scenes of great exaggeration. These sudden shifts undermine our developing emotional link to Sonya and move us toward Verhoeven's views on the events that happen to Sonya.

Verhoeven also uses repetition to make a point. He doesn't talk about a generation gap, but he makes the point about the gap by using Sonya's brother as a reference point. Sonya is always the agreeable child aiming to please her parents. But as we move through events and time, the brother brings home girls to the family who increasingly would be unacceptable to this white, Catholic, conservative family. Again, irony makes the point about family and community hypocrisy, and contributes to the enduring central theme—the loss of innocence that the main character experiences as she gets older and more informed.

Verhoeven also has the narrator/main character break the illusion of believability when she addresses us, the audience, directly. By moving between a dramatic relationship (observing the main character) and a documentary-journalistic relationship (when she addresses us as narrator), Verhoeven breaks the emotional identification that drama can create. This ironic intervention again pushes us toward Verhoeven's voice and away from Sonya as our link to the narrative. Here Verhoeven uses his voice together with irony of character and structure to violate expectations and to create a different kind of narrative experience for the audience.

The Independent Model, the subject of this chapter, is an ideal transition between the Hollywood film and the European and Asian films. We now turn to those European and Asian films in the next chapter, the National Model.

NOTES

1. *The Last Temptation of Christ* was produced independently in the 1980s, but this was because its controversial approach to the story of Christ stirred up opposition in religious circles.
2. See Chapter 15, "The Experimental Drama," in P. Cooper and K. Dancyger's *Writing the Short Film*, Second Edition (Focal Press, 1999).

8

THE NATIONAL MODEL

The most obvious statement I can begin this chapter with is that foreign films, whether they originate in Europe, Asia, Latin America, or Africa have both similarities and differences in comparison to the Hollywood film.[1] Every national cinema exhibits the impulse to appeal to the mainstream (the goal of entertainment), as well as a set of artistic goals (parallel to those of the independent film), all in the context of the particulars of the culture in which the films are made. But this is only a starting point to begin to understand why and how the national models addressed in this chapter differ from the Hollywood film. First, the why of it.

In examining the history of film narrative, one is struck by how quickly film was embraced as an art, particularly in Europe. In the 1920s, in the U.S.S.R., Sergei Eisenstein strove to relate the narrative potential of the new medium to the literature of Dickens, and its formal potential in relation to the form of the Haiku poem.[2] In the same period, in Paris, the Spaniard, Luis Buñuel, was taken up with the influence of the Surrealist painters and its intellectual currency, the ideas of psychoanalysis. In 1930s France, Jean Renoir affiliated his film work in its origins and in its structure to the great novelists of the nineteenth century and of his own day. A decade later, Jean Cocteau synthesized ideas about painting, poetry, and literature in his work. Fritz Lang, in Germany during the Weimar period (1920–1933), explored ideas about architecture, music, and theater (particularly the work of Max Reinhardt) in his work.

The link between the arts and film was far more powerful in Europe than it was in Hollywood. In part this is cultural, but what also must be acknowledged is that film was accepted as art at a very early stage in Europe. In Hollywood, on the other hand, the perception of film as only a form of popular entertainment rather than art extended well into the 1970s.[3]

Another notable phenomenon of the European film was the synergistic impulse toward artistic movements. These creative explosions were instigated both from above, as in the case of the government support for the Russian revolutionary filmmakers in the 1920s (Eisenstein, Pudovkin, Vertov, and Dovschenko), and from below, as in the development of the French new wave out of a group of young film critics (Truffaut, Godard, Rohmer, and Chabrol). Other important film movements included the German expressionists in the 1920s (Murnau, Lang, Pabst, Dupont). Here the influence of theater and design were important.

The Italian neorealist cinema of the post-World War II period was also very influential. Here politics plays a role. The affiliation of the mainstream film industry with the political power of the Fascist government motivated this movement to be different. Its reactive character accounts for its social humanism and its political tendency away from elitism and fascism.

Technology, politics, and the desire for a revolution from below fueled the British direct cinema filmmakers (Reisz, Richardson, Anderson) to move from documentary and virtually to dominate British film of the 1960s. Like Truffaut and Chabrol, Lindsay Anderson was a film critic.

Of course there are other movements that are notable: the Czech new wave of the 1960s; the new German film of the 1970s; the Kung Fu films of Hong Kong; and the new wave of Brazilian films in the 1960s. What is critical about all of these important and influential movements is that they were synergistic and that they propelled film narrative forward in very startling ways. I should add that other cinemas were important but not necessarily characterized by the same short-term explosion. Instead, they were stimulated by other factors: film training in the 1950s in Poland; a sophisticated industrial structure in India and Japan; and a linkage to the literary arts in Denmark (the work of Carl Dryer) and in Sweden (the work of Ingmar Bergman).

Another point of difference should be made here. In Europe particularly there is a connection between the theory and the practice of film narrative. Eisenstein wrote about and made films in accord with those theoretical ideas, as did Pudovkin and Vertov. In France, the ideas of André Bazin influenced Truffaut and other new wave filmmakers to explore and experiment with particular narrative strategies. This impulse to think about film narrative and to experiment with those ideas gave the work an exciting quality that was singularly absent from the Hollywood film. It is true that the Hollywood film was a commercial enterprise and that European film was for the most part produced in the context of publicly subsidized filmmaking. Nevertheless, because of this mix of theory and practice mix, European film and other national cinemas—China, Taiwan, Iran, Hungary—have seemed to mix entertainment values with artistic notions far more readily than the Hollywood film. Because of this mix, we will explore the national model in this chapter.

Although every national cinema has a wide band of filmmaking within its borders, we will focus in this chapter on only a few characteristics within the national film culture. In a sense, I will use a shaping idea to explore each of the sections on national models. Consequently, the sections will be in no way comprehensive. I offer them instead, to provide useful alternative models to the Hollywood film.

One additional comment might be helpful. I will focus on the feature film, the broadest form of film narrative that has moved around the world. This is not meant to diminish in any way the achievements in documentary in France, Canada, and the United Kingdom, nor is it meant to diminish developments in animation in the Netherlands, Japan, and the United Kingdom.

Now we move on to our exploration of the National models.

THE ARTS AND THEIR INFLUENCE: THE CASE OF ITALY

There are many possible approaches to Italian film, such as their aggressive politics and their aggressive aesthetics. But the approach that I will take is to look at three filmmakers and the influence of particular arts on their work.

Although Luchino Visconti adapted novels by Alberto Lattuada, James Cain, Thomas Mann, and Albert Camus in his films, his approach to the screen story was always influenced primarily by his work in opera. As a result, his approach to narrative events and to character was extreme.

Thematically, his most frequently recurring topic is the destructiveness of passion. In *Ossessione* (1942), it is the love of a drifter for a married woman. In *Senso* (1954), it is the love of a younger man for an older woman. In *Sandra* (1966), it is the love of a brother for his sister. In *The Innocent* (1982), it is the obsession of a married man for his mistress, and later for his wife. All of these stories follow the dramatic arc of the operas *Carmen* and *La Traviata*. The course of a doomed love shapes the dramatic arc.

Another theme that recurs in Visconti's work is the corruption of power. This is the theme of his exploration of Nazism in *The Damned* (1968). Here the Aschenbach family, who are German industrialists, is the microcosm for his exploration. As Nazi power grows, the outrageous acts by one member of the family against another increase.

A third theme that Visconti explores is mortality. The changing of the guard is the theme in *The Leopard* (1962). Possessing beauty in another as a stratagem to postpone the moment of physical and emotional collapse and of death is the subject of *Death in Venice* (1972). Dealing with the imminence of death is also the subject of his last film, *Conversation Piece* (1984). Visconti's intense approach to these characters and their feeling states approximates the operatic extremes of passion and loss. Impossible love, forbidden love, the inability to live without love, all these themes that Visconti is attracted to are more often found in opera, but they are very much present in his films.

In the case of Federico Fellini, there are a variety of influences: the melodramas of Roberto Rossellini; the persona-driven political comedies of Charlie Chaplin; and above all, the circus. For Fellini, the circus exhibits certain qualities that he introduces into his narratives: life as a show; the energy and the sudden change of events or programs; the sense of absurdity; the figures of the clown, the dancer, and the grotesque—all of these elements are experiential qualities that Fellini borrowed from his love of the circus and interjected into his films.

Fellini, for example, tells a story of a young woman, Wanda, enamored with a newspaper cartoon character in *The White Sheik* (1952). She decides to meet the actor, Fernando Rivoli, who plays the White Sheik when she visits Rome where she has traveled for her honeymoon. Her new husband, Ivan, is the opposite of the White Sheik. He is practical, and the Sheik is daring and romantic. The narrative is about how fantasy sometimes gets people in trouble. But this situation comedy is treated very gently, and the characters are allowed to display their foolishness, lose their dignity, and nevertheless change according to the demands of the situation and their characters. These rapid shifts are not realistic, but rather how we must change our mood for the different acts in a circus. Here the life of Wanda, her troubles, and her marriage are treated as if the different situations were different acts in an afternoon at the circus. Fellini follows exactly the same narrative rhythm in his *La Dolce Vita* (1960).

In *8½* (1962), a film about a famous film director who is having a personal and a professional crisis, Fellini conceptualizes these crises around the production of his latest film production. He positions the point of view as that of the ringmaster. His main character, the director Guido, orchestrates a series of scenes, real and imagined, as if they were circus acts. There are comedic acts; there are frightening acts; and there are those in between. These scenes are again presented narratively almost as stand-alone acts. They have their own internal logic, and their own differing energies, just as circus acts do.

A final element of Fellini's films that has been much commented upon is his penchant for the grotesque. This tendency recurs sporadically in his early work, but it is fully exploited in a film such as Fellini's *Satyricon* (1969). Set in ancient Rome, the film follows the journey of two young men searching for something lost—a lover, a slave. But the journey takes them to a barbaric place where they lose the one thing they had—their friendship with each other. In other words, they lose all but their physical selves. Along their journey, every degradation one might imagine is visited upon them. Freaks of nature and human mutations have always gone to the heart of the fear and attraction of grotesques at the circus. All those fears and attractions are referred to in *Satyricon*.

There are numerous other directors we could refer to in relation to the arts, but perhaps it is most fitting to refer to Michelangelo Antonioni. His work is philosophically influenced by the existentialist Camus, but his aesthetic reference point is to postmodern architecture, to its powerful alienating influence on behavior. Whether it is the alienation of a young woman from the sterile moneyed world in which she lives in *L'Eclisse* (*Eclipse* [1962]), or the imposition of the psychic pressure of the industrial landscape on a marriage in *Red Desert* (1964), or the vacuous fame of the photograph in *Blow-Up* (1966), or the incompatible clash of the modern and the ancient in *The Passenger* (1975)—in every case the main character is defeated by his or her environment. It's as if modern architecture and modern thought imprison the character, and there is no exit.

THE ART OF POSSIBILITY: THE CASE OF FRANCE

Although there is a powerful classical impulse in France, as represented by a film such as Claude Berri's *Lucie Ambrac* (1999) or Claude Lelouche's *Les Miserables* (1995), there is also an impulse to what is possible in the medium—the impulse to push, pull, and challenge the medium. It is this impulse that we address in this notation on French film.

What is possible in the thriller form? This is the question Claude Chabrol poses in his work over the course of a forty-year career. He has often been compared to Hitchcock, but it would be a mistake simply to consider his work and the few thrillers of Truffaut (*The Bride Wore Black* [1967]) as an homage to Hitchcock. Instead, I think it's more useful to frame the discussion in terms of the thriller as a form that attracts Chabrol, and then as a form he explores in order to discover what is possible in the form.

The thriller is a plot-driven genre comprised, in a sense, of a chase. The main characters are ordinary people caught in extraordinary circumstances. They may not understand the why of it, but they must gain that understanding in order to halt the relentless antagonist from destroying them. They are victorious first in understanding and then in overcoming the antagonist. They are reluctant heroes, realistic but very human heroes, in the end.

Chabrol plays with all the elements of the genre, such as the innocence of the main character and the nature of the antagonist. The plot layer may be modified by a character layer, and the dramatic arc may not lead to a heroic conclusion. All the elements are up for grabs. He does, however, maintain the realist tone we expect in the thriller.

For example, in his *La Femme Infidele* (1969) the main character is a husband, Charles, who suspects his wife, Helene, of infidelity. At the end of Act I, he finds out it's not only jealousy; she is in fact having an affair. Charles then has to decide what to do, but this isn't so easy. He loves his wife. As he struggles with the problem he decides to see his adversary, Victor, but when he does he is so overcome with emotion that he kills Victor. All that's left to find out is if he gets away with it. He doesn't; the story ends with his arrest. But we understand Charles. He is a man in love caught by his pride in his capacity for self-control when, of course, he can't control himself in the end. In this case, Chabrol is challenging our propensity for identifying with the main character in the thriller. How do we feel about caring about a murderer?

In *Le Boucher* (1970) he again invites us to care about a murderer, this time the antagonist. And rather than have the antagonist chase the protagonist, he has him courting the main character. The main character is a schoolteacher, Helene, the headmistress of the school in a small provincial town. The plot is that there is a serial killer killing women. We learn the local butcher, Popaul, is an angry guy and that, being good with the knife, he is the likely killer. By the end of Act II Helene knows this as well. Nevertheless, she continues her courtship with Popaul. In the end Popaul can't bring himself to kill her. He loves her, and he ends up killing himself. In this case a sympathetic antagonist and a powerful character layer replace the expected plot. These are Chabrol's challenges to our expectations for the thriller in *Le Boucher*.

In *L'enfer* (1994) Chabrol explores a marriage. Again the main character, Paul, is an unsympathetic, possessive husband. But in this case, the wife, Nelly, is faithful. The fear that Nelly isn't being faithful is all in the husband's imagination. But his paranoia becomes the plot, and the tension derives from what will happen when his possessiveness turns to violence. Will the wife survive? By making Paul's emotional state and his descent into "hell" the plot, Chabrol challenges our usual expectation of plot—instead of the physical world, he takes us into the inner world of the main character, and instead of physical violence, he uses emotional violence. *L'enfer* is a difficult, intense narrative that in many ways gives its audience no relief. The realism of the thriller is maintained, but Chabrol has stretched our sense of the genre. He does so without resorting to the manifest violence of Polanski's *Repulsion* (1965), for example, which moves beyond the thriller and into the horror story. By maintaining the orthodox story frame of the thriller, Chabrol continues expanding what is possible in the thriller.

In the case of Eric Rohmer, his interest is principally in the comedy and in romance. His narratives are not outright situation comedies like Josiane Balasko's *French Twist* (1995), nor are they outright melodramas like Erick Zoncka's *The Dreamlife of Angels* (1998). Although the situation comedy and the melodrama are flip sides of one another, Rohmer has chosen to move between them. His subject is the chase of a man after a woman, or the reverse. His subject is also the state of being chaste, or how one's moral stance (the cerebral) is at war with the senses (the physical). Since he uses irony and interjects his voice into these narratives, Rohmer allows us to side with either the pursuer or the pursued, or with neither. The result stretches our experience of the romantic comedy and creates something about the time, the place, the age, and the society. The sum in Rohmer's work is far greater than the narrative parts.

In *Claire's Knee* (1969), which one of the films in the series he calls "The Moral Tales," an older man is obsessed with a teenager's knee. Although Jerome is engaged to Aurora, a beautiful, age-appropriate woman, Claire triggers something in him—the need for yet another conquest. If he could only touch her knee, he would feel that he has made that conquest. But he has competition—her young beau, Vincent. Rohmer creates the requisite tension with the two triangles: Jerome-Claire-Aurora, and Jerome-Claire-Vincent. The absurdity of the goal, to touch Claire's knee, ironically points out the power of the cerebral to try to fool the senses.

In Rohmer's *L'ami de Mon Amie* (*Boyfriends and Girlfriends*) (1988) the couplings are age-appropriate for the main characters are young adults. But here the temperaments of two young women couldn't be more opposite. Blanche is shy while Lea is exceedingly outgoing. Lea has a boyfriend, Fabien, and through Lea and Fabien, Blanche comes into contact with Alexandre, a handsome womanizer. Naturally, Blanche wants what is inaccessible and impossible. These four characters and their inappropriate love choices (opposites attract) form the core of the narrative. There will be two dramatic triangles: Lea-Fabien-Alexandre, and Blanche-Fabien-Alexandre. In each triangle the women are inevitably drawn to the inappropriate choice first and gradually to the more appropriate choice. By default, Blanche and Lea end up with the more appropriate choice: Fabien with Blanche and Alexandre with Lea.

L'ami de Mon Amie is from a series Rohmer has called "Comedies and Proverbs." The subtitle tells us the genre—comedy. It also implies Rohmer's voice. He is playing with human nature, and with the attraction of opposites. He is also exploring whether or not this attraction is false, since it is those who are most similar who get together in the end: the two insincere narcissists and the two serious outdoors types. In this film, Rohmer is playing with a tight group of four young people in an ultramodern suburb of Paris. At one point another woman states that Fabien and Alexandre are the only two "worthy" men in the suburb, and so we have an even smaller net. Although the narrative positions the two women as main characters, the two men are initially antagonists, then helpers for the two women. This shifting between negative and positive—the polarity we move through with all the characters—bolsters Rohmer's meditations on love, chemistry, and the chase.

The chase is also the subject of *Autumn Tale* (1998), the last of Rohmer's series "Tales of the Four Seasons." But this time the two women are middle-aged with grown children. Isabelle has a full family, while Magali, a vintner in the south, is alone. Her children have left home. Isabelle decides to place a personal ad in the paper for her friend. She will audition the man, pretending to be available herself. If the man passes the test, she will confess and have him meet Magali. At the same time, Magali's son's girlfriend, Rosalie, with whom Magali is quite close, persuades her to meet her ex-lover, Etienne, her former philosophy professor. The plot in this film consists of the various deceptions two women go through to rescue Magali, a woman they care about, from loneliness. Since this screen story is a comedy, the plot works and the suitor captured by the ad is very interested in Magali, and the narrative ends optimistically with their newfound relationship.

As in *L'ami de Mon Amie*, the central conflict in *Autumn Tale* may be found in the gap between a character's spoken intention (sincere or not) for another character, and the actual outcome of that intention. Isabelle indulges in a lie (insincere), but her intention and the outcome are positive (sincere). Rosalie, in her efforts to set up Magali with her former philosophy professor, seems sincere in her intention, but it is clear that Etienne remains interested in Rosalie and that Rosalie's interest in him is not altogether altruistic (insincere outcome). So behavior and intention seem to be at odds in the case of the flirtatious young woman, as they were in Lea's case in *L'ami de Mon Amie*.

To consider Rohmer's work to be comedies of manners (satire) is to overstate the case. We care too much for Magali in *Autumn Tale* and for Blanche in *L'ami de Mon Amie* for the stories to be satires. In this sense Rohmer is reminding us that looks are deceiving; they are attractive but easily false. Character that is honest or moral is rewarded in Rohmer's world. And in each case, characters get the relationships they deserve. In Rohmer's world, dreams can come true, but they need a little help from your real friends.

WORKING WITH GENRE:
THE CASE OF THE UNITED KINGDOM

British, Swedish, and Irish films have long had a fascination with genre filmmaking. A number of genres originated, or matured considerably, in the United Kingdom: the thriller and the work of Hitchcock; the docudrama and the work of Watkins and Loach; and the satire and the work of MacKendrick. Serious contributions have been made to the action-adventure in the work of Alexander and Zoltan Korda, and to the epic in the work of David Lean. And the distinguishing quality of voice is powerful in the Irish work of Neil Jordan (*Butcher Boy* [1998], *The Miracle* [1996]), and in the Scottish work of Bill Forsyth (*Gregory's Girl* [1981], *Local Hero* [1983]). In this section however we look at classic genre films made in

the U.K. What is particularly interesting is that these genres have national affilia-
tions—the gangster film with the United States, the melodrama with Germany.
Nevertheless, these genres have developed in the U.K. in their own powerful
fashion. And filmmakers looking to distinguish themselves have begun to stretch
the limits of these genres. We turn first to the gangster film.

Mike Hodge's *Get Carter* (1970) is the story of Jack Carter, a mobster from London. He goes north to Newcastle because of his brother's death. The narrative follows his search to discover that the death was not an accident, and his consequent revenge for the death. What is notable about *Get Carter* is that it is
exceedingly violent and paced like a thriller. This means that the traditional family character layer is present, but it is abbreviated to allow for a larger plot layer.
The dramatic arc follows the traditional rise and fall shape. The resolution is the
death of Jack Carter.

Stephen Frears' *The Hit* (1984) follows the same shape. A member of the mob,
Willie Parker, betrays the mob. Ten years later the mob sends out Braddock, a hit
man, and an associate to Spain to find and kidnap Parker. They do so and pick up
another hostage: a witness (Laura del Sol). But they had to kill her lover, and as a
result, the police are in pursuit. As in *Get Carter*, the character layer is smaller and
the plot is more prominent. This does not mean the characters are stereotypes.
On the contrary, in both *Get Carter* and *The Hit* the characters are individuated
and strong. And although the hit man Braddock in the end kills Willie Parker and
his associate, he doesn't kill the witness and this is his undoing. As expected in
the rise and fall shape of the genre, the film ends with Braddock being killed by
the police.

In John MacKenzie's *Long Good Friday* the main character is Harold Shand, the
king of the London underworld. He is about to link up with the top American
gangsters to convert London's Dock into a major gambling center. But there is a
power struggle going on. Whether it is the Americans or his rivals, Harold does-
n't know, but he will find out. In the end he will discover that his opposition is the
IRA and that he can't topple this political terrorist organization. As in the other
two examples, the rise and fall shape of the gangster film is at the core of the *Long
Good Friday*. And as in *Get Carter* and *The Hit*, the plot layer is emphasized, although the *Long Good Friday* has more of a character layer than the other two
films.

These three films are very much gangster films, but they seem more intense in
their presentation than their American equivalents. In part this has to do with the
romantic quality in the American gangster film that derives from the main character's sense of displacement as an immigrant wanting to become part of the
mainstream American power structure. In the British version, the outsider position of the gangster is not an issue, and consequently our empathy for the character is not automatic. In fact, the gangsters in each of these U.K. productions are
nasty characters. The result is that the character layer is diminished and plot is ac-
celerated. The result is a much more visceral experience of the story.

A parallel sense of experience is achieved in the melodrama. This is accomplished by merging the traditional melodrama with an issue of the day. Melodrama can stand on its own very well by dealing with the classical core conflict:

the powerless person struggling against the power structure. *Once Were Warriors* from New Zealand and *Character* from the Netherlands are family melodramas without reference to an issue of the day, as is the great American melodrama *A Place in the Sun*.

By attaching the narrative to an issue of the day, the audience experiences melodrama much closer to home. Antonia Bird's *Priest* is a good example of this impulse. *Priest* (1996), set in a poor Northern city in England, is the story of a Catholic priest whose dilemma is the orthodoxy of his belief. Greg Pilkington wants to be a priest in the cerebral sense, a professional priest. But to do so he must deny his own physical self. He is homosexual. The dilemma for him is to reconcile the professional self and the personal self. The issue of the day, then, is the Catholic Church's position on celibacy. A second issue that challenges the main character is the confession by a young girl that she is being sexually abused by her father. Does the priest break the confidentiality of confession and turn over his knowledge to the authorities? The dogma and practice of Catholicism is challenged in the narrative from the point of view of a priest.

A second example would be Mike Leigh's *Secrets and Lies* (1996). A Caucasian woman, Cynthia, gives up her black baby at birth and has to live a life in which she is an abysmal failure. The critical moment is the grown black daughter, Hortense's decision to find her mother. When they meet it is quite clear that the life Cynthia has led and the family she has had is an abnegation of her transgression. The narrative follows the mother-daughter relationship and the healing power it has on Cynthia. In the end, Cynthia is far more whole for having brought Hortense back into her life. The issue of the day, of course, is the status of relations between blacks and whites in British society. Leigh's viewpoint on the matter is quite clear.

More ambiguous but no less interesting is Udayan Prasad's *My Son the Fanatic* (1997). Parvez is a cab driver in a Northern city. Originally from Pakistan, he is quite acclimatized to England. He even cultivates a relationship with a white prostitute. The problem is his son Farid, who is embracing Muslim beliefs in an orthodox fashion. This clash with his son, which is a generational issue, as well as the clash between secular and religious views of belonging in society, are the issues in *My Son the Fanatic*. How does one reconcile being a new Briton with the old culture (Pakistan)? This take on multiculturalism is very much an issue of the day. The writer of *My Son the Fanatic*, Hanif Kureishi, has taken up this issue of acculturation before in *My Beautiful Launderette* (1985) and *The Bhudda of Suburbia* (1993). Again, what makes the melodrama so vivid in the U.K. case is the linkage of the classic melodrama to issues of the day.

A third genre that is powerfully dealt with in film is the biography. A biography is essentially converted into a film when there is a memorable personality, such as a Virginia Woolf or a Winston Churchill, or an association of a person with an important or memorable event, such as the creation of the Church of England or an Olympic event. The event or the role the person is famous for forms the plot of the biography. But it is the character layer that is emotionally inviting to the audience.

There have been many biographies of important people, but rarely is there a biography—or an autobiography—of a little boy. John Boorman's *Hope and Glory* (1987) is his own story about growing up during 1939 to 1945 in war-torn England. This was a formative experience for Boorman. He grew up to become a writer-director—*Point Blank* (1967), *Deliverance* (1972), *Excalibur* (1981), and *The General* (1998) are a few his films—and his fascination with movies and imagination abound in the film. But perhaps most important about this biography is how innocence and cruelty, sexuality and violence cohabit in his world. Even though his family loses its London home to fire, Billy Rohan, the young Boorman, is always observant and resourceful. Forced to join his grandfather in the countryside, Billy forages for bird eggs and fish when the family complains of insufficient food. He refuses to participate in the humiliation of a young teenage girl by his friends. He remembers that she just lost her mother in a bombing. When his sixteen-year-old sister throws her lover's engagement ring away, it is Billy who finds it for her. He doesn't always understand what is happening around him, but the events make him more observant and as a result more resourceful. In a sense, *Hope and Glory* is about growing up in almost impossible circumstances, and yet finding worthwhile the experience. Billy is not traumatized, he is inspired. The implication is to overcome the barriers of life circumstance and to reach for your dreams. This is precisely what Boorman did and he became an unusual filmmaker of considerable power.

Shekhar Kapur's *Elizabeth* (1998) is the biography of Queen Elizabeth, daughter of Henry VIII, who succeeded her Catholic sister Mary and reigned over England for the glorious 50-year period that was known as the Elizabethan Age. The narrative follows only those years that stabilized her crown, to the point of consolidating her power on the throne as the Virgin Queen. The plot is presented as a religious struggle between Catholics and Protestants, with the Catholic powers, France and Spain, supportive of the enemies of Elizabeth. But what is far more interesting is the character layer—Elizabeth's struggle to be a woman and a queen. She realizes in the end that she must choose, and she chooses to be a queen.

Finally, we turn to the example of Richard Attenborough's *Grey Owl* (2000). Attenborough was already a famous film biographer, having made biographies of Churchill, Ghandi, and Chaplin. In *Grey Owl*, he tells the story of an Englishman who pretends to be an Indian in the Canadian wilderness. It is also the story of an important environmentalist whose book championed a way of life in harmony with the environment.

The plot follows the career of Archie Grey Owl through his career as a trapper and a writer during the 1930s, and through the publication of his book, *Pilgrim in the Wilderness*. On his famous tour of England he becomes a spokesperson for the environment. During his tour in the screen story, we also learn the truth, that he is an Englishman who was born Archie Belaney and that he has misrepresented himself to his public. The story ends gently with his confession of his true identity to his Indian wife, Pony, and to the discovery of his secret by a newspaperman. His true identity was kept secret for the remainder of his lifetime. What was accepted by Indians, his wife, and the newspaperman is that what he had to say was more important than who he was, and that according to those who were closest to him, he had become what he had dreamed of becoming.

The character layer of the story relates to his relationship with Pony. Here the issue is one of identity—is he a trapper? Is he a fake? Or is he something else? Through the relationship with Pony he becomes an environmentalist and gives up trapping. Her love for all living things, particularly the beaver, is transformative, and he chooses to give up trapping. This relationship, a love story but also an identity story, is at the core of the narrative. What happens with Pony becomes the basis for the book, his statement about the wilderness and how the Indian can live in harmony with the wilderness. His book and his speeches are a plea for all people to live in harmony with the environment.

What is different about these British treatments of biography is their connections to issues of the quality of life. They are not transient issues of the day but rather core issues—the importance of the environment in *Grey Owl*, the war between men and women in *Elizabeth*, and the impact of war on the quality of life in *Hope and Glory*. These are stories that transcend the character they are about; because of the breadth of the core issues they deal with, these films become biographies that resonate powerfully.

CHALLENGING GENRE: THE CASE OF AUSTRALIA

Australia has produced classical storytellers such as Bruce Beresford (*Breaker Morant* [1980]), Peter Weir (*Gallipoli* [1981]), and Phillip Noyce (*Dead Calm* [1989]), as well as individualistic feminist filmmakers such as Jane Campion (*The Piano* [1992]) and Gillian Armstrong (*My Brilliant Career* [1980]). But the group I would like to focus on in this section is a group of storytellers who take a genre and try to bend it. This is different from the eccentric treatments of narrative such as Paul Cox's *Man of Flowers* (1984) and Jocelyn Morehouse's *Proof* (1991). Rather I want to look at genre treatments and how they have been amplified or altered to provide a different experience for their audience. A starting point for this examination is the first film by playwright Nick Parsons, *Dead Heart* (1996). *Dead Heart* is a police story set on an outback settlement populated principally by an aboriginal population and a white bureaucracy—a minister, a teacher, a policeman, and their dependents. The usual shape of the police story is crime-investigation-solution, with the policeman as the main character and the perpetrator as the antagonist. The form is essentially plot-driven.

In *Dead Heart*, the crime is committed by the Aborigines against one of their own. A young Aborigine has been having an affair with the minister's wife. He takes her to a sacred site and has sexual relations with her on this site. For taking a nonbeliever to the site, he is killed. This is the crime at the core of the narrative.

The white policeman (Bryan Brown) is a man who bends the law to achieve justice. He will respect Aboriginal law—such as an Aboriginal punishment against his Aboriginal deputy for the suicide of an Aborigine in police custody— but he will withhold or embellish evidence to get a conviction. He is a drunk, and he is generally in trouble with his superiors.

What Parsons has done here that is different from the genre expectations for the police story is that he has introduced ambiguity at the level of the main character and at the level of the antagonist. Because this is a narrative that crosses two cultures, the Aboriginal and the white cultures, and because the character cast as the protagonist, a white policeman, and the character cast as the killer, an Aborigine, are from two different worlds, the usual clarity of the police story is lost. The policeman is no longer "the hero," and the perpetrator is no longer "the villain." Both are ambiguous. The result is that we experience the clash of goals of the main character and of the antagonist as a culture clash rather than as a conflict with the good-evil clarity of the police story form that yields closure and resolution. Parsons' take on the police story leaves us in a far more awkward and discomforting place, as was its intention.

Bill Bennett's *Kiss or Kill* (1997) presents itself in tone as film noir, but actually it is a gangster film. In the gangster film there is a crime that is intended to improve the criminal's status. Whether the antagonist is a policeman or another criminal, the dramatic arc remains a rise and fall shape with a character layer generally focusing on family. In *Kiss or Kill* we have two protagonists, as in *Bonnie and Clyde* and *Badlands*, but they are far less ambitious in their career than the gangsters in those films. They are young swindlers, Nicole and Alan. She gets the victim drunk; he robs them. But during the evening, the victim dies of a heart attack, and this time they find a videotape that implicates a retired national sports figure, Zipper Doyle as a pederast. And so the search is on for the killer of the heart attack victim and by Zipper for the tape. The plot then is a chase across Southern Australia. An additional complication is that wherever the twosome stops, people die. The plot concludes with the capture of our two swindlers. Zipper dies in a car crash. Nicole and Alan are arrested. There is sufficient evidence for murder charges, and thanks to Alan's father's efforts, they get suspended sentences for theft.

The character layer explores their relationship, and here is where the film noir enters. Traumatized by a childhood fire, fueled by anxiety, guilt, and anger, Nicole is unpredictably explosive. Is she the perpetrator of all the murders en route? Will she kill Alan? (An appropriate ending for film noir.)

In terms of genre expectations, we expect the gangsters to be punished at the end and they are not. In terms of tone we expect realism; what we get is the overheated expressionist tone of film noir. And in terms of the character layer, we get a much more ambiguous set of choices. The relationship that in the gangster film is presented as a positive polarity, family, is here presented as a pathological option. All of these changes make the experience of *Kiss or Kill* far more ambiguous than the traditional experience of the genre.

A third example of challenging genre is Shirley Barrett's *Love Serenade* (1996). *Love Serenade* is a situation comedy in which the goal of the two main characters, two young women, Dimity and Vicki-Ann, is to secure a man. Since the Hurley sisters live in a small town their chances are slim, until a disk jockey from the big city comes to town and moves in next door. One of the sisters is outgoing and the other is painfully shy. There is no plot in the film, but the character layer explores the relationship of the two young women with their neighbor, a well-known disk jockey, Ken Sherry. Vicki-Ann becomes his mistress. Dimity remains frustrated by her failure to hook the desirable Ken Sherry. But how do two sisters share one man? Since men always disappoint, and Ken Sherry is no exception, they decide that the best resolution is to kill him. They do so, thus remaining together.

What is interesting about *Love Serenade* is how the structure of the situation comedy is altered. In the traditional situation comedy, where a wished-for romantic relationship is the character layer, the resolution is that the main character gets the object of desire. The relationship comes together, producing the happy ending. In the case of *Love Serenade*, the ending is altered by the sisters doing away with the object of desire. The dramatic logic may be that the real couple consists of the two sisters, or that life disappoints, especially in a small town. Whichever explanation is plausible, the eccentricity of all the characters who are treated ironically by Barrett moves the story toward the darker direction. We have seen this tendency in P.J. Hogan's *Muriel's Wedding* (1994), but Hogan opted for realism whereas Barrett goes much further towards the darkness of the narrative.

There are many additionally interesting characteristics in exploring the national models: the attraction of the epic in the Hungarian work of Jansco and Szabo; the odd mixture of super realism and surrealism in the Polish films of Wajda and Kieslowski; the aggressive irony in the Yugoslavian films of Makavejev and Kusterica; the omnipresence of the political in the Russian films of Kanevski and Mikhalkhov; the literary impulse in the Swedish films of Ullman and Bergman; and the influence of the popular arts in China in the films of Xiang Yimou and Chen Kaige.

There are many rich throughlines in the examination of national models. In many ways this is why so much influential work today is coming from Belgium, Denmark, Hong Kong, Taiwan, and Iran. The great contributors to the national cinemas, including Japan, Germany, India, and Spain, continue redefining themselves. Together with these smaller countries, they are providing the models for global storytelling.

NOTES

1. For a preliminary discussion on these differences and similarities, see Chapter 11, "The Primacy of Character over Action: The Non-American Screenplay," in K. Dancyger and J. Rush, *Alternative Scriptwriting*, Second Edition (Focal Press, 1995).
2. S. Eisenstein, *Film Form* (Harcourt Brace Jovanovich, 1977) and *Film Sense* (Harcourt Brace Jovanovich, 1975).
3. The emergence of auteurs such as Francis Ford Coppola and Martin Scorcese paved the way to American reconsideration of the film as other than a form of entertainment.

9

NEW MODELS

In this chapter we look at narrative models that have become important in the last twenty years. They don't really fit into the Hollywood model, although some of them have been produced in Hollywood. Nor do they fit into the independent model or the national model, although some of them have been produced independently or in Europe or Asia.

In part these narrative models have developed out of the constant search for novelty in an essentially conservative medium. The paradox of wanting both to have a mass audience and to challenge that audience, to surprise that audience is at the core of the development of these narrative modes. These narrative modes—which I call myth, MTV, women telling stories, and nonlinearity in narrative—are now certainly more than a passing phase, and so we have to contend with them as narrative models. But before we do we should try to understand why they have developed.

The first point to be made is that the past twenty-five years have been a period of tremendous technical innovation. Technology in production has advanced in every area to the point that film and video have blurred in their distinctiveness with the consequent growing influence of television on film and of film on television. Production techniques have been enhanced by the digital revolution to the point where every characteristic of a single image can be added to or subtracted from. The result is a totally malleable image, a virtual reality, and a tremendous range of visual and aural possibilities in production. That process of amendment continues in postproduction where nonlinear digital editing allows for further enhancement or subtraction in the organization of images. These advances in technology have enhanced the power of the medium to create, distort, and entertain its audience. Simultaneously, it has encouraged skepticism about the veracity and the intentions of this growing power. This is the backdrop for the development of new forms and intentions that attempt to deal with, use, and in many cases, subvert this new technological reality with a narrative experience that reestablishes its connectivity with its audience.

This might mean narratives that are throwbacks to primitive or earlier forms and formulas, films that portray a myth, such as George Lucas's *Star Wars* (1977) or Luc Besson's *The Messenger* (1999). Or the narrative might be a reaction to formula where the filmic storyteller attempts to create a new myth, as in Julio Medem's *Cows* (1989) or Martin Scorsese's *Kundun* (1997). What is clear in all of these examples, formulaic and antiformulaic, is that the narrative trajectory is essentially nonverbal, a fact that takes us to the second observation about these new modes.

This same period of twenty-five years has seen a new level of internationalization in media penetration. The nonverbal travels across language and cultural barriers far more effectively than does the verbal narrative. This is why MTV has been so powerful a force in creating an international audience. This is why reality TV, popularized in Europe, has become so rapidly widespread in North America. Television, principally cable television, has been the subversive delivery system that has rapidly internationalized the market for film narratives that are new and different. The result is a receptivity for MTV narrative and for nonlinear storytelling.

Paradoxically, the technological changes together with the internationalization of the market has produced two extreme impulses—the democratization of the medium and the search for a new elite in narrative. Democratization has led to modest productions such as *The Blair Witch Project* (1999) having tremendous success. And it has led to a scale of technological elitism (Cameron's *Titanic* is the best example of this impulse), a scale of production that taxes the resources of two production studios simultaneously. Whether this paradox will skew in one direction or the other is unclear, but the success of the Dogma 95 films such as Vinterberg's *The Celebration* (1998) is encouraging. See Chapter 12, "The Search for New Forms," for a full discussion on *The Celebration*.

One last point must be made before we look at these new narrative forms and that is the growth of nonlinear narrative. In a sense, the nonlinear narrative is a strong reaction to the Hollywood film. Rather than the energetic goal-directed character in a plot-driven narrative that moves from critical moment to resolution and closure, the nonlinear film has no single main character, the characters have no goals, there is no plot, and there is no resolution. It almost sounds as if there is no story. But there is. It's a story that requires a far more active role for members of the audience. They have to work to fill in the narrative gaps, to make sense of the behavior and the intentions of the characters in the story, and somehow to find a worthwhile purpose to the experience of the nonlinear narrative.

This is very different from the traditional three-act structure, with its plot and its character that are readymade for us to identify with. The interesting question is why these narratives, films such as Paul Thomas Anderson's *Magnolia* (1999) and Quentin Tarantino's *Pulp Fiction* (1993), have been as successful as they have been. I think the answer also lies in the changes of the past twenty-five years—in the cross-pollination of the film and television industries, in the internationalization of the market for film and television, in the simultaneous drive for formulization and the reaction to formula. It's a different, discontinuous, fractured, global world, and the experience of the young audience (ages 15–30) especially differs from the experience of the previous generation. MTV, computers, and increased mobility have provided a different life experience for this new generation, and the nonlinear narrative manages to capture the fragmentation that has been so much a part of their mode of experience. The consequence is that the nonlinear film can be experienced as a more believable narrative than a traditional linear narrative, which is experienced as quaintly old-fashioned. So the nonlinear narrative form is a form that is new and that may not be as transient or trendy as it was initially thought to be. Now let's turn to these new modes of storytelling.

MYTH

Whether the new narrative impulse is a formulaic myth or a new form of myth, this form has particular characteristics that will make the main character a larger figure—either the ultimate hero or the ultimate victim. In order to create enough dramatic amplitude to establish the hero or victim the dramatic arc often looks like a journey. In the more predictable interpretation of myth, this would mean a super-antagonist, but myth is not predictable and so the antagonist per se is not equivalent to the antagonist in the action-adventure film. Rather, the dramatic amplitude comes from the clash of the outer world of plot and the inner world of the main character's psychological struggle. Generally, those two worlds are incompatible, with the consequence that the struggle seems far more inner-directed.

In a sense, David Lean tries to create a myth in his *Lawrence of Arabia* (1962), as does Bille August in his film *Jerusalem* (1996). But the Lean character struggles with the personal identity issue while the August character struggles with obligation. Lawrence's deeper struggle helps create the mythical proportion of the character, while Ingmar's promise to his father in *Jerusalem* is not personal enough to make Ingmar's struggle carry the dramatic amplitude needed to create myth. Ingmar agrees to take care of the family and the community. His father, as leader of the community, has this sense of obligation, naturally. To hoist this obligation on to a young boy is to designate him a future leader. Ingmar respects his father but events and characters pull the community toward other leadership and to destruction under that leadership. Ingmar simply doesn't have the depth to understand and meet the needs of the community. He is too caught up in family and personal challenges and so he fails to fulfill his promise to his father.

To bolster the sense that the main character's journey is distinct, the plot is important. It needs to pose almost impossible challenges to the character's goal. In *Lawrence of Arabia*, the potential success of the Arab revolt in the desert is considered impossible. But just as important in the creation of the myth is the positioning of the other characters. They are skeptical about the goal of the main character, even those secondary characters whom we consider to be helpers. In this sense, the main character's journey is a solitary one, a journey that is not understood even by those who support the main character.

Luc Besson's *The Messenger* (1999) is a narrative treatment of the Jean of Arc story that recreates the mythic character and the myth of Jean. The story is well known. Jean is a young woman who claims to be instructed by God to lead France against its British invaders and to reclaim France for the King of France. For her efforts and her successes Jean is turned over to the British who have her tried as a heretic and burned at the stake. But the tide is turned, and eventually the French defeat the British who retreat permanently from French soil.

Besson structures the story in three movements: Jean as a child; Jean's obsessive efforts to mobilize the Dauphin and his forces against the British at Orleans, culminating with the crowning of the Dauphin as the king of France at Reims; and finally the betrayal of Jean and her spiritual struggle leading to her physical death. She dies at age 19.

In the first movement, Jean as a child is obsessed with confession. (Although one could use the Act description, movements imply the myth in operation. Acts humanize the character too much.) She is deeply religious. She has visions. One day she finds a sword in a field. That very day the British invade her village. She is saved by her sister whom she watches as she is brutally killed and then ravaged. The most powerful quality of this movement is the profound religiosity of Jean. It is presented almost as a madness, which is not understood by her family. It is also a possession that is not understood by the young Jean. She only understands that she is kinetically moved by her relationship to religion, to its power. For Jean, confession is an outward expression in the world of the power of her sense of religion. The death of her sister, its cruelty, in no small measure narratively establishes the British as the antagonist force, the expression of earthly evil that will embody the antagonist in the second and third movements.

In the second movement the nineteen-year-old Jean rides to rally the Dauphin, to request that he give her an army to march on Orleans. The Dauphin, skeptical and fearful of earthly plots against him, plays a game with Jean. He pretends to be a member of his court while he places one of his associates in his place. If Jean accepts the associate as the Dauphin she is false. But Jean does not fail the test. She identifies the Dauphin in spite of his disguise. Perhaps she is as she claims, a messenger from God.

Privately, Jean shares her plan with the Dauphin, to inform the English they must leave France. If they do not, she will march to Orleans, which is presently besieged by the English, and liberate the city. She is neither a seasoned soldier nor a powerful political personage. According to the Dauphin's advisors, she is mad and dangerous, and it is an act of naivete and madness to entrust the army to the command of this maid. But the Dauphin, feeling he has tried all else, supports Jean. She goes immediately to Orleans. There the army is under the command of the cousin of the Dauphin. He and his nobles are soldiers and men. They want to humor Jean, but her forcefulness and her mystical bond to the common people who populate their army temper their contempt for Jean. They lie to her about the timing of the battle, but in the end she takes command by the force of her will. She is wounded, but the next day she again takes command, surprising the English who assume that she is only a woman. Whether it is the politics at the Dauphin's court or the gender politics of the leadership in the French and English armies, Jean is always opposed. Nevertheless her belief is so great that in the end she overcomes the impregnable defenses and the skepticism of the French leadership and retakes Orleans. The movement ends with the crowning of the Dauphin as the King of France.

The third movement focuses on the betrayal of Jean at the gates of Paris. She has been promised reinforcements but envy in the new king's court shifts the monarch's loyalties and he betrays Jean. He now thinks that it would be better to negotiate with the English. The sacrifice of Jean will be the signal of goodwill in those negotiations. When Jean is taken, the Burgundian bishops are encouraged to set up an ecclesiastical court to try her for heresy. Although the English want her burned to eradicate a military and political threat, the Church fears being seen as a pawn of the English. If she acknowledges her sins she will not be burned. But Jean, who possesses the religious belief that has been her core, does not recant. She tells the court that she is a messenger, and the message is that she must deliver her people from the tyranny of the English. The King of France must lead his people to push the English out of France. Jean is a believer; she is not a witch. And the voice of God speaks through her with a political message.

Throughout this movement Jean carries on a dialogue and a debate with a priest. Is he a figment of her imagination? This test of her faith is an internal test just as the ecclesiastical trial is ongoing and external. In the end, Jean is burned because she is a threat to the English, but the bishops have clearly been unsettled by the vigor of Jean's belief. Finally, that belief is converted into national action as the French act in accord with Jean's message.

The story of Jean of Arc has been told many times on film. It works least well when it merely echoes the historical facts, as in the Otto Preminger version, *Saint Joan* (1957). It works best when the writer-director establishes the internal struggle of Jean over issues of faith and politics, as in Carl Dryer's *The Passion of Joan of Arc* (1929) or in this version, Besson's *The Messenger* (1999). Both achieve the level of the myth of Jean of Arc.

Martin Scorsese's *Kundun* (1997) is also a narrative about faith and politics, in this case the story of the current Dalai Lama, from the point of his discovery as a three-year-old boy to his departure from Tibet. As in the case of *The Messenger*, Kundun is organized around movements: the discovery of the boy; his leaving home for Lhasa, the capital; his education; his personal losses; the invasion of Tibet by China; his efforts to peacefully coexist then negotiate with China; and finally, his nonviolent protest against the Chinese occupation—his departure for India.

Throughout the film, the spiritual is constantly in conflict with the practical, whether it is with his love life, his leadership role in Lhasa, or in his visit to Beijing to meet with Mao Tse-tung. It is as if the making of the Dalai Lama is an internal spiritual journey and the plot, the invasion of Tibet by China, tests the Dalai Lama's values for himself and for his people. In many ways, the sequences progressively reveal the maturation of the inner life of the spiritual leader of his nation. In contrast, the behavior of his advisors and of the Chinese sets the Dalai Lama apart. Everyone seems far more political than he is, which makes his sense of spirituality all the more powerful. What makes *Kundun* a myth is the inner certainty of the Dalai Lama that spiritual values are higher and more enduring than temporal values such as politics and the behavior political power implies.

A good contrast to the myth of *Kundun* is Bertolucci's *The Last Emperor* (1987), a melodrama whose main character, the last emperor of China, becomes a victim of the power struggle between Nationalists, Communists, and the Japanese for the control of China (the plot). The experience of the two films couldn't be more different.

THE MTV NARRATIVE

The MTV narrative is essentially storytelling that is influenced by the music video. Rather than a linear story constructed in three acts, the MTV narrative is constructed along a linear frame, but rather than three acts, the narrative proceeds along a series of set pieces. As opposed to a sequence which could be 30 minutes or longer, a set piece could be quite brief—2 to 4 minutes—and so the entire film might be made up of 30 set pieces. The set piece is equivalent to a music video. Each set piece has its own tone, its own emotional core—a sensation or a feeling rather than an event that contributes to a progression of plot and character toward resolution. The set piece, because of its intensity, actually disrupts and undermines linear progression. That discontinuity extends to our sense of identification with the main character—if there is a main character.[1]

Oliver Stone's *Natural Born Killers* (1994) is an example of this style of narrative. *Natural Born Killers* is the story of Mickey and Mallory and their careers as serial killers. A good contrast to a similar story is Terence Malick's *Badlands*, which has a traditional gangster film approach to the narrative (a rise and fall shape), with a character layer that explains how personal relationships and family life contribute to the making of a gangster. Stone's treatment is far less conventional and utterly influenced by the MTV notion of set pieces. The story frame of *Natural Born Killers* is the career of Mickey and Mallory, including the night they met, Mallory's father's sexual abuse of her, and how getting away from her father essentially kick-starts their career, their capture, their imprisonment, and their escape, which concludes the narrative. Another important story element is the role a reality-TV journalist plays in the creation of the myth of Mickey and Mallory. He also facilitates their escape from prison.

What is important about the intervention of the MTV style is that the set pieces are small narratives in and of themselves. The opening set piece, for example, is set in a diner. Mickey has ordered himself some pie and Mallory has put a coin in the jukebox. Some hunters enter and they find Mallory's dancing provocative. One insults Mallory verbally, another insults her visually. In short order the killing starts, and before it's over three hunters and two restaurant workers are dead. A lunch break has turned grimly violent, set to pulsing music.

Soon we shift to a background set piece on how Mickey and Mallory met. The scene is presented as a situation comedy for television. Artificiality dominates. The scene quickly turns to emotional violence and physical violence. We quickly get the sense that these two young people may be very much in love, but they have a nasty habit of resolving conflict in a deadly fashion. The persecution/retribution theme proceeds through all the set pieces.

One of the side effects of this style of narrative is that we tune out for relief. This makes a sustained emotional experience impossible. The result is quite the opposite from the experience of the classical three-act structure.

Another example of the MTV style of narrative is Roberto Benigni's *Life Is Beautiful* (1998). Here is the story of a Jewish waiter, Guido. World War II is about to begin. Italy is a combatant and Guido has a family. The problem is that he is a Jew. When Italy loses its status as an ally to Germany, Guido and his family are deported to a concentration camp. In order to sustain his son's spirits in the concentration camp, Guido is as playful as possible—everything is a game. By pretending, he instills an attitude in his son that is life-affirming rather than life-threatening. In the end, Guido sacrifices his own life to sustain this attitude in his son.

Both the pre-war narrative and the narrative in the concentration camp are developed as a series of set pieces. The overriding theme of those set pieces is that attitude can overcome any tragedy, and that play and laughter is life-supporting. The set pieces are thus all about tragic or accidental events whose outcome is blunted by the positive attitude of Guido. Is he a naïf or does he know something we don't know? The feeling created by those set pieces unfolds the plot, the progress of the Nazi war against the Jews of Europe.

A description of one particular set piece will give you a sense of Benigni's approach. The scene is early in the narrative. Guido has arrived in the city and he wants to open a bookshop but he needs an official to sign his application. The secretary is discouraging. He will wait. The official will not sign in spite of Guido's protestations. Its lunchtime. He'll have to wait for the next official to arrive in an hour's time. All he wants is a signature. He is outraged. The official suggest he file a complaint and leaves.

Guido is outraged and begins to dictate a complaint but the secretary is indifferent. He rushes to the window and shouts after the official. In his zeal, he drops the window plant on the official. It shatters on his head. Apologetic Guido chases after the official but the official isn't accepting the apology. He tells Guido to forget a bookstore; his request will never be approved. The official then mistakenly picks up Guido's hat (a hat filled with eggs). The contents of the hat, the eggs, shatter and the infuriated official now threatens murder. Guido runs off stealing a bicycle to evade the infuriated official. He rides off but doesn't get too far before he virtually runs over a young woman who had given him the farm eggs the day before. Rather than chastise her or she him, they reconnect in a flirtatious manner. We know this isn't the end of the relationship (she will later become his wife).

This set piece, which has a narrative content, keeps twisting toward comedy, then farce, then hooks into a future narrative opportunity—a love relationship. None of it is rational, but it is entirely reasonable for a fable, which *Life Is Beautiful* is.

WOMEN TELLING STORIES

There are many female directors who do not endeavor to differentiate themselves very much from their male counterparts. Katherine Bigelow's *Point Break* (1991) and Mimi Leder's *Deep Impact* (1998) exemplify this impulse. On the other hand, there are women whose narrative approach differs markedly from that of men, enough so that a case could be made for the notion that women tell stories differently.[2]

The range of difference is, I believe, significant. From the edge of the mainstream, the work of Angelica Huston (*Bastard out of Carolina* [1996]) and Diane

Keaton (*Unstrung Heroes* [1994]) focuses on character over plot, to the other extreme, the work of Su Friedrich (*Sink or Swim* [1990]) and Clara Law (*Autumn Moon* [1992]) opt for the experimental narrative form to voice their stories. Somewhere between these two extremes there are a number of film storytellers, particularly in Europe, who exemplify how differently women tell their stories.

Agnieska Holland, who is originally from Poland, has made films in America as well as France. Her film *Olivier, Olivier* (1993) is particularly unusual. It is the story of the effect of the disappearance of the youngest child on a family of four, and the consequent impact upon the remaining three when he reappears seven years later. Basically, the trauma of the original disappearance disintegrates the family. The father, a veterinarian, goes off to work in Africa, and the mother essentially falls apart, while the preadolescent daughter blames herself for what has happened. When a young teenager appears, claiming to be the disappeared boy, the family heals. The father returns, the mother is energized with hope. Only the daughter suspects that he is an imposter. He is. Olivier's body is found. A neighbor had molested and killed him. The film ends posing the question, What will happen to this family now?

What makes this narrative so interesting is that Agnieska Holland opts for four main characters rather than one. The traditional approach would be to experience the story through the mother, with the plot (the disappearance) proceeding as an important layer of the structure. By privileging all the characters—the mother, the father, the sister, and Olivier (whether the original son or the imposter)—their perceptions occupy the whole narrative. The subjective power of identification, as well as the force of plot, are all blunted, and what we are left with is the trauma for the whole family and the question of what we would do under such a tragic shadow. By opting for multiple points of view Holland has made the film a story of adults and children. All are vulnerable, and there is none of the closure that derives from the linear three-act approach to narrative. The open-endedness and the vulnerability of all the characters leaves us vulnerable.

Another important filmmaker is German Margarethe Van Trotta, whose film *Marianne and Julianne* (1981, also known as *The German Sisters*) is a story that also sidesteps a linear narrative. It is the story of two sisters in the troubled late-1960s, Julianne is a social pacifist and Marianne is a terrorist and an anarchist. The film opens with the suicide of Marianne's husband and closes with the impact of her suicide on Julianne. Von Trotta structures a series of concentric circles around the two sisters through time. We move into the past in a number of these circles, learning that their religious and repressive father was a Nazi and that Marianne and Julianne, each in her own way, had to reject the values of the father. In a sense, their suffering and anger has everything to do with individuation and generational strife. The more compliant daughter, Marianne, became an anarchist, left her child and husband (he commits suicide later), and eventually destroyed herself. The more responsible sister, Julianne, still suffers from the guilt generated by her rebellious adolescence. Each sister is trapped by the past.

The use of concentric circles rather than acts allows Von Trotta to reveal the feelings and the bond that connects these two sisters in spite of the divergent paths each has chosen. Instead of the linearity of the act structure, Von Trotta uses temporal scenes moving back and forth through time. Theses circles of reve-lation lay out the nature of the relationship. Because of this structure, the bond that unites the sisters becomes the lifeline for each that pulls them through per-sonal and political trauma. The circles also serve to cut off events and other char-acters from becoming more than they are. By its structure, the film is really con-fined to the relationship of Marianne and Julianne, and the result is a powerful evocation of sisterhood.

There are other female filmmakers whose work is of great interest from a more didactic feminist perspective: Liliana Cavani (*The Night Porter* [1974]) and Lina Wertmuller (*Swept Away* [1974]) in Italy; Diane Kurys (*Entre Nous* [1983]) and Agnes Varda (*Vagabond* [1985]) in France; Sandra Goldbacher (*The Governess* [1998]) and Antonia Bird (*Priest* [1996]) in England. Although these women direc-tors do approach their material in a far different manner than do their male coun-terparts, they balance their interest in the character layer with a greater attention to plot than either Von Trotta or Holland. Their work however does merit your attention.

THE NONLINEAR STORY

The nonlinear narrative, as I stated earlier, is the opposite of the linear three-act narrative. Whereas the three-act story has a goal-directed main character moving through a catalytic event to resolution, resisted by an antagonist and challenged further by the plot, the nonlinear story has none of these characteristics. There is not, in all likelihood, a single main character. The characters do not have appar-ent goals. The likelihood of a plot is remote, and if there is a plot as in *The Thin Red Line*, the progress of the war is distant from the narrative purpose of the majority of the characters and consequently, it may not have an apparent linkage to the characters. The narrative elements—character and structure—are united by a far more powerful sense of voice than is usually evident in a conventional three-act story, but beyond that, the cause-and-effect tightness of classical narrative is sim-ply not in operation. However, there are other narrative devices that can help shape the narrative—a shared feeling or feeling state among the characters, for example, or a particular time or a special event that justifies the characters being in the story together. An example of a shared feeling becoming the common thread for the characters is operating in Paul Anderson's *Magnolia* (1999). In Julie Dash's *Daughters of the Dust* (1992), it is a time-frame/event frame that pulls to-gether the narrative. The majority of the family will be emigrating from an island to the mainland that very day. Both a place and a premise pull together the three stories in Milcho Manchevski's *Before the Rain* (1994).[3] The place is Macedonia and each story tells an interreligious love story that is in the end destroyed by reli-gious hatred between Muslims and Christians.

The most famous and the most influential of the nonlinear films is Quentin Tarantino's *Pulp Fiction*. Ostensibly a gangster film, the narrative is framed at its beginning and end with a prologue and an epilogue that occur in a restaurant. A couple, Ringo and Yolanda, decides to rob a bank in the prologue. In the epilogue, two gangsters, Vincent Vega and Jules Winfield (John Travolta and Samuel L. Jackson), stop the robbery and move on to their daily activities, which are the subject matter of the first story. After the prologue we have three stories. They occur out of chronological order. If time were the organizing principle, they would follow the order of prologue, epilogue, story one, story three, story two. The linkage between the stories is primarily the characters—the two gangsters, Vincent and Jules, their boss, Marcellus, Marcellus' wife, and a boxer, Butch, who has the nerve to rip off Marcellus. The narrative events of the first story are split between two tasks—to execute some young malingering drug dealers who have failed to pay Marcellus in a timely fashion, and for one of the two gangsters to accompany Marcellus' wife for the evening. Marcellus is away. These two incidents, one plot, the other character layer, don't really provide more than a pretext to characterize the hit men. They have jobs, but they are uncertain about their identities, and so the narrative becomes a study in behavior under the pressure of high expectations.

The second story, the last chronologically, focuses on Butch, a prizefighter, who not only doesn't want to throw a fight for Marcellus, but he also cashes in on this fact. His betrayal of Marcellus and his consequent effort to escape Marcellus; his encounter with a Neo-Nazi gun dealer; the rape of Marcellus by the dealer; and the rescue of Marcellus by Butch—all constitute an essentially absurdist plot that makes no sense in terms of the rise and fall expectations of the gangster film. In fact, the plot arc here is one of victory rather than death, except for Vincent who is killed by Butch. In the second story, an absurdist plot, a focus on plot over character, and the shift in focus to a totally different character, have nothing in common with the first story—nothing but the tone. In both stories there are references to classic gangster films attitudes and behavior, and in those references the tone is humorous and ironic. Where we expect action, there is dialogue. Where there is action, it's absurdist rather than realist (as in the rape of Marcellus). The irony, the humor, and the running editorial comment on the genre unite stories one and two.

In the third story, which chronologically follows the first story, one of the drug dealers is being taken to Marcellus. Accidentally he is shot and the shooting makes a mess of the car (evidence to the police of wrongdoing). The hit men are directed to the home of an associate, where the car is cleaned up for the appearance of propriety (legality) so the hit men can proceed back to Marcellus. These are the narrative events, and they provide the opportunity for Jules to meditate on his chosen profession. This deliberation leads him to decide to leave the profession. The focus then shifts to identity, and once again the rise and fall shape of the gangster film is discarded. The absurdist tone links story three to the prior two stories, as does the appearance of the same characters, Vincent and Jules, in stories one and three.

What we are left with by the end of the film is a meditation on the gangster genre. The irony comments upon the values expressed in the classic genre and claims that the characters are modern gangsters, that they need a deeper sense of job satisfaction, that what they do is not terribly secure and there is no union, and that maybe they should find another line of work (before they die, as Vincent does, suddenly and without purpose). This is the tonal shaping device that unites these three stories. But the lack of a main character to follow leaves us to bring shape to the experience. That shape is open and will differ from person to person. Whether this is the result that was sought, we don't know, but it is the upshot of the nonlinear narrative experience.

In the case of Atom Egoyan's *Exotica* (1995) the shaping device is a place, a strip club called Exotica. As in Anderson's *Magnolia*, the characters in the narrative all share an emotional state: they are all wounded characters, traumatized by an event or person from their past. There is a modest plot about smuggling exotic eggs illegally into Canada, but the plot does not really contribute to understanding the behavior of the characters.

There are five characters that we follow. Thomas is the smuggler. He runs an exotic pet shop. Francis is the accountant who uncovers irregularities in the shop. Chloe is the pregnant owner of Exotica, the strip club, and Eric is the disc jockey of the club, who is the father of the baby the owner is carrying. Christina, a young dancer at the club, is the former lover of Eric.

We are also gradually told about a traumatic event in the past—the body of a young girl was found. Three of the five characters are marked by this incident. We only discover at the end of the narrative that the traumatic event shared by three of these characters is that the young girl was Francis's daughter, Christina was the girl's baby-sitter, and Eric was involved in the search for the young girl. In fact, Eric first met Christina on that search.

In their contemporary lives, these characters deal with their wounds by fabrication. Thomas evades his homosexual desires by smuggling. Francis pretends his daughter is still alive by having his niece "baby-sit" her. His fixation on Christina, his former baby-sitter, also keeps the affiliation with his daughter alive. Chloe is pregnant, but she sexually desires Christina rather than Eric. Eric was useful only to impregnate Chloe. Eric is wounded because he can't possess Christina who he wants to possess, but he can enter a sexual business relationship as the father of the unborn child.

There are no turning points in *Exotica*. It is a single act where people gather in a club and through their actions reveal their pain but not their goals. We don't really understand them or their actions until the end of the story. At that point we are left with the sense that shared pain is a form of mutual support. Even though these characters are not going to develop what I would call conventional relationships—marriages, even friendships—they do belong to the same club, so to speak: the club of being damaged people. In a moment at the end of the narrative, Eric and Francis embrace. In that surprising gesture, these two men emotionally acknowledge their common bond—the impact of the trauma in their lives—the loss of a daughter for Francis, and the loss of his lover, Christina, for Eric. In that acknowledgment, there is a humanity that has been devoid from our experience of these two characters.

Whether Egoyan's goal was to look at the seamy side of life—strip clubs and smuggling—and find humanity there, or whether his goal was to look at the acute pain the characters in this narrative, this post-modern world, suffer, is difficult to conclude. As in the case of all the nonlinear narratives, the capacity for interpretation is as individual as the audience. Closure and linearity both yield a specific interpretation; nonlinearity yields the opposite.

NOTES

1. For a more thorough look at the MTV style, see Chapter 11 in K. Dancyger, *The Technique of Film and Video Editing*, Second Edition (Focal Press, 1996).
2. A detailed discussion of women telling film stories can be found in K. Dancyger, *The Technique of Film and Video Editing*, Second Edition (Focal Press, 1996), pp. 175-181.
3. A full discussion of nonlinear storytelling can be found in Chapters 12, 13, and 24 in *The Technique of Film and Video Editing*, Second Edition (Focal Press, 1996).

EXPERIMENTS IN VOICE

Voice, the editorial prism through which writers and writer-directors filter narrative characters and events, creates a uniqueness of story; voice also can echo similarity to other stories. At one extreme, the writer-director who involves us in a genre according to genre expectations submerges his voice. At the other extreme, the writer-director who distances us from character structure and story form elevates her voice. In Chapter 5, "Tone," for example, I discussed how the use of docudrama, hyperdrama, and satire exemplified the most overt set of devices to create a direct line between the writer-director and the audience. Numerous writer-directors have experimented between these two extremes, and those experiments are the subject of this chapter. In order to understand the contemporary ascent of voice, which is taken up in the next chapter, these intermediate steps need to be explored.

In order to position oneself between these two extremes, the choices are varied, but they exploit two general strategies: to engage or invite us to identify with the main character and with structure and form that puts us in the position of deepening involvement; and the opposite, to distance us from character, structure, and form so that there is a clear line between the narrative and the voice of the writer-director. To position us, the audience, where in part we are involved, yet on another layer we are distanced, requires a mix of narrative strategies that will engage us on one level and disengage us on another. Before this begins to sound like an introduction to the scriptwriting equivalent of faith-healing, a practical example will illustrate how this works.

THE CASE OF *THE MANCHURIAN CANDIDATE*

John Frankenheimer's *The Manchurian Candidate* (1962), written by George Axelrod, proceeds on one level as a realist thriller with a plot focused upon political assassination at the highest level. Power politics at the national level fuse with cold war politics to give this thriller the sense of global threat in line with the cold war paranoia of its time. Together with an unsympathetic assassin and the theme of the psychology of brainwashing (our own unconscious fear of being influenced by the other) there is much to engage us in the narrative.

Raymond Shaw, the main character is the obnoxious son of an overbearing mother and stepson to a U.S. senator, John Iselin. Since his mother is actually a communist agent wearing the marriage and her attitude, she acts as if she is a Daughter of the American Revolution; she is instrumental in forcing Raymond out of a love relationship and into the Army. The time is the Korean War and anti-communist feeling runs high.

While on a patrol in Korea, Raymond's whole company is captured by the Chinese. They are whisked off to be brainwashed. Although all the members of the patrol, including the commander, Captain deMarco, are brainwashed, it is Raymond Shaw who is given special attention. In order to test the depth of control, Raymond is commanded to kill two members of the patrol, and he does so, without remorse, or memory of the event. The patrol is then returned to America; Raymond is given a Congressional Medal of Honor for his bravery during an action where two of his fellow soldiers were killed. Now in the United States, Raymond Shaw is ready to be turned over to his U.S. operative, his mother, for the real assignment—to assassinate the Presidential nominee at the political convention.

But there are complications. Captain deMarco keeps having bad dreams, as does a black sergeant who was also on the patrol. It's the same dream. Another complication is the girl, whom Raymond's mother sent him into the Army to desert, Josie Jordon, comes back into his life. The past keeps challenging the agenda of the plot—for Raymond to kill the Presidential nominee.

On another level, Frankenheimer's film is rife with distancing devices and irony. The Caucasians dream white dreams and the blacks dream black dreams. These dreams illustrate the effectiveness of the brainwashing. The dreams locate the action at a garden party that devolves into a brainwashing session. The opening to Captain deMarco's dream is a white garden party, and the black sergeant dreams of a black garden party. This narrative joke in the midst of a scene that establishes that Raymond Shaw can kill on command is shocking and humorous.

Another example is the sense of humor of the Chinese scientist who brainwashes Raymond Shaw. His speech is peppered with television references from Lucky Strike commercials and other Americanisms. How is a Chinese scientist so familiar with America? Later he talks of going shopping for his wife at Macy's, an American shopping institution. He is more "American" in his speech than the Americans, an irony of character.

Another character irony is that Raymond's American operative (the top Chinese agent) is his mother, the wife of a U.S. senator. An ironic incident is that Raymond Shaw, under the control of his mother, responds to a Queen of Hearts playing card. When he sees a Queen of Hearts he is in the control of his foreign agents, or the Queen can free him from the control of the agents. At a masquerade party, having been "secured" by his mother, he sees the love of his life, Josie Jordon, at the party. He hasn't seen her in years. And what is she masquerading as? The Queen of Hearts! And so he falls out of "control by his mother" and into the arms of his former lover. He promptly marries Josie and for a short time becomes a "normal person." But murder is in the cards. Raymond will be "recaptured" by his mother, who orders him to kill his father-in-law, Senator Jordon. Because she is present, he also kills Josie. Tragedy has come full circle. It is these narrative or character shifts that push us out of the story toward the voice of

Axelrod and Frankenheimer; and then very quickly the thriller (the form) and plot bring us back into the narrative.

The question then for us is what are the strategies that bring us into the narrative, and what are the strategies that push us out of the narrative? Clearly the choices available have to do with character, structure, the plot layer, the character layer, and form. What also needs to be added to this mix is the issue of reliability versus unreliability. How to consider this issue is the notion from documentary of a narrator. The narrator can be first person or third person (distanced, sometimes referred to as the voice of God). Both forms of narration can be either reliable or unreliable. What's important is that the unreliable narrator is distancing, particularly when what we see is out of accord with what the narrator is telling us. The voice-over in *Apocalypse Now* (1979) is a good example of this strategy. The narration is confessional and seems personal, but it's misleading as well, particularly about the evolution of the mission. This notion of unreliability can move us toward the voice of the writer-director, and away from character, structure, and form. We turn now to this issue of experiments in voice.

THE INTELLECTUAL VOICE:
MIKE NICHOLS AND FRANKLIN SCHAFFNER

We saw in Chapter 8, "The National Model," a number of good examples of experimentation in voice. The comedies of Eric Rohmer suggest his particular notions about personal behavior and honesty of intention, and Bill Bennett's work in *Kiss or Kill* takes a realist genre, the gangster film, and gives it a much darker hue akin to film noir. These are examples that set the parameters for this chapter—experiments that lie between genre expectations and the voice of the writer-director. This chapter, in turn, will set up the parameters for the chapter that follows, the ascent of voice where genre expectations, in particular character expectations, are violated for the primacy of voice. To understand more fully this transition, we begin with two filmmakers who respect genre expectations but who do not hold to its orthodoxy in order to leave some space for their voice. These filmmakers also exercise a bigger viewpoint that contextualizes their narratives within their societies. I call theirs the intellectual voice. We turn first to the work of Mike Nichols.

Mike Nichols from the outset was interested in the relationships of men and women. Unlike some filmmakers who will take a particular perspective, such as George Cukor and Vincente Minnelli and their capacity to empathize with women's point of view, and filmmakers such as Robert Aldrich and Richard Brooks who are very interested in presenting the male point of view, Nichols is interested in a number of points of view. He is sympathetic to the points of view of both a young man and an older woman in *The Graduate* (1967); he is sympathetic to the married couple in *Who's Afraid of Virginia Woolf?* (1966); and he's sympathetic to men on the prowl as well as to their prey, young women, in *Carnal Knowledge* (1971). If there is a deeper position that he takes it's that all of us, men and women, are trapped in the roles families and society expect of us. He respects how men and women can help each other overcome that trap, whether it's love, respect, or intelligence that is the key. His voice is respectful of the individual goals of men and women and how they can help each other in relationships. This is the key to the outcomes in *Who's Afraid of Virginia Woolf?* and in *Regarding Henry* (1991). Simultaneously, Nichols is making melodramas or situation comedies that maintain their genre characteristics so that we can emotionally remain with his characters. Two examples that could push the satirical edge or voice further don't—in order to maintain that emotional relationship with the audience.

Working Girl (1988) is the story of Tess McGill, an ambitious secretary. She has taken business courses, has a degree, has ideas, but her working class background and the attitudes of her bosses conspire to hold her back. The catalytic event is that her new boss is a woman, but as she discovers at the turning point of Act I, the boss, Katherine, says she will help Tess but in fact she is using Tess's business idea, an acquisition of radio stations for Trask industries. In Act II, with Katherine laid up with a broken leg, Tess promotes the idea herself via a merger expert Jack Trainor. She is successful with the idea, and with Trainer. Although Katherine tries to take all the credit, and Trainor, at the turning point in Act II, Tess will overcome these obstacles and be promoted in business by Trask and in a relationship with Jack Trainor.

Mike Nichols has respected the characteristics of the situation comedy in *Working Girl*. We identify with the goal-directed Tess. Her path is challenged by an effective antagonist, Katherine. The character layer offers options—her working class boyfriend and the upper-class Trainor. And the plot layer, the acquisition strategy for Trask Industries, is a daunting challenge to Tess' goal. The genre works as one expects the situation comedy to work. But there is something extra here, the voice of Mike Nichols around the issue of relationships. There is love and there is sexuality in the Tess-Trainor relationship. But there is also a tremendous empathy for both of these people. Part of this empathy is achieved negatively, as in the betrayal of Tess by her boyfriend. She finds him in bed with another woman in their apartment. There is also the betrayal of Tess and Trainor by Katherine who claims that Tess' idea is her own. Her lies again for the sake of ambition make her betrayal twofold: she betrays and lies to Tess as an employee, and she doubly betrays and lies to Tess as a woman. The balance of empathy is derived from the decency of Tess and Trainor. They are respectful of one another and of others, as in Trainor's awkwardness when he has to tell Katherine that he can't marry her.

Nichol's opportunity for genre violation is even greater in *Primary Colors* (1998), the film about the 1992 Clinton campaign for the Presidency based on the novel by Joe Klein. All the elements are present for the kind of treatment found in Mamet's *Wag the Dog* (1998), which is essentially a satire. That's not how Nichols treats the story of the campaign in *Primary Colors*, however. He treats it as a mix of melodrama and situation comedy, essentially realist, where the candidate, Governor Jack Stanton (John Travolta) and his wife, Susan Stanton (Emma Thompson) are characters who are charismatic and goal-directed; they want to win the nomination and eventually the election. They have lots of opposition, as one would expect. But Nichols focuses on how the internal issue—the candidate as his own worst enemy via his "extracurricular activities"—is dealt with by his wife as well as by his advisors, including his former campaign manager, Libby Holden (Kathy Bates). If there is a character who is a main character here, it's actually his black political advisor, Henry Burton, who is coming to grips with his own ambition throughout the campaign. For Henry, however, the premise is idealism or ambition. And the experience of the plot, the campaign, is treated as a loss-of-innocence melodrama.

Again Nichols is interested in relationships—the marriage, the relationships within a campaign that are so intense they are like a marriage. Can the candidate maintain any dignity after all that is uncovered and undertaken to achieve power? The answer given is yes, if that power is achieved. Again Nichols could have gone the route of satire, but the fact that he chooses the melodrama/situation comedy mix illustrates again that men and women in relationships, their behavior and their individuality, are more important than the singular skewering of the political figures that the novel *Primary Colors* was based upon.

If Mike Nichols is interested in men and women in relationships in the positive and negative senses, Franklin Schaffner is interested in the behavior of men. His interest is broader than the testosterone vision of men in Oliver Stone's work, and it is also broader than the unique comradeship of men as portrayed in the work of Sam Peckinpah. Perhaps the filmmaker that Schaffner most closely resembles is Howard Hawks, although Hawks' focus was on the importance of rites of passage for men. For Hawks, circumstance, age, and culture would determine the frequency of such a rite, and genre would determine how eccentric males can be. Schaffner's choice of genres and approach is more reality-bound than Hawks; but the focus on men and their need for a code to moderate their behavior is a primary element in Schaffner's work. His affection for realist genres, however, moderates his voice, as was the case for Mike Nichols.

Schaffner's main characters have a powerful sense of entitlement. His Patton is a man who feels that he himself descended from Julius Caesar. Taylor in *Planet of the Apes* (1968) feels he is at the top of his game in the human department and consequently he is condescending to his colleagues, to the woman he takes up with on the planet of the apes, and to the apes themselves. In *The War Lord* (1965), set in eleventh century England, the new lord of the domain (again Charlton Heston) takes advantage of his right—to bed a village bride on her wedding night. After that he decides not to return her to her new husband. Papillon in *Papillon* (1973) believes that he was framed for a crime and sent to Devil's Island—even though life as a criminal might lead someone to believe that prison was a real possibility. And the sculptor in *Islands in the Stream* (1977) believes that his work and the environment, physical and emotional, supersedes issues of family, children, community, and society. Consequently, he is entitled to proceed with life decisions that support his work above all else.

If entitlement were all there were, these men would be selfish indeed. These characters all have a talent, a gift, and they have a passion that makes them charismatic and also comprehensible in their actions. The opposite to such figures is the Oliver Stone male character whose actions are passionate but incomprehensible—and thereby less worthy of our empathy. If Stone's men are feeling all the time, Schaffner's men are thinking and feeling all the time. Schaffner's War Lord is a dutiful knight who is relentless in battle, but knows he's left a void in his personal life. Patton is aggressive tactically and projects a sense of invulnerability in war, but he is impervious to feeling too much. If he did, he could not proceed to fulfill his destiny. Taylor in *Planet of the Apes* believes so strongly in his mastery that he lives while his two colleagues end up dead and stuffed. He also convinces the scientist ape who works with him to allow him and his mate to escape. The sculptor in *Islands in the Stream* is a great fisherman and protective of his drunken friend. And Papillon has a will of steel. Isolated in darkness, he keeps his mind and body sound enough to continue in his escape plans. All these men infuse their relationships with passion—passion for a woman in *The War Lord*, passion for freedom in *Papillon*, passion for a young son in *Island of the Stream*, but none of them relinquish their intelligence in doing so.

These men need some kind of code to check and to channel their drives. Patton needs the military code. Papillon needs the penal code. The sculptor needs the survival code of war in *Islands of the Stream*, and the War Lord needs the code of his duke to check his impulses in *The War Lord*. All of these male characters challenge but need more powerful external codes to keep their powers in check. This limitation is viewed as a good thing. Without it the men who are talented would deploy their talents too indulgently and the outcome would be their own destruction.

Franklin Schaffner works principally in melodrama, although *Planet of the Apes* is science fiction and *Patton* is a war film. Nevertheless, his treatment of the dramatic arc is always as a melodrama's arc—the struggle of the powerless character against the power structure. He uses genre within a realistic mode, whether it is melodrama or science fiction. His voice is consequently masked by our relationship with the main character. But it is in his treatment of that main character, a male, and in his treatment of the dramatic arc for that character, that Schaffner's voice is present and clear.

THE MORE ASSERTIVE VOICE:
ARTHUR PENN AND ROBERT ALTMAN

When I was a film student, no American director after Orson Welles was more admired than Arthur Penn. He had made a psychoanalytic western, *The Left-Handed Gun* (1958), and he had made an intellectual thriller, *Mickey One* (1965). From these two works one could see a director looking for a style that was at odds with the narrative elements of character and structure, so that we would be shaken out of our genre expectations into something far more uncomfortable. It's as if Penn wanted to warn us about appearances. "It's not what you think. You're being lulled. Wake up. Think. Act." In his own way, Penn saw his films as his own form of political action—and that is the voice of Arthur Penn, the voice as expressed more specifically in the work that was to follow.

In *Bonnie and Clyde* (1967) that voice finds its path in the tonal shifts that are powerfully juxtaposed. *Bonnie and Clyde* is a gangster film that follows the expected rise and fall dramatic arc, the career of Clyde Barrow and Bonnie Parker. Penn positions the two main characters as well-defined characters caught up in an adolescent relationship with one another. The robberies initially arise out of Bonnie teasing Clyde and of Clyde's desire to impress Bonnie. They have the naivete and cruelty of adolescents—they rob and they kill if they have to. But they are very much adolescents, and thus they seem too involved with their relationship's progress to weigh the consequences of their actions. As their career progresses, they enjoy their outlaw adulation. At last they are getting attention. The fact that it is the kind of attention that will lead to their demise is superseded by their adolescent pleasure in the attention.

The first half of the narrative is peppered with humor. There is Clyde's sister-in-law; a kidnapped accountant; the politeness of the thieves toward their victims—then the occasional shock of violence, such as a bank teller killed, is a bucket of cold water on the illusion of innocence and play that pervades these early criminal activities. But in the latter half of the narrative the killing of Clyde's brother and the wounding of his sister-in-law set up the brutality of the killing of Bonnie and Clyde that concludes the narrative. This tonal shift from the humor of play in the first half to the extreme brutality of death in the latter half, is the area where Penn establishes his voice. The result is a surreal treatment of an essentially realist genre, the gangster film. Whether Penn is commenting on criminality in American society, or upon the mythology surrounding the gangster as a public figure and a media figure, or whether the brutality in the narrative links up with the war in Viet Nam, or all three, the film is a wake-up call to its audience.

The same can be said of *Little Big Man* (1970). Here the subject is another American mythological figure, the westerner, the white man as the white knight of the West. The centerpiece of the film, the Sand River Indian massacre and the consequent massacre of General George Custer and his seventh cavalry at the Little Big Horn are two famous (or infamous) events in the history of the conquest of the West by the forces of the U.S. government. The main character, Jack Crabb (Dustin Hoffman), is introduced to us as an old man being interviewed about these two events. In order to present his viewpoint, he tells his personal history and the context for his involvement in both events. He was adopted by the Cheyenne Indians as a young boy. He was a survivor of an Indian attack on his family, and he grows up the adopted son of the Cheyenne. When he is rescued, he doesn't feel like a white man. He feels more Indian than white. He marries an Indian woman only to lose her in the Sand Creek massacre. He meets helpful white men—Wild Bill Hickcock, a swindler named Merriweather—but most whites are like George Custer, self-centered and self-serving. The Cheyenne are represented by his grandfather, Chief Dan George. The grandfather calls the Cheyenne human beings. He feels that in the end the Indian way of life will be destroyed because there is an endless supply of white men but a limited number of human beings.

Jack Crabb lives somewhere in between the white world and the Indian world. He is the narrator of the story. Is he a reliable narrator? Since Penn mixes so much humor with the brutality once again, as in *Bonnie and Clyde*, we are caught outside genre expectations. In the western the classic struggle of primitivism versus civilization proceeds with the Indians representing the virtues of primitivism and the whites representing civilization, the negative polarity in the western. Generally in the western, civilization means materialism. In *Little Big Man*, civilization means cruelty, exploitation of the environment, and a general meanness of spirit that is represented by the swindler Merriweather. He swindles people but sees it as a good business risk with good rewards. Whites are seen as cruel members of the military, or as civilian prostitutes, such as Mrs. Pendrake (Faye Dunaway). There is no good corner here on civilization. By alternating humor with super-realism in the context of a poetic pastoral genre, Penn again asserts his voice.

Ten years later Arthur Penn made *Four Friends* (1981), Steve Tesich's meditation on the legacy of the 1960s. This time the genre is melodrama and the struggle for the main character, Danilo, a Yugoslav-American, is either to be like his father, a steelworker, or his own man, an American. For Danilo this means breaking away from his family and going away to college. He does so in Act II. He leaves his friends behind and tries to be a real American. He becomes engaged to Adrienne, his roommate's sister. A complication is Adrienne's incestuous relationship with her father. At the wedding party that ends Act II, the girl's father, Mr. Carnahan, shoots Adrienne and Danilo. Danilo survives. Act II is over, and the great experiment of being American is over. In Act III he goes ethnic, but this doesn't work either, so in the end he chooses to take up with his high school girlfriend (a hippie), Georgia, and to become a college teacher. But en route he goes through social protest, the sexual revolution, the drug revolution, and the anti-American revolution, all in Act III, and in the end comes to appreciate that in America you choose to be who you choose to be. Penn is far more realist in *Four Friends* than in his other films, but he always displays great empathy for the struggle of the main character to find himself.

Penn still resorts to shock—the shootings at the end of Act II, Georgia's acid trip in New York—but the gap between humor and brutality in Penn's work has closed. It's as if more realism and less tonal shift was necessary when *Four Friends* was made.

Robert Altman also uses genre violation to accentuate his voice. Altman is best known for his satires—on war in *M*A*S*H* (1970), on politics in *Nashville* (1975), on fashion in *Pret-à-Porter* (1994), and on ultra-urbanization in *Short Cuts* (1993). Of course, humor is critical in satire as is irony. Altman mixes irony together with humor to fuel his satires. Irony can be created by structure, as in *Short Cuts*. It can be created by the contrast in the behavior of characters, as in *M*A*S*H*. And it can be created in the dialogue, as in *Nashville* (1975). To see how Altman highlights his voice let's look at the operation of irony in three different genres. First the western.

McCabe and Mrs. Miller (1971) is the story of McCabe, a businessman, gambler, and gunman. By framing this character in the western, Altman is working in a genre where the main character is positioned as a hero who represents primitive or pastoral values (morality, justice, harmony with the environment) in a struggle against the materialist values of civilization. The first source of irony or distancing in the narrative is how Altman positions the main character. As a businessman, McCabe represents the values of civilization.

The second irony is that although McCabe is known as a gunman, he is not differentiated from the other men presented in the narrative. He is scrambling for his share of prosperity in a nascent town, as are the others. Instead of the presentation of the western hero as an individual, as in Sydney Pollack's *Jeremiah Johnson*, for example, McCabe is a character in line with the turn of the century Northwest and its population.

Altman follows a similar approach to his main character in the detective story, *The Long Goodbye* (1972). Here Phillip Marlowe is an extension of the drug-hazed Los Angeles of the 1970s. Marlowe in Edward Dmytryk's *Murder By Sweet* (1944) is individuated; he is neither a policeman nor an affiliate of grey characters, as the Paul Newman character is in Robert Benton's detective story *Twilight* (1998). The first concern we have about Marlowe in *The Long Goodbye* is how will he be able to solve a crime when he can't outfox his cat about the brand of cat food he is serving her. In fact, the story will proceed to see this Marlowe as someone who is continually victimized by the police, by the mob, and by his friend Terry whom he drives to Mexico at the outset of the narrative. When he kills Terry in the end, we understand it not so much as the solution of a crime but as the bitter result of feeling betrayed by his friend. Instead of the heroic Marlowe of earlier film versions, Altman's Marlowe is a victim, just as McCabe was a victim in his *McCabe and Mrs. Miller*. In both *The Long Goodbye* and *McCabe and Mrs. Miller*, character and the treatment of the character together with the arc of the narrative undermine genre expectations. The result is to satirize the form and, indirectly, the society of the day that commands that genre proceed according to expectation.

Altman's voice also raises another aspect of reframing the main character in the western and in the detective film as a victim. In a sense, doing so is the equivalent of having an unreliable narrator as the main character. Since we do not trust the character or find the character insincere in a treatment that goes against genre expectation, we are distanced from the character and, as a result, we experience the voice of Altman rather than identifying with the main character.

This impulse is carried even further in Altman's *The Player* (1992). In this satire on Hollywood values (the more you mistreat people, the higher you go, and if you murder them, you could become the head of a studio!), Altman is focusing on a main character, Griffin Mill, a studio executive, who is being threatened by a disgruntled writer, David Kahane. At the end of the first act he kills Kahane; at the end of Act II he is dismissed as a suspect in the murder investigation; and by the end of Act III, he is married to June, the writer's girlfriend, has moved up in the studio, and discovers that he killed the wrong person. He is still being threatened. Here Griffin is always positioned to be victimized: he is caught, harassed, about to be fired, or charged with a crime. So here we have a reversal—an evil man is being treated in the narrative (structurally) as if he is an innocent. This reversal parallels Altman's treatment of the cowboy McCabe in *McCabe and Mrs.*

Miller and detective Marlowe in *The Long Goodbye*. Again, the treatment of the character forces us into an ambivalent relationship with the main character. Once more the unreliability of the voice or and our identification with that main character pushes Altman's voice into the foreground. Here again irony serves the purpose of elevating the voice of the filmmaker.

THE ASSERTIVE VOICE:
STANLEY KUBRICK AND QUENTIN TARANTINO

Stanley Kubrick has been a genre filmmaker, but he has adapted these story forms in a way that has allowed him to aggressively put forward a distinctive voice. He has done so by experimenting, in his gangster film *The Killing* (1956), for example, with the use of a narrator who distances us from the action. He also altered the balance of the plot layer and the character layer in favor of plot. In *The Killing* Kubrick began his meditation on human failings, a theme he would pursue to the end of his career.

In *Paths of Glory* (1957), Kubrick's first war film, he experimented with the placement of the main character in the plot. That plot, set in World War I, is the attack on a German position called the Ant Hill and its aftermath, the execution of three French soldiers for cowardice in the face of the enemy. The plot involves two parties that are, if you will, the protagonists and antagonists. Contrary to expectation, the antagonist in this war film is not the enemy, the Germans, but rather two French generals, and the protagonists are the three soldiers who don't survive the punishment designated for them by their leaders, the generals. The main character who leads the attack and also acts as the defending lawyer for the three soldiers is Colonel Dax (Kirk Douglas). Because his life is not at risk as the lives of the three accused men are, Colonel Dax is the voice of reason in the midst of the insanity of war and power politics among the general staff. He represents Kubrick's voice.

In *Dr. Strangelove or How I Learned to Stop Worrying and Love the Bomb* (1964), Kubrick uses humor and absurdity to find his voice with respect to the subject of accidental nuclear war. In *Lolita* (1962), his adaptation of Nabokov's novel, he uses the dissonance between unrealistic desire (Humbert Humbert) and a paranoid humor (Claire Quilty). Quilty, the entertainer, succeeds in seducing Lolita where Humbert keeps trying and fails to be more than a pawn for Lolita. The tonal shifts between characters create the space for Kubrick's voice. In *2001: A Space Odyssey* (1969), this is accomplished by the sheer audacity of setting the classical struggle of technology versus humanity, the core of the science fiction film, against the narrative sweep of the entire "history" of humankind, including its future. In *Full Metal Jacket*, Kubrick's voice emerges from the structural focus on a two-act plot and Joker, a main character who like Colonel Dax is positioned on the periphery of the action of the plot. Joker too provides a character who observes and comments on the destruction of his fellow soldiers at the hands of their officers as much as at the hands of the enemy.

To yield an appreciation of how powerful that voice can be, I turn to Kubrick's two least "successful" films, *Barry Lyndon* and *Eyes Wide Shut*. Kubrick's *Barry Lyndon* (1975) is his adaptation of the Thackeray novel. This portrait of an Irish young man who, through his lack of means and his impetuous nature, falls from grace, marries a rich widow, exploits her, abuses her son, and is eventually seriously wounded by that son. He ends his days poor. Kubrick means to point out once again the disappointing nature of human frailty, and he does so with a profound sense of inevitability and a profound sense of tragedy. Kubrick distances us from Barry Lyndon by essentially creating a person it is impossible to admire. Barry, even when given the opportunity, never rises to the occasion. He spoils his own son with a gift that eventually kills him. The boy is killed by Barry's kindness, just as Barry's humiliation of his stepson kills Barry's relationship to the wealth and name of his wife's family. Barry is not a victim of others, he is a victim of his own character. This is the human tragedy played out in Kubrick style.

In *Eyes Wide Shut* (1999) a successful New York couple live a life that is materially rich but spiritually empty. *Eyes Wide Shut* is the journey of the main characters, Dr. Harford (Tom Cruise) and his wife, Alice, (Nicole Kidman) in search of self-gratification. Their self-love, whether wrapped in his altruistic cloak or her restless self-intoxication needs to be fed. An incident at a high society party begins a fevered journey for Dr. Harford. Alice plants a seed of doubt in his mind that there is another man in her life, which in turn fuels her need for excitement and his doubt that he can meet her needs. What follows is a figurative hallucination that he can find the key to excitement, to the mysteries of sexual ecstasy. He tries a prostitute. He visits a pornographic party for the rich. The castle merges the pleasure principle with sadism. A woman who tries to help him is killed for her kindness. The journey has turned into a nightmare. Although we stay with his point of view, in the end it is Alice who voices resigned disappointment. In the end, she is reconciled to their relationship, with its limits of reality (they are parents). But it is a disappointment, and who knows what lies ahead for this couple. Again Kubrick is focusing on human frailty and disappointment in this narrative, even in the midst of wealth and material well-being and status. It's as if the film narrative verifies Freud's conclusive views on the potential for psychoanalysis. The patient is cured, but now they have to wake up to the misery of everyday existence.

Quentin Tarantino is a writer-director who has focused his voice on a narrower band of genres, principally the gangster film. Nevertheless, he has used structure and character to assert his voice. In *Reservoir Dogs* (1992), *Pulp Fiction* (1994), and *Jackie Brown* (1997), Tarantino has used the rise and fall shape of the gangster film as his preferred form. But he has played with the form using nonlinear structure in both *Reservoir Dogs* and *Pulp Fiction*. And in each of the three narratives he has preferred to focus on low-level characters. None of them are the masters of their fate, and as a result they are not driven by ambition but rather by issues of loyalty, of belonging. The consequence is that plot, so central in the genre, is played down, and behavior or the character layer is elevated.

Because there is no single main character in either *Reservoir Dogs* or *Pulp Fiction*, creating goals to move us through the narrative is a challenge. The characters in *Pulp Fiction* and *Reservoir Dogs* have a short-term goal, but they don't seem to have a long-term goal. The consequence is the sense that they are characters in search of an identity. Even Jackie Brown needs the better part of the narrative to articulate a longer-term goal for herself.

Tarantino's voice is powerful because he focuses on the less powerful presentation of the gangster character. In fact, he focuses on characters who are powerless and look to their peers (the group) for definition, for meaning. Whether they get that momentary power or not will depend upon the forces of rivalry and betrayal in the group. The betrayer might be the mob boss in *Pulp Fiction,* or an undercover cop in *Reservoir Dogs*. Whereas the classic gangster film is intended to explore ambition and the American success story in a gangster frame, Tarantino is working with the idea that gangs are traps, and only when you break free from loyalty and group pressure can you have a future. Jackie Brown manages to do this. Jules (Samuel L. Jackson) in *Pulp Fiction* manages to walk away. So the goal of Tarantino's voice is to find the limits in the gangster myth as an American success story. His view is far darker.

By resorting to a nonlinear structure and by emphasizing the character layer over plot, Tarantino forcefully moves us towards his revisionist position on the important urban myth of the gangster. He serves as an apt transition to the very forceful and often dark assertion of voice that we find in Joel and Ethan Coen and in Tod Solondz, the subjects we now turn to.

PART III

THE INTERNATIONALIZATION OF STORYTELLING

THE ASCENT OF VOICE

There have always been film storytellers whose voices were more dominant than the stories and their characters. Luis Buñuel and Jean-Luc Godard are among the most important. As we saw in the last chapter, Stanley Kubrick and Quentin Tarantino have been very assertive in using structure and character to focus their ideas—about power in the case of Kubrick, and about the influence of the media in the case of Tarantino. What is notable in the past twenty-five years is that film-makers are far more bold about their own ideas than was the case in the past. This may be because of the perceived power of the medium. For the longest time, particularly in the United States, film was considered an entertainment medium, and consequently the level of ambition of its storytellers was circumscribed by their perception of the medium. Chaplin and Welles were exceptions. Today there are far fewer exceptions, and the consequence is that there are far more film storytellers who view character and structure as the means to express their own views, particularly about society and power in that society. This ascent of voice is not only an American phenomenon. We see it in many other national cinemas as well. It is to this ascent in voice that we now turn.

JUZO ITAMI—THE SOFT SATIRIST

Juzo Itami stands apart from the formal aesthetic and exotic layers of film story-telling in Japan. I have labeled his approach soft satire, but it is actually richer than that label suggests. His voice is quite distinct. We will look at his films *The Funeral* (1986) and *A Taxing Woman* (1987) to illustrate that voice. Later in the book, Chapter 12, "The Search for New Forms," we will also look at his film *Tampopo*, which combines the themes and narrative strategies he explores in *The Funeral* and *A Taxing Woman*.

On the surface, *The Funeral* seems to be a straightforward film. It begins with the death of the patriarch of a family and concludes with the end of the post-funeral family gathering. The narrative could almost be viewed as an anthropological document of the process. But that is not Itami's intention. Although he focuses on the salient events—the death, the identification of the body by the family, choosing the casket, organizing the formal funeral in a manner respectful to the deceased and the family he has left behind—Itami is more interested in the gap between grieving in a personal sense and the public acknowledgment of the loss. In that gap he satirizes the selfishness of individuals who are too wrapped up in their own loss to do more than pay lip service to the dead. In the course of doing so he poses questions about the meaning of the public process of burying a person. For Itami, burying and mourning are different, and in the film the burial implicitly overshadows the mourning.

To make his point, Itami uses humor. In the prologue, Mr. Amamiya at that point alive returns from a doctor's visit. He was pronounced in good health, and consequently he has bought his favorite foods—barbecued pork, avocado and eel—a cholesterol-heavy feast on which he gorges himself. Shortly thereafter he falls ill with severe chest pain. His wife, with the help of a neighbor (a psychiatrist), organizes a cab to the hospital. Mr. Amamiya walks into the cab on his own. At the hospital, Mr. Amamiya has another heart attack and dies. The approach Itami takes suggests that this sixty-nine-year-old man challenged his system, it rebelled, and he died. In other words, the victim brought on his fate.

The family is alerted, and when they gather they don't seem overwhelmed. They seem distracted. This sense of distraction finds its apogee when his son-in-law's mistress comes to pay her respect at the country home where the wake will take place. What she really wants is reassurance that the son-in-law still loves her. And so he must reassure her, missionary-style, in the woods adjacent to the house where the father-in-law's body lies.

This level of self-absorption is prevalent among the mourners. They can't wait to get the formalities over with so that they can return to their careers and to their possessions. If there is a prevailing voice in *The Funeral* it is that selfish people don't experience feeling; they go through the motions and do what is expected rather than what is more deeply respectful. Itami makes this point in as bawdy a manner as possible.

If *The Funeral* is treated as a situation comedy, *A Taxing Woman*, which is also very humorous, adopts the form of the western—the struggle of primitive or virtuous values against civilization or materialist values. The hero is a female tax inspector, Ryoko Itakura, who is zealous in catching and reforming those who defraud the government. Gordo, the antagonist of the narrative, is everything "the bad guy" should be in the western. He is cruel to his mistresses. He is insatiably cunning and greedy. His schemes to avoid taxation require a team of accountants and powerful people. He doesn't ride a horse, but he is driven in a white Rolls Royce. As in *The Funeral*, Itami is bawdy in his humor and aggressive in the cruelty of the antagonist. The ritual character of "the gunfight" is replaced by the ritual of the tax raid. Although the film is set in modern Tokyo, the narrative structure is the frame of the western. The frame also allows Itami to mock the values of Ryoko, the tax collector, as well as of Gordo, the tax evader. His voice—his use of soft satire—takes up a national pastime, tax evasion, and skewers it and the members of the society on both sides of the issue. The real target for Itami is the social behavior of individuals in a society where public behavior masks private intention. This is his real target.

For those of us in the audience, our connection to Itami is enhanced by the lack of an empathic character for us to relate to. In *The Funeral*, Mr. Amamiya, the victim of the heart attack, as well as the members of his family, are in turn held up to scrutiny and a measure of contempt. In *A Taxing Woman*, the narrative shape, framing a modern tale of tax fraud in terms of the old-fashioned western with its heroes and villains, also distances us from Ryoko and Gordo. They become caricatures to be moved away from identification and toward service to the satirical view of Itami. Both form and character are used to enhance the voice of criticism—all are held up to ridicule by the filmmaker.

NEIL LABUTE—THE CRUEL SATIRIST

Neil LaBute, a playwright as well as a writer-director, has made his reputation on the basis of two films, *In the Company of Men* (1997) and *Your Friends and Neighbors* (1998). Both are contemporary narratives about relationships, and both present their subject from the male point of view.

In *In the Company of Men* two corporate males, Chad and Howard, are temporarily transferred to a big city in the Midwest. To amuse themselves they make a wager to see who can bed, Christine, the least appealing woman in the company, in this case a young woman who is deaf. They proceed to compete with one another for Christine. The more aggressive of the two, Chad, wins, although Howard really falls for Christine. Before leaving, but after making commitments and securing favors, Chad confesses to Christine that it was all a hoax, he doesn't really love her. He leaves her crushed and moves on, out of town, back to the real jungle, presumably to continue in his predatory ways.

It would be very easy to conclude that the film is misogynistic and hateful in its cruelty. In a sense it may be. But on another level LaBute is making a comment about the war between men and women, a war that's been in high gear since the sexual revolution. What he's saying is that men have to assert who is in control more than they need the relationship. It's about power. Who better to illustrate your power over than a woman who is made powerless not only by virtue of a lower position in the company but also by her physical impairment. And the fact that Christine can't hear makes Chad and Howard more bold in their open cruelty.

This is not a very flattering portrait of a man. Indeed, LaBute is rather scathing in his lack of sympathy or empathy for Chad and Howard. They are scavengers. LaBute's real target is the cult of male behavior that feeds on conquest, humiliation, and manipulation. The fact that wagers born out of boredom are used to excite Chad and Howard also suggests a level of narcissism that is plainly destructive. Whether it's corporate life or something more systemic, LaBute doesn't find redemption or hope in this behavior. Quite the opposite. The behavior is likened to the behavior that led to the fall of the Roman Empire—read American Empire. Not a very pretty picture.

It doesn't get any better in *Your Friends and Neighbors*. This time three couples are involved. Jerry and Terri, Barry and Mary, and Cary and Cheri may be couples, but they don't seem to derive any solace from being together. Indeed, when the three men get together they are competitive, but nevertheless there is a greater bond or trust than is present in the relationships of the couples themselves. As the couples migrate in and out of each other's beds we get the sense that sex itself doesn't quench appetite and need. There is dissatisfaction with the self here, and the different characters adopt a quantitative strategy to a qualitative problem. What we are left with in the end is a portrait, again cruel, again from the male perspective, of man as predator and woman as victim.

It's as if LaBute is using chess as his narrative model. In the end there is only one winner. But when checkmate is declared, LaBute is using the concept ironically. There is only the satisfaction of winning; the characters are alone spiritually and consequently lonely. It's an empty victory.

As in *In The Company of Men*, the male characters in *Your Friends and Neighbors* are not very sympathetic. The level of self-absorption, manipulation, and cruelty distance us from them, particularly from Cary, the most assertive and cruel of the males. What is interesting structurally is that there is no plot, only character layer, and that the structure has a loose, nonlinear shape. The result is episodic and inconclusive. The absence of plot also places disproportionate narrative expectations on character complexity and dialogue. Here LaBute is as cruel as he is elsewhere. The dialogue is manipulative, evasive, parrying, and not at all confessional as the characters present it. LaBute does not let them off lightly. Nor does he let us off lightly. His voice is aimed directly at contemporary, self-absorbed men and women. These are people who don't trust others and can't seem to develop nurturing relationships that will sustain them. The self is too protected. This is the tragedy of his characters and his view of the tragedy of contemporary American life. We are the target of his cruel satire.

NEIL JORDAN—THE VOICE OF TOLERANCE

Neil Jordan has been prolific and ecumenical in his work. He has moved through various genres, ranging from horror in *Interview with a Vampire* (1993), the gangster film in *Mona Lisa* (1985), the political thriller in *The Crying Game* (1992), a class melodrama in *The End of the Affair* (1999), and the unorthodox melodrama *The Butcher Boy* (1996). Perhaps the quintessential Jordan film, the film that illustrates his tolerance beautifully, is his romantic melodrama *The Miracle* (1990).

James, the protagonist of *The Miracle*, lives in a small coastal town that is a train ride from Dublin. He is a musical teenager who overcomes his boredom by making up literary stories about romance in the life of the least likely citizens—a group of nuns, for example, or a lonely elderly gentlemen. The setting is romantic, but the population isn't. James, however, is romantic, and his view of the world is that everyone else is as well. This is a suitable projection for the views of the main character. A real woman comes into James' life. She comes off the train from Dublin. She is beautiful. She is mysterious. James and his girlfriend speculate about this mysterious woman. Before Act I is over, James has spoken to the mystery woman and she has kissed him. The act turning point poses the problem. The woman who James has fallen in love with is the mother whom he thought was dead. He will find out who she really is by the end of the second act, but before he does, James pursues her with passion. His alcoholic father tries to warn her off, but she too is drawn to this boy-man who is her son.

I have suggested that Jordan is the voice of tolerance because he is very willing to explore a taboo—incest without judgment. James is an innocent romantic boy. His mother is also a romantic, and a bit foolish, but she is accepted by Jordan as is the son. James does fall out with his mother when he discovers the truth. He is angry, but in the end, he resumes his romantic outlook. Jordan has simply conveyed that love, romance, and passion do not know boundaries and that that state of unfiltered love is important in life.

Jordan displays this same tolerance for the main character in *The Butcher Boy* (1998). A twelve-year-old boy with the face of an angel, Francie, a boy whose alcoholic father and suicidal mother leave him unable to face life realistically, turns to making up a life. But in the course of this created life, he finds a negative polarity: a middle-class woman who overprotects her son.

As the narrative progresses, Francie's life goes from bad to worse. There's his father's alcoholism and abuse, and then there is the deteriorating state of his mother. At one point, she is hospitalized. Clearly her way to deal with her life situation is to manically bake. But her manic phases are always followed by depression. After hospitalization, she is better but a visit from a former lover and relative sets her back. Neglecting to take her medication, she commits suicide. And Francie's father sinks deeper into alcoholic rage toward Francie.

As Francie's real life situation deteriorates, he constructs greater internal fantasy. But he also focuses on a real target for his rage. That target is a schoolmate who has a real family. He loathes the boy for being nurtured (and overprotected), the opposite of his own family life.

Francie particularly views the schoolmate's mother with disdain. First he is only insulting, but later as his own inner life becomes chaotic, he externalizes that chaos and hatred upon this target, the mother of a boy who is receiving what he himself needs, but doesn't receive from his own family.

In the end, Francie murders her. Actually, he butchers her. This insane act is the irrational act of a boy whose life has been scarred continually by loss. His anger finds its outlet in a target.

Although the narrative is dark and tragic, Jordan uses a voiceover to present the inner voice of the main character as a creative and imagined antidote to his reality. It's not confessional, it's compensatory, seeing the world as a better place that it is; its invented it's created, and in being so Jordan lightens the darkness of the narrative. We hear Francie and we wish, as he does, that life had been better, but for Francie it hasn't been. Again Jordan tolerates the intolerable.

Jordan's capacity to empathize is also notable in the conversion of Fergus, a killer into a loving man in *The Crying Game*. It's worth mentioning that, without irony, Fergus falls in love with Dil, the transsexual lover of his actual victim, Jody, a black soldier. By moving the heterosexual Fergus into a homosexual love affair and relationship with Dil, Jordan is pushing the notion of tolerance forcefully but nevertheless believably. The film conforms to the realism necessary in both of its layers as a thriller and as a melodrama.

The fact that the gangster, George, in Jordan's earlier film, *Mona Lisa*, falls in love with the black madam, Simone, he chauffeurs around town, and the fact that in the end he saves her from death by killing Mortwell, his own employer, highlights how far people will go when they care about others. This is particularly poignant because when we are introduced to George at the opening of the story he is violent and apparently racist. For George to save Simone, a black woman at the narrative's conclusion is a transformation very much in keeping with the Jordan voice of tolerance.

Before we leave Neil Jordan, it's important to mention that passion, romance, friendship, and loyalty are all dimensions of tolerance taken up by Jordan in his work. But to achieve a believability factor, Jordan always sprinkles pixie dust in the environment or in the behavior of his characters. There's always a little magic in the air in Jordan films. It's an enabling magic that makes more believable that tolerance does exist.

SPIKE LEE—THE TEACHER/PREACHER

Spike Lee has from the outset of his career favored educational over entertainment goals. In his most powerful works, *Do the Right Thing* (1989) and *Jungle Fever* (1991), there was a fervor about the ideas, about racism and its consequences, and about interracial marriage, that added a zealous sense of outrage to the work. It is this dimension of the work that I view as Spike Lee the preacher. Spike Lee the teacher is on best display in his pro-family ideas expressed vividly in *Crooklyn* (1994) and in *Clockers* (1995). Both dimensions come together in his film *Summer of Sam* (1999).

Although *Summer of Sam* has a plot, a series of killings in New York in the summer of 1977, the plot, including the apprehension of the killer, the son of Sam, forms the background to a mood in the city that can only be described as a fear so palpable that it unleashes personal behavior more in keeping with the plot of *On the Beach*, the post-nuclear holocaust novel by Neville Shute. The behavior of the characters in *Summer of Sam*, then, is impulse-driven and emotionally violent, and the behavior is out of proportion to the life circumstances or personal choices made by the characters.

The characters are a tight group of twenty-something young adults, particularly Vinnie and Richie and Dionna and Ruby, Italian Americans who grew up together in a small Italian neighborhood near the beach in Brooklyn. The film narrative focuses on two relationships within a larger peer group. That peer group is macho, racist, and aggressive. What binds these young men is the notion that if you are in any way different you are the enemy and have to be brutally excluded. The two men who are the focal points of the narrative are Vinnie, a hairdresser and Ritchie, a would-be musician. Vinnie (John Leguizamo) wants to belong to the group. Ostensibly he is the main character as conformist. He is married to Dionna, but he is obsessively unfaithful. Women for him are "Madonnas" (mothers and wives) or "whores." This ideology and behavior cements his membership in the peer group.

Ritchie (Adrian Brody) is the non-conformist in the group. He takes up with Ruby, the local prostitute, and treats her respectfully; here is a real male-female relationship in the making. This nonconformist behavior makes him a threat to the group. Taking up with the local "whore" and treating her like a "Madonna" is unacceptable, and he is punished by the group with the accusation that he is the Son of Sam.

In this community at this time, 1977, given the unprecedented heat and the paranoia around the actions of the Son of Sam, society is upside down. It's upright citizens, such as Vinnie, the philandering hairdresser, become betrayers of their families (his wife, Dionna) and of their friends, such as Ritchie, and Ritchie is punished because the other, the outsider, has infiltrated the community and must be purged.

There is no character here that we can hold up as a victor; everyone loses. This is the fevered message of the preacher Spike Lee. When values become subverted, the individual and the community suffer. There is no tolerance here. The group hates Ritchie because he's different from them. Dionna hates Manhattan because it's an uncontrolled environment. Its music and its drugs loosen the social constraints under which she's lived. And Vinnie has lost himself in the obsession of proving that he's a man and in his confusion about Dionna as a Madonna and somehow different from other women. Lee the preacher is saying that betrayal and murder occur in an environment, a community that has lost its values.

Spike Lee the teacher, in the same narrative, points out a society obsessed with celebrity. The night clubs, bar, and parties seduce the characters, particularly Vinnie as the epitome of manliness and importance, arriving in Manhattan in the right set of wheels. Lee the teacher treats Vinnie and Dionna as novices, innocents, in our advanced class in cool behavior. The wife-swapping that follows is too much for both Vinnie and Dionna, and on the journey home the marriage dissolves right before Vinnie's eyes. Lee uses the couple's breakup to illustrate how playacting at sex has serious consequences. Lee the teacher is making the point that relationships require less playacting, less lying, and a more honest exchange between the parties. If this isn't present, the relationship will fail as it does here, with a ripple effect that is unforeseen. The implosion of the other layers of Vinnie's life, both personal and professional, are a direct result of the failure of the marriage. The failure is the moment of truth for two characters who have been avoiding the truth throughout their relationship.

Summer of Sam provides Spike Lee with an opportunity to synthesize both dimensions of his voice, teacher as well as preacher. He does so with enormous force.

THOM FITZGERALD—THE VOICE OF
SEXUAL DIFFERENCE

There are very few films that defy interpretation, but Thom Fitzgerald's often do. Thom Fitzgerald's film *The Hanging Garden* (1998) powerfully evokes a sense of fable. Fitzgerald has used the hyperdrama form to make a statement about sexual difference.

The narrative swings between a past story and a present story. The character that links them is a young man, Willy, in the present story and an obese adolescent in the past story. He is the same person. Is he real or imagined? There are three "chapters" to the film: The Lady on the Locket, Lad's Love, and Mums. The first and the last are in the present, and the middle chapter takes place in the past. The first chapter focuses on the wedding of the main character's sister, Rosalie. We are introduced to the family. The father is an angry alcoholic; the mother supervises the events of the family, and then once the father is put to bed, she literally leaves the home for good. Willy has returned from the city. He clearly is gay, and his sister's husband seems more interested in him than in his wife. At the center of the wedding party there stands a tree, and the body of an obese adolescent hangs there. It is Willy as an adolescent. Current references made to his weight suggest they are one and the same.

The middle chapter focuses on the obese adolescent. Here Willy is abused and belittled by his father. His mother, who is worried about his sexuality, pays a local woman to sexually initiate her son and dissuade him from his sexual preference—being gay. He does have a sexual encounter with the young man who in the earlier story marries his sister. The story ends when, again belittled by his father, Willy hangs himself in his father's garden.

In the third chapter we return to the present. The mother has left. The father is lonely. The newly married couple are not on steady ground as the husband has a sexual encounter with Willy. In the end, Willy cuts down the body that has hung in the garden and buries his dead self. And then he leaves with his young sibling, Violet, beside him to prevent the destruction, at the hand of the father, of a sibling who also has a blurred sense of gender.

A family tragedy is generated from being different and not being accepted. That tragedy has hung over and destroyed the family, and forced its members to leave where they have grown up. This is the moral of Fitzgerald's hyperdrama—if sexual differences are not accepted, families and lives are destroyed. If the father had accepted the adolescent Willy, had accepted his gender blurring as well as his physical appearance, Willy would not have been destroyed. So, too, with the rest of the family, who could not live with the consequences of Willy's fate.

CLARA LAW—THE MODERN TRADITIONALIST

Clara Law is a Hong Kong filmmaker who has made at least two films about the place where the past, with all of its traditions, meets the future, with its globalization and its postmodern disconnectedness. These films, *Autumn Moon* (1992) and *Floating Life* (1996), examine present relationships under the pressure of the past and the anxiety about the future.

Law uses a nonlinear structure and an ironic humor to examine these relationships. *Autumn Moon* takes place in Hong Kong: not an overcrowded Hong Kong but an almost lunar landscape version of Hong Kong—cool, cerebral, and empty. Two characters are equally central: Tokio is a Japanese tourist, Lui Pui Wai is a Chinese schoolgirl. The film begins with his arrival and ends with his departure.

The two meet while he is fishing by the harbor and she is en route to school. They can't speak each other's native language, so they resort to English to communicate. Tokio is hungry for good food. He asks Li to take him to her favorite restaurant. Li takes him to MacDonalds. Tokio is a tourist—materialistic, acquisitive, and unhappy. At one point he gestures that he has a broken heart. Li, on the other hand, is happy. She lives with her grandmother, for her parents have already immigrated to Canada. She will follow at the end of the school year.

By spending time with Li and with her grandmother, Tokio is nurtured by what I will call tradition. His materialism is tempered by this experience. Whether Tokio is altered by the experience remains unanswered. But he definitely is the beneficiary in the relationship.

Li gains a preview of adulthood. It's not a very appealing preview, but this too is left unresolved. In the encounter, however, Clara Law is exploring the virtues of tradition, of family ties, and ironically pointing out the price of detachment, the price of being a tourist in life. The price seems very high. In this sense she seems to be validating the benefits of family ties and traditions.

This thesis that tradition is valuable is even more strongly stated in *Floating Life*. Here the film begins with the elders of the Chan family together with their two young sons leaving Hong Kong. The Chans are migrating to Australia. The film ends with a semblance of adjustment to their new home in Australia. In between, we follow the lives of the diaspora of this particular family—the daughter is already in Australia, the oldest daughter is in Germany, and the adult son remains in Hong Kong. Each of these lives is braced by a husband or lover, but because they are apart, all the members of the Chan family, including the parents, are diminished. They are unsettled by virtue of being outsiders in cultures that may not welcome them or that they don't understand. The responses of the children differ: the oldest daughter in Germany worries constantly and feels guilty that she is not taking care of her parents. The daughter in Australia is a neurotic en route to a total breakdown. And the son in Hong Kong has become a libertine living in the moment. The two youngest sons are rushing to assimilate, and the parents in Australia feel lost and in despair, particularly the mother.

What saves these members of the Chan family are the other members of the family. When they embrace tradition, whether it be about their ancestors or about herbal remedies or superstitions, they progress, they adjust, they go on productively and with an aura of knowing and believing in a future. The despair lifts.

Although Law uses irony and humor in both films, her voice is clear: that traditions strengthen the members of the family. It should not be abandoned as they become internationalists. In her narrative approach, Clara Law is avant-garde, modern, but in terms of her voice, she is very much a traditionalist.

TOD SOLONDZ—THE SCREAM AS VOICE

There is no writer-director who has more powerfully personified the ascent of voice than Tod Solondz. In his two films *Welcome to the Dollhouse* (1995) and *Happiness* (1998), Solondz has pointed his lens at suburban American life, first through the eyes of a single character, an unpopular teenager desperate for acceptance in *Welcome to the Dollhouse*, and then toward an entire suburban family in *Happiness*.

Although Solondz deploys irony and humor in *Welcome to the Dollhouse*, his position remains vested in a single character, Dawn Wiener. Her parents are presented as preferring the "angelic younger sister," Missy, or the oldest child, "the male brain," Mark, all of which leaves Dawn, the middle child, a pubescent girl, as an outsider even in her own family. What is clear in the presentation of Dawn is that she is also isolated by virtue of being creative relative to her parents and her younger sister. Her peers are also presented as conventional rather than creative. Essentially, the main character probably wouldn't fit in no matter what adaptive strategies she might undertake. We have to assume that she is the stand-in for the writer-director, Solondz.

In *Welcome to the Dollhouse*, Solondz relies on the conventions of positioning the main character as a victim wanting to be victimized no longer. Dawn is a typical teenager in her desires. How the other characters push the narrative away from realism is their propensity to be over the top. The Wieners in their adoration of the youngest child; Mark's devotion to his band in spite of the lack of talent demonstrated by the band; the banal good looks of the lead singer, Steve, who she idealizes—all of these characterizations are excessive and consequently ironic rather than realistic and available to us in a manner with which we can identify. These are not characters we can identify, which leaves only Dawn as worthy of identification. In terms of characters, then, we have a schism—a main character who is victimized with the consequence that we care about her, and a set of other characters who are separate from the main character in the sense that they are ironic.

When we look at the story line we see the same schism. There's nothing wrong with Dawn's goal—to be accepted. It is understandable. But it is the aggressive reaction of the others to her that isolates her further and makes her efforts ironic and futile. *Welcome to the Dollhouse* mixes realism and irony, thereby making the film available to us with a clear voice of the writer-director, criticizing family and community for its indifference, its insensitivity, and its cruelty to an important member of the community, an artist in the making, the main character.

If *Welcome to the Dollhouse* functions as both melodrama and satire, Solondz' next film moves far from melodrama and, in its way, beyond satire. I would suggest that *Happiness* is Solondz's voice as scream, a scream about family values, about suburban life, about therapy, about communication, about honesty, and about hope. *Happiness* is as dark a vision of American life as we have seen; as dark as Fritz Lang's *Fury* (1935); as dark as Billy Wilder's *Ace in the Hole* (1951). It's useful to examine *Happiness* in relation to Sam Mendes' *American Beauty* (1999). Both are focused on the inability of the members of a suburban family to help one another. They live together, but that's as far as one can go. Both culminate in a death or the acknowledgment of responsibility for a death. Both have satiric and melodramatic layers. But if *American Beauty* is a satire about the ineffectiveness of the family to satisfy its members, and about the tragedy that befalls the member who calls the family a charade (the enlightened one), *Happiness* is the cri de coeur: the

Jordan family is more than a failure, it's the purveyor of illusion and those illusions destroy people. There is enormous pain and anger in *Happiness*. It is a profoundly troubling experience, and it is important for us to understand how Solondz moves from the satiric voice in *Welcome to the Dollhouse* to the voice of something else, what I have called the scream.

Only Luis Buñuel in *Un Chien Andalou* (1929), Pier Paulo Pasolini in *Salo* (1975), and Nagisa Oshima in *In the Realm of the Senses* (1976), have managed to create the sense of outrage Solondz does in *Happiness*. To do so he has had to move us over the edge of taste, and to utilize a number of narrative strategies to subvert our expectations. Those narrative strategies begin with a nonlinear structure; there is no main character, and if there is a stated goal, it is to find happiness in a relationship—within a family or outside the family. Solondz also adopts an MTV approach to the scenes—each has an intense feeling state as its goal. A therapy session fuses the aggressive sexual fantasy of a patient with the boredom of the therapist. A visit of two sisters, Joy Jordan and her married sister Trish, moves between Joy's loneliness and Trish's aggressive rivalry, all under the guise of help. The dinner breakup of the relationship of Joy Jordan and Andy Kornbluth fluctuates between social convention and aggressive payback.

An elaboration of the MTV style is to make the dialogue intensely aggressive while the body language, the visual, is the opposite. Another elaboration is to give fantasy—aggressive, sexual, or both—space to overtake other feelings, such as love and compassion. The result is that each of the individuals presents as self-absorbed. They are incapable of being genuinely with the other, whether it's a sibling, a son, or a neighbor. Finally, there is the issue of boundaries. Solondz doesn't recognize boundaries. And so Bill Maplewood, a therapist who is a pedophile is a pedophile with his son, Timmy. A lonely obese woman sees men as predators rather than as potential companions. For her, murder and dismemberment are not too good for men. The narrative events themselves are so shocking, so naked in their desperation and anger, that they are not funny as irony can be, they are not sad as melodrama can be, they are not imaginatively creative as powerful satire can be; they leave us without resources or recourse. This is the upshot of Solondz's scream.

THE SEARCH FOR
NEW FORMS

Although nonlinear stories have occupied the most pronounced direction in the search for new filmic narrative forms, more traditional alternate models have also seen a revival. The utilization of a theatrical frame, or the frame of the novel; the renewed search for television forms as a frame; and finally, the reworking of filmic genre frames, have all served to present films in search of an international audience in a novel or heightened manner.

Whether this adoption of an unexpected frame is a hook to capture audience interest or whether it is a new exciting narrative development is our subject in this chapter. What can be said is that the degree of adaptation of new frames certainly suggests that new forms can help a conventional story seem fresh or less conventional with the consequence that old stories seem new. We will look at each of the following: theater as a model, the novel as a model, and finally film as a model.

THEATER AS MODEL

Theater has always been influential on film and scriptwriting. Shakespeare has been a historic reservoir for adaptation. Indeed, a play like *Hamlet* has had a half-dozen film adaptations, running from the psychological (Lawrence Olivier) to the literal (Kenneth Branagh). The availability of readings that diverge illustrate the richness of the original work.

Theater has also generated great screenwriters, from Harold Pinter to Clifford Odets, Ted Tally, John Guare, and David Mamet. It is likely that this generation of talent will continue.

Add to this the notion that the frame of a play, the literary allusion of theater and it's prestige, can, if applied to the story form of the film, provide something novel or new. How this works can be illustrated in the Mike Newell (director) and Richard Curtis (writer) film *Four Weddings and a Funeral*, in which the veneer of theatrical structure is the frame of the story. The frame is to shape the entire narrative around five events—four weddings and a funeral. The shape gives the story a quality of ritual, as if it were unfolding along the lines of that set of rituals.

Because the frame is theatrical rather than a journey, a relationship, or a single event, the artifice is apparent and in a sense non-filmic—or to put it more positively, theatrical. What I propose is that by adopting this theatrical structure, the film seems novel and new, when in fact the actual narrative is something more familiar: a romantic comedy that proceeds along far more classic lines.

Four Weddings and a Funeral is in fact a story with a main character. The main character, Charlie (Hugh Grant), has a goal—to avoid commitment. In Act I he meets an American girl, Carrie (Andie MacDowell). He spends the night with her, and they like each other, but at the end of Act I Charlie cannot commit to more than a one-night stand. At the end of Act II Carrie marries, and Charlie now understands the depth of his mistake—he is totally dedicated to her. In Act III, Charlie tries to marry a former girlfriend but realizes when Carrie comes to his wedding to tell him she's left her husband that he can't marry today. The narrative ends with Charlie's confession in the rain—Carrie's the only one for him. Charlie has overcome his goal. They are together.

The frame, the four weddings and a funeral, is nothing more than a theatrical shell overlaying a traditional romantic comedy. The form packages the traditional story to make it appear to be something other than it is. The form makes an old story seem new.

Even more elaborate is the form adopted in the John Madden (director) Marc Norman, and Tom Stoppard (writers) film *Shakespeare in Love*. Here a play within a play within a film is the form taken. The narrative is the story of young Will Shakespeare. The plot is the writing of *Romeo and Juliet*. The problem is that Will is experiencing writer's block. The character layer is to discover a muse, naturally from the other side of the tracks. Playwrights and actors are workers; the muse is a young woman, Lady Viola, whose family has a mercantile fortune. She does not, however, want to be a lady of the manor. She wants to be a lady of the theater.

An additional complication is that ladies in the theater are played by men. As herself, she becomes Will Shakespeare's muse. Disguised as a young man, Thomas Kent, Viola auditions for the play he is trying to write, a comedy. As she begins to pretend to be a man, to be a player, and then as her real life imposes the impossibility that she will remain the mistress, the love of Will's life, the play Shakespeare is writing turns to tragedy. Act III is the enactment of the tragedy of Romeo and Juliet, with Viola playing the Juliet role overcoming the prohibition that no woman shall play a woman on stage. This enactment of the play echoes the tragedy of Will and his lover who will now be apart forever, Viola to return to her social class and a mercantile marriage, he to carry on her memory in writing his next play, *Twelfth Night* (a woman pretends to be a man, but reveals her true identity to love the man who owns her heart, the stand-in for Will).

The cleverness of integrating the writing and production of a play as a theatrical device that parallels the filmic narrative of the impossible love relationship between Will the writer and his muse, layers the narrative in a more elegant and naturalistic manner. The consequence is that *Shakespeare in Love* uses the form within a form to invite the audience into the construction of the narrative. It's as if the writer lets the audience in on the joke as he is telling it: knowing and experiencing makes the experience all the more pleasurable. Here the adaptation of a form within a form, in this case the use of theater as the borrowed form, enhances the basic story and makes *Shakespeare in Love* a new experience of knowing for its audience.

THE NOVEL AS A MODEL

Novels have long been a mainstay for film adaptation, but more recently film-makers have used a novelistic structure in the film narrative itself. What I mean by this is best illustrated by two distinct characteristics of the novel relative to film. First, the novel tends to be capable of more than one voice. Whereas we experience film through the point of view or voice of the main character—or when that identification is subverted, through the voice of the writer or writer-director—in the novel we can experience the voice of the writer and of the main character, or through more than one character.

This presence of more than a single voice in a film narrative is film taking on the novelistic narrative form. One can experience this in a subtle way in the Ruth Prawer Jhablava (writer) and James Ivory (director) episodic treatment of the novel by Kaylie Jones about her father James Jones. The script focuses on the father-daughter relationship in *A Soldier's Daughter Never Cries* (1998), as well as each of the family relationships. The adaptation even resorts to the use of chapters to further emulate the novelistic approach. It also makes a point of privileging a number of points of view—Channe, the daughter, Bill Willis, the father, Marcella Willis, the mother, Billy, the adopted son, and the real mother of the adopted son. The experience is consequently loose and episodic. Eventually we are involved in the narrative, but the multiple points of view slow down the process of identification and alter the goal-directed expectation with which we enter the film.

A more accessible novelistic-style narrative is *Croupier* (1998), written by Paul Mayersberg and directed by Mike Hodges. *Croupier* is about a character who wants to be a writer. Jack Manfred's not very successful. At the advice of his father, a manipulative, deceitful character, Jack takes a job at a London casino as a croupier. He's very good at this job. He's honest, or tries to be, while all those around him cheat and beat the system. Jack begins to live on two levels: he tells himself he is honest, but he allows himself to be influenced first by Max, a colleague at work, and then by Jani, a woman he meets while she visits the casino. With these two characters he participates in their dishonesty. Jack begins to live in his head (honest) and in the world (dishonest). This schism destroys his personal life, but it does allow him to write a book about being a croupier. It becomes a bestseller, but the author remains anonymous. The story ends with the impression that his father has been effective in manipulating Jack, first with the job itself, and then in an effort to rob the casino. Has Jack functioned effectively only as a writer? He certainly has not been effective as a person. Here it's his father who has been effective. These paired points of view—inner-outer world, son-father, effective-ineffective—are the two perspectives that dominate *Croupier*.

A similar duality pervades *The Limey* (1999) by Steven Soderbergh, but here the two points of view are the past and the present. Wilson is a gangster who loses his daughter. He is both to blame, because in the past he was a neglectful father, and to expiate his guilt in the present he wreaks havoc on those who are responsible for her death. The result is two time frames and two perceptions, each informing the other. Together they form two perceptual layers, two points of view.

Soderbergh worked with a similar notion in his *Kafka* (1991), an original screenplay by Lem Dobbs; but in *Kafka* there are two perceptions of events, one imagined and one real. Together they pose the question whether the main character is paranoid about the world or whether in a terrifying world paranoia is the appropriate response. Again the two points of view seem to confuse us about the narrative, but in fact they are narrative departures borrowed from the novel form—departures that pose two perspectives in a medium more accustomed to a single perspective.

Perhaps the most successful novel-like approach to film narrative is M. Night Shyamalan's (writer-director) *The Sixth Sense* (1999). Here two points of view dominate the narrative, in effect telling the story with two main characters. It's not a shared point of view, as in a multiple-character narrative such as *Mystic Pizza* (three main characters but one point of view because of the shared goals). In *The Sixth Sense*, the first point of view is that of Dr. Malcolm Crowe, the child psychologist (Bruce Willis). The second is the point of view of a young patient, Cole Sear (Haley Joel Osmont). Dr. Crowe's story is that he feels guilty because he once was unable to help one of his patients. That patient, now grown, shoots him at the outset of the film. Dr. Crowe gets a second chance to help Cole, a disturbed young boy who is frightened because he sees ghosts and fears being labeled crazy. Cole is also afraid of his experience of the ghosts. The young boy's point of view is fully elaborated in his experience of what ghosts share with him. Late in the story, Cole actually uses that knowledge to save someone. Gradually, Dr. Crowe is able to convince Cole that his ability to see ghosts doesn't make him crazy; in fact, it is a gift that can help rather than harm. Cole uses this perception to share a message for his mother from her dead mother. When Cole sees the healing impact upon his mother, he changes from being a troubled young boy to a boy who has a gift and feels it is a gift.

At this point we learn that Dr. Crowe himself is a ghost, and that the shooting that opens the story was fatal. He was unable to face his own reality, his own death. His work with Cole has helped him accept his fate—and, of course, he could only help Cole because the boy sees ghosts.

M. Night Shyamalan has presented *The Sixth Sense* through two distinct points of view. Each story and each character intertwines and informs the other, but we don't understand it fully until the end. At that point, the distinct points of view finally do make sense.

TELEVISION AS A MODEL

Television has had numerous influences on film. The early Beatle films were documents of performance strung along an absurd story line. Using the variety show notion of performance, director Richard Lester applied documentary film techniques to make the musical numbers dynamic. The absurdity of the story line was inconsequential. Borrowing from another television standard, the TV news provided a documentary-like style that could be readily applied to film narratives that wanted to be perceived as "documentary" or realism-based. Haskell Wexler's *Medium Cool* (1969) and Michael Ritchie's *The Candidate* (1972) both exemplify this style. More recently, Oliver Stone borrows freely from MTV in the form and substance of *Natural Born Killers* (1995).

But today the relationship of film and television have a different, more immediate relationship. Because of the intense competition for audience and the proliferation of delivery systems, television has gone into overdrive in its search for novelty. Reality television is just the latest manifestation. What makes these innovations even more influential is their international influence. Reality television has moved from Sweden, The Netherlands, and the United Kingdom to the United States in eighteen months. And the novelty has found an audience. This has not been lost on film writers, directors, and producers. The opening sequence of Steven Spielberg's *Saving Private Ryan* (1998) owes much to the impulse and power of reality television. But nothing has quite captured the attention of writers and directors worldwide as much as the reality television-oriented series of Dogma 95 films from Denmark.

This cluster of films—Lars Von Trier's *The Idiots* (1999), Thomas Vinterberg's *The Celebration (Festen)* (1998), Soren Kragh-Jacobsen's *Mifune* (1999), and Kristian Levring's *The King Is Alive* (2000)—have particular stylistic characters that essentially echo reality television: handheld cameras, no artificial light, no artificial sound (e.g., music), and a writing style that essentially emulates realism in a less-shaped fashion than melodrama. These films are not quite docudrama, since they don't highlight the point of view or voice of the writer-director; they are films that are almost anthropological in their view on behavior. The more genuine the behavior seems to be, the closer to the sense of actuality that goes to the heart of the Dogma philosophy. Before I turn to the strongest example, *The Celebration*, I would like to suggest that Dogma 95 links to the cinema vérité movement that was so influential on the docudrama and which is alive and well in the work of Ken Loach (*My Name Is Joe*, 1999). In this sense reality television and the Dogma 95 films echo that earlier affiliation between film and television, a relationship that peaked in the work of John Cassavetes and which now has come back under the aegis of Dogma 95.

The Celebration is the story of a family reunion in honor of the 60th birthday of the patriarch of the family. His three surviving children arrive from various parts of Europe. The narrative will follow the next twenty-four hours. We discover in Act I that the eldest, Christian, had a twin sister who died. We see that the youngest son, Michael, is boorish and aggressive, and that the surviving daughter, Helene, is insecure and dependent upon drugs and alcohol to cope with the stressful family situation. We also learn that everyone kowtows to the father. He is not only the patriarch, he is a feared patriarch. In Act I there is considerable attention paid to characterizing each of these people behaviorally. Interestingly, the mother seems marginal and taken up with appearances. The Act I turning point is the toast of Christian to his father. There, before all the guests, Christian congratulates his father, sharing with the guests his family secret: that his father raped him and his sister persistently from his preteens into his teenage years. He warned them not to tell anyone. At this point we understand that his twin sister committed suicide in the very home she never left.

Act II proceeds with the shock waves of this revelation among the two other children—the youngest son defending the father, the daughter full well knowing the truth. She carries on her rebellion with the arrival at the party of her black lover. The mother remains in profound denial and tries to keep up the public front. But a process has begun, and the momentum is unstoppable.

In Act III the tables turn. The younger son leads the attack to restore family dignity. He moves against the father, and it's as if the truth has set him free. The angry young man becomes thoughtful and a leader. The sister is grateful that she now has siblings who are not perfect but are as flawed as she has felt. The last to come around is the mother, who at the morning-after breakfast banishes her husband for his past deeds. She is now together united with her children. Christian has accomplished what he needed to do—to publicly share his pain and, in the process, heal, even if the healing is modest.

There is no plot in *The Celebration*, but there is a great deal of drama. This is generated principally from the secret and its revelation. But even more palpable is the reality television approach to observing behavior and what that observation reveals about the characters. In each case we in the audience feel we are voyeurs watching the most personal or private revelations about these characters. In the case of the oldest brother, an old girlfriend from the town, this evening a waitress at the party, asks if she can shower in Christian's room. She is open in her affection for Christian, and she is provocative in her desire for him. But Christian is unresponsive. He is flat, claims fatigue, perhaps depression. But his response to her also reveals preoccupation. Only later do we realize that he is preoccupied with his should-I-should-I-not decision about the revelation of the secret. He is also very much in mourning for his dead twin. This scene doesn't reveal anything direct that propels the narrative forward, but in an observational sense, it tells us a great deal about Christian's state of mind.

In the case of his sister, Helene, there is an equally observational and revealing scene. She is assigned the room of her dead sister. A hotel employee takes Helene to the room. There is little question that he is trying hard to be professional, but he is nevertheless somewhat unnerved by the notion of Helene staying in the room of her dead sister. Helene, on the other hand, is fascinated. It's a chance "to be with her sister." She moves about the room doing what she believes her sister will do. The bathroom where she killed herself was clearly a haven, a place to escape while lying in the bathtub. As Helene moves through her sister's spaces, she finds a note in a fixture above the room. Helene has found the last communication from her sister. She has achieved her goal—"to be with her sister"—this last time. She is comforted by the experience, but by now the clerk is totally unnerved by the "reunion."

In the case of Michael, the behavior is impulsive and rather hysterical. He blames his wife for not bringing his black shoes. How can he appear before his father in a black tuxedo and brown shoes? His hysteria and his anger flow. His wife must return home, a few hours away, and retrieve his black shoes. She refuses and explodes in anger herself. Michael's anxiety and anger are escalating. Suddenly, Michael is demanding in the opposite direction. He needs reassurance. He needs sex, but he waits, and when she signals agreement, he all but attacks her. The sex is not loving but rather desperate, a reflection of his character and his state.

Each of these scenes in Act I is observational and very revealing about the emotional state of the three siblings. None involves the father directly but each enhances the sense of actuality, the veracity of these characters. This behavioral narrative is at the core of the link between reality television and the Dogma films.

Denmark is not the only center where reality television and film narrative connect. In France, the work of Eric Zoncka, such as *The Dreamlife of Angels*, is very influenced by behavioral observation. Here Isa and Marie, two young, marginalized women are the center of the narrative. Their narrative arcs diverge. Marie who is self-destructive enters a relationship that in the end feeds her self-hatred and she commits suicide. Isa, who forms a relationship with a young accident victim in a coma, has her sense of hope, even belief, restored by this almost impossible relationship. Throughout the narrative, the observation of behavior is the focus, as opposed to furthering the narrative arc. And as in *The Celebration*, the actual events are modest in and of themselves, so we are left with being with the characters. Whether this positions us as voyeurs or as privileged observers into the inner or deeper level of the characters, the result is very intense. These notions about film and character relate directly to the intensity and novelty television needs to generate to maintain its audience. Television emphasizes reality, current events. The look of the Dogma films capitalizes on this sense of appearance of actuality. We see this relationship repeated in the Belgian films *Rosetta* (1999), by Jean-Pierre Dardenne and Luc Dardenne, and *An Affair of Love* (2000), by Frédéric Fonteyne (*A Pornographic Affair* is the title in Europe). We also see it in the modest narrative approach of Cedric Klapische in his *When the Cat's Away* (1996) (France). How this burgeoning relationship between television and film will next turn is of great interest, since the intense pursuit of audience in television is promoting a rate of change, novelty, and innovation that will continue to influence the more gradualist approach to narrative in film.

FILM AS A MODEL

It may seem strange to consider film as a form imitated by film in its search to appear fresh. But this strange pattern is indeed ongoing and growing, as I will explain. Of course most films approach narrative in a manner that is either expected according to genre or commercially proven. The notion that I propose in this section is that a number of films, in an effort to appear fresh, have adopted a film form notable perhaps in another genre or have applied an overmodulated genre approach to a narrative of the same genre. This has in each case made an old story seem new.

The first and most startling example is *The Blair Witch Project* (1999). Its writer-director team, Daniel Myrick and Eduardo Sanchez, borrowed freely from reality television in their approach and style. The narrative itself is simple. Three students with a video camera go into the woods to look into the local myth of the Blair Witch. Eventually they're lost, first one and then the two others. The style implies their destruction by the witch. All that is left is their footage. The film itself is framed as a documentary about their disappearance. The footage makes up the basic scenes of the documentary—or, since it's staged, we should call it the mockumentary.

In fact, *The Blair Witch Project* is a horror film with the three characters eventually succumbing to the ghost. Horror films tend to follow precisely the arc that this film follows: a chase in which the main character is victimized by a monster, or by a manifestation of his or her own sexuality and aggression. The horror film is also plot-driven, as is *The Blair Witch Project*. Where this film diverges from the usual horror film is in its tone. The horror film presents itself with an over-the-top tone. Whether we call it baroque, passionate, or expressionistic, it is intense and far from realism.

The tone in *The Blair Witch Project* is exactly the opposite—a form of excessive realism. There are no monsters, no special conjurings of violent deeds via special effects. Borrowing freely from cinema vérité and Dogma 95, the style is documentary-like. By adopting this approach, the horror film is presented as a documentary, a form that masks the real genre and proposes another. The result is to subvert genre expectations: it's not a nightmare movie, it's a movie nightmare. The results speak for themselves, although it's dubious that audiences will fall twice for the same trick.

Juzo Itami's *Tampopo* (1987) has a similar surprising effect. The narrative is framed by an audience of financiers watching a movie. The producer is distracted. He is more interested in his mistress and the food being served. The implication is that what will follow must be very strong to capture his interest. What follows is the story of how a truck driver with a Paul Hogan hat and attitude and a passion for food will become the mentor for a woman who runs a small diner. Her goal is to make better soup or, to put it another way, to be a success as a chef. His goal is to help her become a champion in the making of soup and a successful restaurateur. He will succeed as will she, with many interludes: scenes about eating, restaurants, and the social factor in restaurant behavior. The totality of the effect is eccentric, but by borrowing the frame of the western—heroes and villains, as well as ritualized confrontations—Itami creates an ironic treatment of a simple story. He also makes the mentor and the cook heroes, western heroes. The irony that she is, after all, only making soup, does not diminish her achievement.

Itami's treatment echoes Kurosawa's *Yojimbo* (1961) and Sergio Leone's remake of *Yojimbo*, *A Fistful of Dollars* (1964), except that those tongue-in-cheek versions actually dealt with the western hero amidst good and evil sides with the attendant ritualized shootouts. Itami's confrontations, the making of a better soup, is a long way from life and death, or good and evil. The result is an original approach to a narrative that in its barebones is a melodrama. By providing it with the overlay of the western, the narrative becomes more mythic and more memorable.

Guy Ritchie's *Lock, Stock and Two Smoking Barrels* (1998) is a gangster film that alters the traditional balance of plot and character levels to such an extent it becomes a genre film and a parody of the genre simultaneously. Gangster film tends to have a rise and fall shape with a plot that follows the gangster's career, and the character layer following the character's family life. *Lock, Stock and Two Smoking Barrels* has multiple main characters, a young cluster of "criminal" entrepreneurs, a traditional gangster "godfather," a group of drug-glazed dealers, and sundry employees and employers and parents of these groups. The film has a surplus of characters, a surplus of plot, and a resultant tone that veers between realism and parody.

Beginning with the young entrepreneurs, Tom, Soap, Eddie, and Bacon, putting together a large sum to play poker in a crime boss' high-stakes game, they believe their player is unbeatable. Although he is warned by his father, JD, Eddie has the charm and gullibility of youth. He is cheated in the game and loses not only his stake but ends up owing Hatchet Harry $250,000. Eddie and his colleagues have a week to come up with the money or else. They plan to steal the money from the drug dealers next door. Various enforcers, rivals, and bosses get into the fray. And somewhere in the mix, the mafia boss commissions the theft of two antique shotguns worth £300,000. The money and the shotguns circulate. Many die. Eddie is rescued in the end by JD, and the enforcer, Big Chris, who is as much a concerned parent about Little Chris, as he is an enforcer, survives. Most of the other players kill one another.

There is so much plot in *Lock, Stock and Two Smoking Barrels* that the narrative virtually becomes a parody of itself. This results from the over-plotting. The family references for Big Chris and Eddie echo *The Godfather* in the genre's paean to family. But the character layer is so modest relative to genre expectations that it is no more than a nod to expectation. In this film, overstuffing the narrative with film references has helped create a parody of the genre.

Using film as a model can be used for parody, as in the case of the gangster *Lock, Stock and Two Smoking Barrels,* or it can be used to deepen the voice of the writer. Pedro Almodóvar is a filmmaker who has always used melodrama to explore social tolerance for personal and sexual diversity. But when he adopted one of the great melodramas, *All About Eve* (1950) by director Joseph Mankiewicz, as the basis for *All About My Mother* (1999), he transcended the impact of his earlier work.

All About Eve is a film about the struggle between career and personal life. The main character, Margo Channing, cannot have both, and in the end she chooses to give up stardom for her personal goals—family life. The film uses the plot of the rise of a new star, Eve Harrington, to put pressure on the older star, Margo Channing, to make the choice.

All About My Mother is also about the choice between a career or a personal life, but it broadens the definition of personal life to include motherhood and womanhood. For Almodóvar the mother is a nurturer. The story begins with a mother,

Manuela, losing her adolescent son, Esteban, in a car accident. Manuela travels back to her former home to tell the father that he has lost Esteban. There she finds the father, an actor who is now a transvestite and transsexual with breasts, and tells him that he is no longer a father. The father is also dying of AIDS. She also takes under her wing, Sister Rosa, a pregnant nun who, rejected by her family, is cared for by Manuela and her friend, Huma, an actress-transsexual who was a man. Together, they reconstitute to create a new family for the newborn child. Sister Rosa, however, dies in childbirth. So both mothers and fathers die in each case here, through an expression of their sexuality, but children always need a mother. And so, as in *All About Eve*, the main character chooses a personal life as a mother over a career as an actress, a choice made for Esteban and now again for the newborn baby.

The story unfolds as a melodrama, vigorously mixing the world of the theater and the world of ordinary characters, as in *All About Eve*. Almodóvar, in his own fashion, is celebrating the classic film, the genre of the melodrama, and his own views about sexual diversity and creative and human continuity. Both impulses come together in *All About My Mother*.

Oliver Stone has a vastly different intention than Pedro Almodóvar. Oliver Stone's *U-Turn* (1997) is not a typical Oliver Stone film that presses a particular perspective or theory. Instead, *U-Turn* is a gangster film with the shape of the gangster film and the tone of film noir. It references both genres with an irony and a cruel humor that makes the film noir tone inevitable. Along the way, it references both genres. The gangster film has a rise and fall plot with compensation in a character layer that offers a positive perspective on the main character, the gangster. Film noir, on the other hand, offers a far darker interpretation of the character layer. In fact, the main character is destroyed by the negative results of his character's choice. This is the end result for the main character in *U-Turn*.

Bobby Cooper, a petty thief on the run, has to pay a debt in Las Vegas. En route his car breaks down in a small Arizona town. He has chosen a fork in the road at the onset of his car troubles. The result is a town where the mechanic is an extortionist, where the local Indian does not offer sage advice, and where the local beauty, Grace, is not only married and seductive, but she is married to the man who fathered her. This is not a sleepy town; it's a dangerous town, and it's a lethal town. Bobby Cooper gets into financial trouble when the money he's been transporting to Las Vegas is incinerated and he is bled upon in a botched robbery at a 7-11—where his only goal was to buy a cold drink. To restore his financial status and pay the extortionist to recover his car, Bobby agrees to kill Grace. Her father/husband, Jake McKenna, has commissioned the kill. A dangerous town indeed. Bobby finally gets out, only to be killed by Grace.

Bobby has not been dishonest or disreputable; he simply suffered from being in the wrong place at the wrong time. The town is lethal, and from the outset, the populace has been unwelcoming, even aggressive. In the end, they get him. By referencing the gangster film and film noir, and by adding an ironic tone, Oliver Stone has created a rather unique amalgam of two genres. Unlike so many of his films, *U-Turn* is rather relaxed in its pace. Perhaps it would be better to characterize the pace as inevitable. *U-Turn* owes much to the gangster film and to film noir, but by a distinct tonal approach, and by positioning Bobby as an innocent, Oliver Stone has converted *U-Turn* into a meditation on both genres.

The war film has had many manifestations, but the most enduring is the use of the battle as the story frame and the ordinary soldier as the basic character. What has varied is the writer's voice. Lewis Milestone has worked in this area from an antiwar perspective in *All Quiet on the Western Front* (1930). John Huston has explored the psychology war imposes on the ordinary person in *The Red Badge of Courage* (1951). Robert Aldrich has attacked the hierarchy of class and political privilege in *Attack* (1956). Steven Spielberg has explored the price of personal and personnel sacrifice in *Saving Private Ryan* (1998). What is interesting about Terence Malick's *The Thin Red Line* (1998), based on the 1962 novel by James Jones, is that he references all these thematic interpretations.

The battle in *The Thin Red Line* is the battle for a Pacific island in the war against Japan. Malick follows various characters in a single regiment. But because he has a variety of goals he takes a nonlinear approach. There are multiple main characters, and he takes a random access approach to the battle. Sequences do not indicate a chronological, progressive approach to the battle. Rather, the narrative is organized around the mini-narratives of specific individuals. What drives these narratives are the internal goals of individual men: an ambitious commander, an overly responsible subordinate, a pragmatic sergeant, a risk-taker, a self-sacrificing character, a poet, and a dreamer. Whether schemer or poet, whether responsible or irresponsible, these characters are very human. Their view of the enemy depends on their internal life. The environment they find themselves in is beautiful or hostile, for example, depending upon their internal life. The consequence is a fragmented, impressionistic experience.

There are heroes, but none are romanticized or mythologized as, say, a Sergeant York character. They are simply men. There are fearful men, too, even cowards, but they are not demonized. In fact, Malick goes out of his way to humanize all of these men. The result is a fragmented rather poetic experience of men in war. Time doesn't exist, and the enemy is fleeting. What does continue is their internal lives, their memories. These dominate as long as the men live. The outer world, the world of war and battle, exists but not as powerfully as the internal lives and perceptions of these men. The result is an experience that references many other war films, but seems quite unlike any other.

THE STRUGGLE OF STYLE
AND CONTENT

With the ascent of the voice of the writer there is an aggressive search for a form to present the story that will not undermine voice but rather enhance it. In the last chapter we explored the search for forms that would mask voice. In this chapter we look at the use of style to highlight voice. The result very often is a struggle between the style of the film and its content. This is not an entirely new phenomenon, although it's very pronounced in today's more internationalized setting.

THE SUBVERSION OF NARRATIVE:
THE CASE OF BUÑUEL AND GODARD

Although Sergei Eisenstein and Dziga Vertov struggled with this issue throughout their careers, the filmmakers we associate most readily with this struggle are Luis Buñuel and Jean-Luc Godard. For the purposes of this chapter it's best to view style and content in a creative tension with each other. In both Buñuel's work and in Godard's, there is a very powerful voice rooted in an aesthetic position that supported the political perspective of each.

Luis Buñuel, from his first film *Un Chien Andalou* (1929), a short he made with Salvador Dali, took the position that he would play with the propensity of his audience to seek meaning in story. By juxtaposing absurd images ringing with aggressive sexual innuendo, Buñuel was attacking meaning itself. Whether one views his political position as anarchist or surrealist or both, the experience of his juxtapositions was shocking: an eyeball is sliced; the mouth of a woman is transformed into a moth.

This tendency to shock is focused on the sexual hypocrisy of a class of people in Buñuel's next film, *L'Age d'Or* (1930). His last Spanish film for thirty years, *Las Hurdes* (*Land without Bread*, 1932), is an indictment of the Spanish society that would allow the plight of any of its citizens to fall to "subhuman" levels. Buñuel's juxtaposition of the visual and aural elements provided a counterpoint of style and content so devastating that he shortly departed Spain indefinitely. (He was no longer welcome in his homeland.)

Rather than detail his entire career, I will highlight a film from his Mexican period and one from his French period. *The Criminal Mind of Archibald Cruz* (1955) is the story of a man whose childhood trauma frames his view of himself and his relationships for the rest of his life. An incident that provides a prologue sets the tone. Archibald plays willfully with his toys. A governess tries to exert her authority over him as the parents go out for a social event. Archibald is more than angered. He wishes the governess dead. At that very instant a stray bullet from the nascent revolution ongoing in the streets below passes through a window and kills the governess. Archibald believes she is dead because he wanted her to die. The power as well as the guilt he feels follow him into adult life. A developing relationship with a woman is a threat. Will she die as did the governess? Here the absurdity and the logic, together with a straightforward style, highlight the voice of Buñuel. Children aren't innocents, nor are adults idealists. Both have to live with their emotional turmoil. In Buñuel's world desire conflicts with social convention, making the individual a victim of both.

Twenty years later Buñuel made *The Discreet Charm of the Bourgeoisie* (1972) in France. Although he had targeted the social, sexual, and political characteristics of the bourgeoisie in his films *Exterminating Angel* (1962) and *Viridiana* (1961), nothing in his work is quite as nasty as *The Discreet Charm of the Bourgeoisie*. Here fantasy and reality intermingle to portray the self-absorption and venality of a group. Organized around eight eating (or trying-to-eat) sequences, the narrative focuses on a half dozen men and women who arrive for dinner only to find they have come a day early. They move on to an inn to find that the inn is out of food, and on it goes. The nominal leader of the group, Don Rafael, an ambassador, gradually loses any appearance of diplomatic skill. Instead, he evolves into the kind of character who increasingly says what he thinks rather than what he should say. The ambassador's closest rival for power in the group, Msgr. Dufour, is a bishop, but his is a "power of the people." His goal is to prove he is one of the real people—the workers. But in doing so, he is as enraged as the dispossessed tend to be, and he kills a farmer (a man of property). And so a man of God ends up killing one of God's children. This is typical Buñuel.

In the midst of all of this sturm und drang about getting enough to eat, a series of rather surreal dreams range from fear to rage. Don Rafael, for example, dreams of his dinner being invaded by guerillas. Naturally they kill the guests. So although the film is ostensibly about the social probity and seriousness of the bourgeoisie over the social ritual of being together and eating together, the film in fact, through its organization, reveals the underbelly of that social probity. That underbelly is rife with anger and sexual desire, frustration and violence. In this fashion Buñuel counterweights appearance with feeling, style with an alternative content.

Jean-Luc Godard is as polemical and as playful and mischievous as Buñuel. But rather than an anarchistic goal, Godard's goal has a more political shape. As in the case of Buñuel, Godard's work relies heavily on narrative interventions to distance us from character and structure. But whereas Buñuel favored hyperdrama as his genre of choice, together with an ongoing reference to melodrama, Godard moves from genre to genre. His early work in particular is genre-oriented, beginning with his gangster film (*Breathless* [1960]) and quickly moving on to the war film (*Le Petit Soldat* [1963]), science fiction (*Alphaville* [1965]), the musical (*Sympathy for the Devil, Tout va bien* [1969]), and the melodrama (*Two or Three Things I Know about Her* [1967]). The other notable characteristic of Godard was his prolific output. In the first decade of his career he averaged two films a year.

In order to capture the flavor of Godard's mix of style and content, we will look at that first decade—its beginning and its latter phase with his films *Breathless* (1960) and *Weekend* (1967). In the case of *Breathless*, the best starting point is to look at the gangster film it references. Gangster films are rise and fall stories, narratives with a strong plot and a strong character layer. *Breathless* certainly has both. But although this genre has its own sense of veracity to parallel the realism of the genre, Godard's tone is much more playful and kinetic. He is interested in positioning Michel, the main character outside the law, but more importantly, outside the conventions of society. Godard's gangster is a nonconformist, and although Michel does kill, he will in the end be punished for his identity as a free spirit, an energy source too dangerous to bourgeois society, rather than because he is a threat to his fellow man. Just as the main character is kinetic, so too are the directorial choices Godard makes. If Buñuel's characters are inscrutable and disturbed, Godard's characters are emblematic of youth, they are dangerous because they are vigorously individualistic.

The character layer follows Michel, the French main character's relationship with a young American expatriate, Patricia (who sells the *Herald Tribune* to make money), suggests that youth is a dangerous segment of society, youth from all countries (in this case France and the United States). The instability and the sexual energy of this relationship fuel the need for the main character to fall. In Godard's gangster film, it is the character's positive qualities rather than his negative actions that require punishment.

In the case of *Weekend*, Godard takes essentially a nonlinear approach to a journey. On one level, a couple, Corinne and Roland, clearly each using the other, travel from the North to the South. Whether it's a weekend trip or a purposeful effort to exploit family finances for selfish ends, we never find out, because the journey is transformed from the geographical to the metaphysical, traveling from civilization to barbarity. Corinne ends up joining guerillas in the South, feasting on the remains of Roland. Whether this is a feminist position or more generically aimed at the whole race is unclear. Before that barbaric ending, the couple experiences the underside of national well-being—spectacular car crashes, personal pettiness and cruelty, as well as Saint Juste (Jean Pierre Léaud) who dresses and speaks as if he had walked in from the French revolution. These interludes, together with visual, verbal, as well as advertisement inserts about revolution, reveal the voice of Godard—the film is an incitement to abandon your façade and join the revolution. It's eat or be eaten in this world. As with Buñuel, *Weekend* is funny, confusing, and disturbing. Style and content conspire to elevate Godard's voice over the narrative elements of *Weekend*.

What is important to hold on to is that both Buñuel and Godard use a specific story frame that promises a certain kind of narrative. They then proceed to subvert that frame by narrative interventions: the use of irony, and the jump to an alternative or opposite narrative device that elevates their voices by subverting our expectations. This is a pattern continued today by Oliver Stone, by Martin Scorsese, and their contemporaries who have been influenced by them as well as by Buñuel and Godard.

THE SUBVERSION OF REALISM:
THE CASE OF STONE AND SCORSESE

In the case of Oliver Stone, the starting point for his story frame is realism. Whether he is dealing with Vietnam in his trilogy (*Platoon* [1986], *Born on the Fourth of July* [1989], and *Heaven and Earth* [1993]), or with presidents or presidential trauma (*JFK* [1991] and *Nixon* [1995]), or journalism and political or social themes (*Salvador* [1986] and *Natural Born Killers* [1995]), Stone will use a known event (an assassination or investigation), a rock career (*The Doors* [1991]), a career in serial murder (*Natural Born Killers*), or the civil war in El Salvador (*Salvador*). Stone is well known for pushing a particular perspective upon that frame. Here style actually serves to emphasize content. Occasionally, Stone will use style to subvert the frame, as he does in *The Doors* and in the recent *U-Turn* [1997] discussed earlier, but he more powerfully uses style to subvert content, as in *Natural Born Killers*.

The frame of *Natural Born Killers*, as I discussed in Chapter 9, "New Models," is the career of Mallory and Mickey, a pair of serious serial killers. By using an MTV style that creates a series of mini-MTV films—all of different styles—Stone actually moves us away from the frame, from the career of Mickey and Mallory, and towards a consideration of the source of the power of the media. Through the inclusion of a TV reporter who aggressively exploits the killers, as well as his audience, Stone introduces the notion of media and power directly into the narrative. But it is his use of an MTV style that showcases narrative events as if they were a piece of entertainment, rather than primarily the brutal events that they are: the sexual abuse of Mallory by her father; a police riot; an execution. Here style exploits content, the very point Stone wants to make about the power of the media. Through this intervention, the frame becomes nothing more than a vehicle to editorialize about the power of the media.

In the case of Martin Scorsese's best work, narrative and style are in a creative tension that allows style to alter meaning. As I mentioned earlier in Chapter 9, "New Models," *Kundun* (1997) is a biography of the Dalai Lama, but style transforms it into a study in the power of spirituality. In *Casino* (1995), the biography of a casino owner becomes a satire on how the accumulation of money in the casino debases the quality of his personal and professional life in direct proportion to its accumulation. The height of this dialectic is, of course, *Raging Bull* (1980), the biography of Jake La Motta. Scorsese juxtaposes performance in the ring with performance at home. As he rises in the ring, La Motta fails in his personal relationships. Tragically, the ring is replaced by a nightclub stage, but there is no one left, only La Motta rehearsing his lines in the mirror alone. His personal life has been totally emptied.

In order to see narrative and style in dynamic conflict, I turn to the work of Bernardo Bertolucci in his film *Beseiged* (1999).

THE DYNAMIC OF THE OVERWROUGHT TREATMENT OF NARRATIVE: THE CASE OF BERTOLUCCI'S *BESEIGED*

As I elaborated on Bernardo Bertolucci's voice in Chapter 5, "Tone," I will only re-iterate that his obsessions are love and politics from a Marxist perspective, and that his work fluctuates between a sense of betrayal in one area that offsets a level of commitment in another. It's as if a character cannot have both personal con-tentment and political conviction. There is always a dark storm in one area or an-other, and depending upon the time and place, a sense of romantic hope or inevi-table doom will prevail.

In Bertolucci's most recent film, *Beseiged*, we are presented with these themes in their purest sense. There are none of the overwrought passions of *1900* (1976) or the false emotions presented as sexual passion in *Last Tango in Paris* (1972). In a sense, *Beseiged* harkens back to *The Conformist* (1970) for its elegant intensity and its relation to music, dance, and opera as its source of style.

The main character is a young African woman, Shandurai. The film begins with political trauma in Africa. Her husband, a teacher is taken by the police. We learn later that he is imprisoned (we assume that the reason is political outspo-kenness or activity). The sequence that proceeds moves with a swiftness that em-phasizes shock over exposition. The sequence is also interlaced with the perfor-mance of an African chant together with ancient instrumental accompaniment.

The scene cuts directly to Rome, where Shandurai is now a housekeeper to an Englishman, Kinsky. She does so to support her medical studies in Rome. There is no indication about how much time has passed. Kinsky is a piano teacher and a composer. He seems to be a man of means. Very quickly he leaves a ring in the dumb waiter for Shandurai. When she asks what this is, Kinsky professes his love for her. Kinsky is a desperate man, and Shandurai thinks he is mad. She tells him she is already married. Clearly he knew nothing about her. And so the story of these two people and their relationship begins. Out of anger, Shandurai chal-lenges him to secure the freedom of her husband, and this is precisely what Kinsky sets about to do. The narrative will end with the arrival of the freed hus-band at this new home in Rome.

In between, the two protagonists do not speak about their actions with each other. Kinsky will act to do what he can to effect the release of the husband. What we see is that furniture is gradually disappearing from the house. He even sells his mode of being expressive, his grand piano, in order to raise the necessary funds. As Shandurai begins to understand the scale of his effort, she is slowly won over. His is an act of love, and he is giving up all that is meaningful to him be-cause he loves her. Although these two don't understand one another, and even though they come from different worlds, the first world and the third world, his love is colorblind. Eventually Shandurai is overwhelmed by his feeling and returns it. These two very different people do not understand each other's histories, but they have created their own powerful present. What will the arrival of her husband portend for this new relationship? Bertolucci doesn't offer an answer, he simply ends the narrative.

The frame of *Beseiged* is a love story, an impossible relationship. In the course of the plot to secure the release of the husband, and in the course of the two-ships-passing-in-the-night character layer, Bertolucci finds a way to create a love that is so powerful it is unstoppable; it must succeed. It is operatic, and it subsumes the national barriers in the plot and character layers. In *Beseiged*, personal passion is the life force that transcends politics, practicality, daily life, and its minutiae. Music, very different music, expresses the passion of the third world culture and of the first world. Both are alive and filled with feeling. This is what brings these two characters, Shandurai and Kinsky, together, and in the end makes plausible and necessary the passion that overrides difference. If these two improbably paired people can be joined, what of the rest of us? This is the powerful result of the dissonance of style and content in Bertolucci's *Beseiged*.

THE STRUCTURAL CHALLENGE TO CONTENT: THE CASE OF *BEFORE THE RAIN*

Milcho Manchevski's *Before the Rain* (1994) is organized around three stories presented out of their logical time frame. On screen they are presented in the order of story 2, story 3, and lastly story 1. By beginning with the last story first, Manchevski is announcing that real time doesn't matter. This is his first subversion.

The three stories are essentially love stories. The first is set in Macedonia. A young man, Kiril, a priest in training, has taken a vow of silence. A young Muslim girl, Zamira, seeks sanctuary, in the monastery where Kiril lives and works, from Christians who accuse her of killing a Christian. Kiril's silence, and the notion of how a young girl could and would kill a grown man, are the next two narrative subversions. In short order they fall in love, and he hides her from his colleagues and from the armed Christians who search the monastery hunting for the girl. The young priest denies hiding Zamira to protect her, but his lie is discovered, and he and the girl are expelled from the monastery. Now free from his vow of silence, they talk of making their way to North America, but they don't get far before they run into her grandfather, her brother, and a number of armed Muslims. Zamira is treated like a whore rather than a young relative in danger. They have found her with a Christian, which implies her loose as well as disloyal morals. As they send Kiril off Zamira runs after him and is killed by her own brother. The story sets out the premise of the two stories that will follow: racial hatred destroys love.

The second story focuses on Anne, a British woman who has arranged to have lunch with her husband. Her purpose is to tell him she is leaving him for Aleksander, a Macedonian photographer who is her lover. In the restaurant, an argument between a Christian and a Muslim ensues. We assume that they too are Macedonians. The aggrieved party returns to conclude the argument, gun in hand. In the gunfire, Anne's husband is killed. Again, racial hatred kills.

In the third story the main character is Aleksander, the very same Macedonian photographer. He returns to Skopje and then to a Christian family in his village. There he sees his first love, Hana, a Muslim woman. We sense the tension between Aleksander and the woman's father. Later she asks that he find her daughter, Zamira—the same young girl hidden in the first story. He rescues Zamira from the mob mentality surrounding the anger about a murdered relative. They believe Zamira is the killer. He rescues her, but then Aleksander is killed by his own Christian relatives. He rescued the girl out of his love for Hana. Now he is dead, and soon the young girl will be killed as well. Again, racial hatred destroys love.

In *Before the Rain* Manchevski has used a nonlinear frame to tell three stories about the same theme: that racial hatred destroys love. Structurally, each story has a love relationship at its core—one crossing religious or national boundaries. That transgression is lethal. That structure gives each story greater weight than the narrative alone implies. Together, the specific stories seem to be making a more universal statement. Structure gives us the author's voice as well as the depth or passion of that voice.

ALTERNATING STRUCTURES

The Case of *Sliding Doors*

Peter Howitt's *Sliding Doors* (1998) has a simple premise. If time could be stopped even for a few seconds, the outcome would be altered. The story is simple. A young woman, Helen, in London loses her job (the critical moment). She goes home by subway, known as the Tube. On the Tube, the story bifurcates and becomes two alternative stories. In the first Helen misses the train and takes a cab home to find her boyfriend, Gerry, in bed with a cold. In the second story, Helen gets on the subway, meets James, a man on the train, and then finds Gerry in bed, not with a cold, but with Lydia (a former girlfriend). But now Helen has another relationship—James. The film proceeds to alternate between the two versions until each reaches resolution. They then merge back into a single story with an ending that echoes back to the meeting on the train.

The first story is essentially the story of a masochistic woman unable to rid herself of what is clearly a bad relationship. In this story, Helen is the stubborn but victimized character who becomes pregnant by Gerry, has an accident, loses the baby, and only in doing so has the courage to say au revoir to him. But upon doing so she bumps into James from story two who is also in the hospital, to visit his ailing mother. The film will end implying these two people should be together.

In story two, Helen does manage to get on the tube. There she meets James who noticed her at her office (where she has just been fired). James is attentive, witty, somewhat flirtatious. Helen has a boyfriend, but not for long. She goes home, finds Gerry being unfaithful, and breaks off the relationship. Helen begins a relationship with James. She changes. She blossoms and becomes pregnant by James. But there is a complication. He claims to be visiting his mother in the hospital, but she witnesses him there with another woman. When confronted James confesses that the woman is his wife. They are separated, but for the sake of the mother they carry on as if they are a couple. Helen accepts his explanation, steps out into the road, and is hit by a truck. Hospitalized, Helen loses the baby and dies. In this story Helen is hopeful, disappointed, and then hopeful again about a man.

The structure of these two stories that are divided by time provide a life lesson for the main character. Story two, although Helen dies, instructs the character not to give up on men, there are good men out there. Story one ends with Helen meeting the good man from story two. Thus the structure pushes a woman who in story one makes bad choices and is betrayed, to change and be hopeful. The character of story two integrates into the conclusion of story one. She has hope where there was none. The structure in *Sliding Doors* does what she couldn't do—make a good choice, a positive choice. Whether this is fate, wishful thinking, or the voice of the author, structure subverts the content of story one to make another ending possible.

The Case of *Leolo*

Jean Claude Lauzon's *Leolo* (1992) offers an unusual structural variant: it has two character layers, one the real story, the second the imagined or alternative story. The result is a meditation on the real story as well as an echo of what might be.

The actual story is that of a young boy growing up in Montreal in the midst of what can best be called a mentally challenged family. The story is not political, and so their working-class origins are neither romanticized nor vilified. Rather, it's their mental instability that is explored. Depression, limited intelligence, schizophrenia—these are the problems that circumscribe the future for the members of this family. Will the same fate lie ahead for the main character? The answer is yes. The film ends with the main character, Leo, at age twelve, being taken into the psychiatric ward that has housed most of the other members of his family.

The narrative events of this character layer, with its emphasis on primitive behavior and resolutions to life issues, even the most basic, illustrate the limits for the main character. This character layer is filled with frustration, anger, and disappointment.

The alternative or imagined character layer has quite a different arc. Here the boy focuses on being Leolo, he reads, and a mentor encourages him to read, to go to the imagined other world. In this world, life problems are imaginatively resolved. His older brother, Fernand, becomes a body builder; Leo's budding sexuality has an outlet. In this world he also imagines that he is not his mother's son but rather Leolo Lozone, a boy conceived in Italy rather than in Montreal. This notion is elaborated in the birth myth that he has imagined that opens the film—its critical moment. A Sicilian peasant masturbates on tomatoes to be shipped to America. Two days later his mother in Montreal falls on those very tomatoes.

One becomes lodged in her, and this tomato is the go-between in his birth. This imagined beginning opens the alternative or imagined character layer. This layer struggles to compensate for his feelings in the actual character layer. The consequence is a stylistic challenge to the content of the first layer of the structure. The tension between the two character layers fuels the dramatic tension that pulls us into Leo's life.

THE TONAL CHALLENGE TO CONTENT

The Case of *La Haine*

Matthieu Kassiewitz' *La Haine* (*Hate*, 1995) has a very simple story frame: one day in the life of three characters, Vinz, Hubert, and Said. It begins during the trauma of a night of revolt against authority. The immigrant and poor minorities of Northern Paris have revolted against the police and there have been injuries. The older brother of Said has been injured. He is in hospital, and he may die. This is the context for the narrative of *La Haine*.

The narrative follows the three main characters, each male, poor, and angry. Said is Arab, Hubert is African, and Vinz is Jewish. Each is different from the other, but they feel a bond on the basis of their outsider status in France and their anger. The catalytic event is the revelation that Vinz, the angriest of the three, found a policeman's gun the night before. The balance of the narrative poses the question, what will he do if Said's brother dies in hospital? We know that there will be violence. We are not sure, however, what it will be. The resolution of the story is that act of violence. The surprise is that it is the police who kill the armed young man.

The tonal expectations for such a narrative are realism. This is, after all, a classic melodrama. But the tone is almost super-realism (reality TV) alternated with film references. Vinz is introduced mimicking the Travis Bickle character in Scorsese's *Taxi Driver*, in the bathroom mirror. The black protagonist is introduced in a makeshift gym where he is shadow boxing, in a sequence that echoes the introduction of Jake La Motta in *Raging Bull*. This fluctuation between super-realism and film stylization makes *La Haine* experientially fluid, exciting, and in the end shocking. Movies aren't life, and life isn't a movie. When a young man dies suddenly and without glory we are shocked into a super-reality—death doesn't occur as it does in the movies, backed by a forty-person orchestra. This is Kassiewitz' subversion in the experience of *La Haine*.

The Case of *Man Bites Dog*

Remy Belvaux's *Man Bites Dog* (1992) imagines the life of a killer for hire, but the presentation of this portrait is as a film in process. Ben, the killer, is being interviewed by a film crew in the aftermath of his work, and in the end he is killed just as he is being filmed. The crew filming him is also killed, and so the film ends with the work incomplete. But with this stylistic choice, the film portrait allows Belvaux to be inside and outside the life of this killer. The result is an uneasy, funny, and shocking portrait. Is it reality television or a mockumentary? That is for us the viewer to decide. In either case, the experience is unsettling.

In order to portray the killer and his nature, there is a recurring type of scene—murder, often of women and occasionally children, and its aftermath, or getting rid of the body. The killer clinically explains the issue of dead body weight and the weight in stones needed to sink the body. He then dumps the body off of an escarpment. Occasionally his motive for the murder is given—robbery. Again clinically, he explains that killing old people is preferable to the young. The old have savings while the young have nothing. Ben's own sense of sociology as a rationale delights the killer.

And then there is Ben at home—with his family, and with a prostitute with whom he has a long-time relationship. Here he is the height of thoughtfulness and filial consideration. The juxtaposition of behavior and attitude is striking.

Finally, there is the filming. Ben is excited about the notion that his life is being captured on film, and he wants to make sure the crew does a comprehensive job. He shares with them the logic of killing, and he also shares his hatreds—of blacks, minorities, and all outsiders. He has a lot of hate. He also boasts about his sexual prowess, which we witness in his relationship with the aging prostitute. And he wants them to know he is a devoted son. He is coarse and boastful, but there are moments when he displays another side as well—his loneliness. He not only wants to be filmed, he wants to be a friend of the director and his crew. Belvaux portrays the crew to be as amoral and immoral as their subject.

Because the killer is portrayed in a direct sense—he speaks to the camera as well as being filmed doing his job—there is an aura of actuality. It is only in the exaggeration of the character and his behavior, and in the behavior of the film crew, that we experience Belvaux's sense of irony. This approach, of shifting from reality to mockumentary is more often used strictly for humor (Rob Reiner's *This Is Spinal Tap* [1984] is an example). In *Man Bites Dog,* there is an alternative sense of ironic humor and powerful emotion—even horror—at this man's nature and his actions. This fluctuating experience of the character moves us far from the reality-based experience of the gangster film, the genre *Man Bites Dog* is close to. The clash of style and content unsettles us, leaving us wondering, has this been a movie or a real experience?

NARRATION SUBVERTS THE NARRATIVE

The Case of *The Sexual Life of the Belgians*

Jan Bucquoy's *The Sexual Life of the Belgians* (1994) uses as its story frame an autobiography. Bucquoy is telling us his life story, covering the period from 1950 to 1978. The point of view will be the sexual-relational dimension of his story. Because it is framed as an autobiography, the story is very much like a visual diary. It has that personal layer. But it also has an ironic layer because the character is not celebrating his life, rather he is exposing his life. The result is a mix of melodrama and satire. The style, confessional, yields veracity. The content, the prism of sexuality, undermines that veracity and gives the narrative a more sociological quality confirmed in the title. The irony distances us from the diarist, the main character, and raises the question of the narrative as commentary on national behavior rather than personal. The boy, Jan, is simply a vehicle for the story.

The chronology of the narrative—from Jan's first sexual encounter while he is being breast fed, through sexual encounters both homosexual and heterosexual, through Jan's marriage, its failure, and his sixties-seventies free-love phase, and finally ending as he's trying to finish his book about love—is presented as if Jan is involved in and yet also outside of his various relationships. Because the prism is so narrow, we don't really get to know the characters, nor do we get deeply involved with Jan. In fact, the characters remain stereotyped—his mother, cheap, withholding; his wife, status-conscious and withholding; his various girlfriends, unsatisfying. In the end Jan tries to establish a loving relationship on paper, but this too is subverted by the gap between his reality and his ideal—the love between an older woman and a younger man in Nicholas Ray's 1954 film *Johnny Guitar*. It's as if only the maternal figure can provide the love ideal for Jan. He ends the film tentatively—will Jan finish his book? Will he find love? The announcement that ends the film is that Part I is over, implying that the narrative and Jan's search will continue.

The gap between the real and the ideal is supported by a diary style. Often Jan will address the camera as if he is being interviewed. Many of the relationships are examined in a two-person scene that proceeds as a specific slice of life, a moment that captures the essence of the relationship, including the reason for its failure. In addition, the focus on sexuality allows the writer to draw allusions to other writers and storytellers such as Flaubert or Nicholas Ray. The clash of style and content makes *The Sexual Life of the Belgians* both a diary and a satire. The tonal conflict between the two deepens the irony in the narrative.

The Case of Lars Von Trier's *Breaking the Waves*

Although we will mention a dimension of Von Trier's *Breaking the Waves* (1996) later in Chapter 15, "The Centrality of Metagenre," I turn to it here because it offers an extreme example of how style and content can clash to alter the film experience.

On one level Von Trier's narrative is a straightforward melodrama that tells a doomed love story. Bess, a poor, limited young woman marries an outsider, a Danish oil rigger. The sense of place and the sense of people is very realistic, bleak, and even harsh. To provide relief for his audience, Von Trier inserts musical interludes. Those interludes remind us stylistically that we are not in the middle of a documentary. We are experiencing a manipulation, a movie that is artifice. In Act II, the husband asks Bess to sleep with other men and to tell him about it. These experiences are increasingly extreme. If she loves him, she will do as he asks.

In Act III, the artifice takes over the melodrama, and a man who was crippled at the end of Act I can walk again. But he can walk because Bess has prostituted herself for the last time to save him. He's asked the ultimate sacrifice and she's made the ultimate sacrifice. She is murdered, and he is saved. This transformation that he can walk again is entirely an act of artifice. Yet it has been prepared for in this series of musical interludes. As the film changes from melodrama to hyperdrama, from realism to fable, from realistic event to created artifice, we are shocked by the shift. Do we agree? Do we accept the transformation? It is the risk Von Trier takes. It is his way of using style to alter the meaning of content. In its way, it is as bold a moment as the transformation that takes place in Godard's *Weekend*.

The Case of Wong Kar-Wai's *Chungking Express*

Wong Kar-Wai's *Chungking Express* (1995) uses as its story frame the course of a relationship. The secondary frame is that a particular restaurant and food in general becomes the means of expression for the man and the woman in the relationship.

The stylistic subversion of *Chungking Express* poses the Hong Kong environment, in spite of a density that literally throws people together, as a counter force against the possibilities for intimacy. Won Kar-Wai's approach to the characterizations of the man and the woman focus on his anxiety and on her disconnectedness. She relates to The Mamas and the Papas version of California as Shangri La, implying that Hong Kong is quite the opposite. Just as she seems to be running away from the milieu and its citizens, including him, he is simply running— to his job, to eat, to communicate. He seems almost desperate, thus lessening his appeal to women.

This odd couple, however, seem destined for one another. She seems to acknowledge this in her relationship with him via his apartment. She cleans and considers decorating options. But she's not ready for the real thing. When he discovers her there, she leaves her job and Hong Kong, only to return a year later somehow changed and more mature. When they meet at the end of the narrative, we believe there is a chance for this relationship. He, on the other hand, carries on in his habitual pattern. Only the restaurant where they met remains a fixture for him. But after their year apart even that has changed. Only he remains constant.

Chungking Express is about disconnectedness. Not the kind of disconnectedness the characters in Danny Boyles' *The Beach* (2000) exhibit, nor the disconnectedness of the characters in his *Trainspotting*. In *The Beach*, the characters are running away from convention for excitement. In *Trainspotting*, the characters are alienated outsiders and so unconventional behavior is their norm; disconnectedness is their daily state. *Chungking Express* isn't about drug states, it's about spiritual states. In that sense, the two main characters are either alienated from their environment or a victim of their environment. That mood of alienation is the powerful result of a style that subverts the narrative events of *Chungking Express*, a style that creates a powerful tone—not ironic but rather distant.

IRONY AND VOICE

The Case of *Election*

The story frame of Alexander Payne's *Election* (1999), a novel by Tom Perrotta, is a high school election for student government in Omaha, Nebraska. The election for student body president has three candidates and a teacher-advisor, and these are the four main characters in *Election*.

The story begins with only one candidate, Tracy Flick. But because the teacher, Mr. McAllister, hates her, he encourages the most popular boy in the school, Paul Metzler, to run against Tracy. Paul's entry into the race prompts his gay adopted sister Tammy to run as well, and the race is on.

The election provides Payne with the opportunity to look at the behavior of each character and to show that public action differs from private feeling. In the case of Tracy and her teacher Mr. McAllister, their personal desires and antipathies drive each to dishonest behavior. In the case of the teacher, he is trying to have an affair with his best friend's ex-wife, Linda Novotny, who is his wife Diane's best friend. His behavior both with the Linda and with the election (he destroys two ballots to make sure Tracy loses) essentially ruins his life and career, and he ends up in New York constructing a "better" life. Tracy, who is ambition personified, is rewarded for her desire. Her destruction of the election signage of her rivals goes unpunished. She is accepted into Georgetown University and will no doubt run for President in a future sequel to this story.

The tone of *Election* is ironic and humorous, always pointing out the gap between thought and action, between morals and ethics. Each of these characters sidesteps morality in order to promote their agendas. Paul wants to be liked and he is. Tammy wants a love object and finds it by being expelled from school and sent off to Catholic girls school. Tracy wants to win, and Mr. McAllister wants to believe he is altruistic but he isn't. He is a man who always feels the threat of women no matter their age.

The style of *Election*, less linear and ironic, subverts the frame, the election, to make the narrative a meditation on values.

There are other films that are effective examples in which style subverts the narrative frame, such as Danny Boyle's *Trainspotting* and Mary Harron's *I Shot Andy Warhol* (1996). The work of Cedric Lapisch in France (*When the Cat's Away* [1996]) and of Clara Law in Hong Kong and in Australia both exemplify this tendency. The result is to elevate the voice of the writer and director through the very particular strategy of undermining the expectations raised by the frame of the narrative.

14

THE MEDIUM IS THE MESSAGE

One of the palpable characteristics of global storytelling is a recognition of the global power of the media. It is both what binds and separates us. It should not be a surprise, then, that the media itself has become a character in contemporary narrative. In this chapter we will look at the presence of the media in terms of content as well as style, and at how the media consequently plays a role in global storytelling. To do so we first turn to the context, not just Marshall McLuhan's proclamation about the medium being the message, but also the acknowledgment of media power and the consequent caution in his pronouncement.

McLuhan suggested that the medium itself, although powerful, would in its very nature alter human communication between people. It would also alter self-image, the community and the society, which in turn would make that medium seem all the more powerful.

McLuhan's focus was principally on the relatively new form (in the 1960s), television, but his ideas are readily transferable to consideration of the Internet and its impact on how we value human values and technology. Perhaps the most interesting notion about McLuhan is the idea that media can influence how we think.

However we approach McLuhan's ideas, they have elevated the importance of the media and its interaction and influence upon the self, the community, the society, indeed the global community. His phrase, television will create "a global village," has never been more apt and it is applicable to much of the thrust of this book.

THE PRE-MCLUHAN ERA IN FILM

Before the publication of McLuhan's *Understanding Media: The Extensions of Man* (1964), the media, principally newspaper, theater, television, and Hollywood, had been presented in a bifurcated manner. If a newspaper for example was presented in a comedy, for example, it was often a screwball comedy. The film implied the power of the newspapers, but also belittled the power of the people who worked in the media. The male reporter in William Wellman's *Nothing Sacred* (1937) and the male editor in Howard Hawks' *His Girl Friday* (1939) are both duped by women. In *Nothing Sacred* the woman is a "civilian" who is the subject of a story on the bravery of a dying woman. The problem is that she's not dying. In *His Girl Friday*, Hildy, the woman reporter, doesn't really want to leave the love of her life, reporting. And the editor, Walter, doesn't want the love of his life, Hildy, to leave him for another man. The plot will enable each of them to get what they really want. In both cases, the films make fun of the power of the media, represented by the men. Gently, the message is that they are not so powerful, that they are actually more romantically vulnerable than women, or to put it another way, they are professionally powerful and personally weak.

On the melodrama side, we veer toward film noir. Both Orson Welles' *Citizen Kane* (1941) and Billy Wilder's *Ace in the Hole* (1951) show the newspaper mogul, Charles Foster Kane and the ruthless reporter Charles Tatum, respectively, to be power-hungry but deeply flawed characters. In each case the actions taken, whether out of hubris in the case of Charles Foster Kane, or out of desperate ambition in the case of Charles Tatum, result in the fall of the man. This view of the destiny of the newspaperman is later echoed in Alexander Mackendrick's *The Sweet Smell of Success* (1958) and in Federico Fellini's *La Dolce Vita* (1960).

Theater is presented with somewhat more charm. The implication is that theater is not for everyone, consequently its power and its players are less menacing. The positive qualities of theater infuses Vincent Minnelli's *The Band Wagon* (1953) with a sense of joy about performance that is safe. The only drag on Tony Hunter, the main character in *The Band Wagon*, is that he's coming from that other medium, Hollywood film, as if to say you'd be glum too if you had to be in movies. But he does get over it. The pleasure of performance and "the artistic value of theater" are at the heart of the post-McLuhan version of theatrical life in Woody Allen's *Bullets over Broadway* (1994). Allen doesn't tamper with the sense of self-importance and joy carried over from *The Band Wagon*.

Looking at melodrama, the great film about the theater is Mankiewicz's *All About Eve* (1950). The job of performance, the elitist quality of theater relative to the other arts, and the implication that it is a small and rarified world that doesn't have a pervasive influence—these remain as core qualities of *All About Eve*. Consequently it retains its charm, although the caution of the film is that you can lose your head in stardom, and if you do the price may not be worth the exalted reward.

Hollywood, which is more powerful than the theater, does elicit representation that parallels the world of newspapers. Musical and situation comedies often portrayed the naivete and the narcissism of the talent of Hollywood. The quintessential Hollywood film is, of course, Stanley Donen and Gene Kelly's *Singin' in the Rain* (1952). No film has portrayed those qualities in a more charming manner. Preston Sturges went so far as to split his Hollywood film *Sullivan's Travels* (1941) into two parts: initially, it is the humorous tale of John Sullivan, the greatest director of comedies. Sullivan wants to make a serious film. After all, the country is in the middle of a Depression. Pretending to be a bum (to find out what it's really like), the plot twists away from the director, and in the serious second half of the film Sullivan finds himself in a southern prison. Now he's a prisoner on a chain gang, and Sturges won't let him out until he appreciates how important comedy is to prisoners and to working people. Once he gives up his delusions of serious grandeur, Sullivan is freed and happily goes back to directing comedies.

The dark side of Hollywood living is the film noir version of Billy Wilder's *Sunset Boulevard* (1950). The question of how much dignity Joe Gillis, a writer is willing to sacrifice to further his ambition is easily answered; as much as it takes. He rewrites a script for Norma Desmond, a silent screen star, but eventually realizes that he is her companion rather than her cowriter. But Joe's sense of self-deprecation is such that he stays. Only later does he realize how much he's lost— Betty Schaefer, a woman who believes in him! But it's too late. As Joe walks out on Norma Desmond she kills him. His desire for Hollywood success had a high price, and he paid it.

Somewhere between the light of the musical comedy and the darkness of film noir, the Hollywood producer is the subject of Minnelli's melodrama, *The Bad and the Beautiful* (1952). The producer is dissected like a laboratory rat by his mentor (another studio executive), by a director, by a writer, and by an actress. The result is a portrait of Jonathan Shields, a composite portrait using David O. Selznick as its starting point. There is charm here, and there is talent, but there is also a level of self-serving manipulation of those closest to him. They love him and they hate him. They are seduced by him and they are degraded by him. And we are left in awe of him. The Hollywood mythology is positively stoked.

And now we come to the most powerful medium of all, television, and here the trepidation about that power is evidenced early. Television, although discovered twenty years earlier than its debut, does not really become a factor in American life until the 1950s. Variety shows, drama—both live and taped—news, and sports quickly make television a powerful fixture of American life. With the Kennedy-Nixon debate of 1960, the power of television is unforgettably confirmed. Then the development of cable, the VCR, and satellite broadcasting each made television even more powerful and multilayered in its functioning, from the most local level to the global. That sense of power and importance has if anything only increased.

Before McLuhan the cautionary tale about the power of television is Elia Kazan's *A Face in the Crowd* (1957). Marcia Jeffries (Patricia Neal) facilitates the rise of a bum to the status of a TV star via radio. Lonesome Rhodes is charming and self-serving. His rise is due to a tell-it-like-it-is personality packaged as a singer-host of a show. The show becomes so popular that Lonesome begins to wield personal and political power via his popularity, over the people who helped him— Marcia, Colonel Hollister. In the end, however, he is powerful but alone, a man living up to his name. As Marcia sees him and is disillusioned by him, we know that his power is temporal and his needs bottomless. Lonesome Rhodes has charisma, and television lives off the sunshine of charisma. So do films about television. While they revile the abuse of the power of the medium or the practitioners in the medium, they also are in awe of its power. This is the deeper relationship with the narrative of *A Face in the Crowd*.

A similar love-hate relationship is at the core of Sidney Lumet's post-McLuhan take on television, *Network* (1978). Here television is presented as so powerful that it drives out humane and moral judgment. The power makes its holders intoxicated. They will kill for ratings, and they certainly won't flinch at using people or destroying them. Paddy Chayefsky, who wrote the screenplay for *Network*, cut his creative teeth in live television drama. He laments the entertainment impulse in programming. He feels it's run amok and that it constitutes a real threat to our society. That's why he's chosen satire as his genre of choice. He wants to win minds by frightening us, and, as happens in *A Face in the Crowd*, he both succeeds and fails. What audiences remember from *Network* is the power of a mad news anchor, Howard Beal, sticking his head out a window and yelling, "I'm mad as hell and I'm not going to take it anymore." We accept Howard Beal's caution as cathartic entertainment. The power of the medium is confirmed.

These films about the media reflect an appreciation of their power in American life. But their focus is tempered by a sense of the underside of this power—its corrupting influence on behavior and upon character. The players in the media are not characters in the business world, admired for their entrepreneurship, or in the political world, admired for their idealism or their contribution to the society. These characters are more narcissistic and more self-serving. They are more flawed. But their celebrity holds an attraction that has remained irresistible. This quality has only become more palpable and more powerful now that we truly live in McLuhan's global village. And so we turn now to how the media have become characters in contemporary film narrative.

THE POST-McLUHAN ERA IN FILM

The media, particularly the most powerful, television, has become an important influence on how film narrative unfolds. Broadcast journalism, the news as well as the documentary, has been an important feature of those films where actuality or veracity is a central feature. The most direct representation of this quality is in the docudrama. A film like Ken Loach's *My Name Is Joe* (1998) is trying to produce in its kinetic qualities the frenetic, kinetic workings of the mind of an alcoholic, in this case the central character, Joe.

Another area where this presents is in genres that rely on a sense of realism best described as "being there." Vietnam films in particular strived for this quality. But no war film has gone as far as Steven Spielberg's *Saving Private Ryan* (1998). The twenty-minute opening sequence takes us onto the D-Day beach in Normandy. Spielberg does everything he can to give us the feeling that we are there with a captain and his company. (See Chapter 5, "Voice," Chapter 6, "The Hollywood Model," and Chapter 12, "The Search for New Forms.")

Other film genres have crossed over to embrace actuality in order to subvert our genre expectations and replace them with a sense of actuality, of being there with the main character. This is particularly effective in the horror film *The Blair Witch Project*. But it has been equally effective in a gangster film such as *Man Bites Dog*. The sense of actuality makes these dramatized films seem like documentaries. This sense is enhanced in all these films by the acknowledgment of the presence of a cameraperson or crew and of the act of filmmaking. In each case the illusion of actuality is strengthened by the referent point seen so often in the documentary on television—the shadow of the cameraperson, or the mirror reflection of the act of filmmaking itself. These referent points deepen the sense of actuality. Now we turn to the representation of the media in contemporary films, first the journalist, in the media of newspapers and magazines.

As the power of newspapers and journalism has diminished relative to the growth of the impact and immediacy of television and the celebrity of stars and directors, there has been a shift in the representation of the journalist. No longer is the journalist portrayed as he was in Wilder's *Ace in the Hole* (1951). More typical is the romantic view of the journalist as a western hero. This means that the journalist stands in for a set of values somehow lost in the society at large. Examples of this characterization include the two main characters in Alan Pakula's *All the President's Men* (1976), based on the book by Carl Bernstein and Bob Woodward; the photojournalist in Roger Spottiswoode's *Under Fire* (1983); and the print journalist in Roland Joffé's *The Killing Fields* (1984). In all of these cases, the main character represents the moral position, whether the issue is the truth in *All the President's Men*, political morality in *Under Fire*, or the simple sanctity of human life in *The Killing Fields*.

A good recent example of this kind of representation is Michael Winterbottom's *Welcome to Sarajevo* (1998). Here Michael Henderson, the main character is a British journalist covering the Bosnian war. He is so horrified by the savagery of the war that he fixes on a mission, to adopt a young girl orphaned in the war. Michael risks his life to smuggle her out of Bosnia. A major portion of the narrative is devoted to his effort to smuggle her out and to keep her once she is in England. His behavior, personal and committed, is an expression of his humanity in the face of the horrific situation he has to report upon professionally. The main point here is that the journalist is portrayed as a "moral" hero, the kind of main character we find in the classic western.

There has also been an effort to use the reporter as the main character in a situation comedy-melodrama, as in Ron Howard's *The Paper* (1992). But because the power of the newspaper is not what it was when Ben Hecht wrote *The Front Page* (1931), the passions behind the story tend to fall flat. Dramatically, the newspaper has dimmed as a power center relative to the other media, and consequently the plot to enable the character in *The Paper* to appear heroic simply doesn't work. This particular media is not what it used to be.

Turning to the theater, the best representation of the theater as a media character is John Madden's *Shakespeare in Love*. The film, written by Marc Norman and Tom Stoppard, is presented as a work in progress. As I discussed in Chapter 12, "The Search for New Forms," the plot of the film consists of the writing and performance of the play *Romeo and Juliet*. The main character is Will Shakespeare. The character layer poses a muse on one side and a financial backer for his play on the other. The women in this story, both the lady who is muse and Elizabeth the Queen, help further the play and Shakespeare's standing as a playwright, while the pressures of commerce and competition are barriers (albeit mild) to his satisfaction. Norman and Stoppard opt for a situation comedy form, so there is no question that the plot will enable Shakespeare to be what he is destined to be—a great playwright. The broad success of this film suggests that the elitist view of the theater that was so prevalent in the pre-McLuhan portrait of theater and its characters, is now far less elitist and in a sense less class-oriented than had been the case.

The media that are perceived to be more powerful in the current period are film and television. The portrait of these two media is far more complex than the newspaper or the theater. We turn first to film.

In terms of comedy there are a number of films that have addressed film-making and the values associated with a career in film. Barry Primus' *Mistress* (1992) is the story of an independent director who is given a chance to produce a film if he will employ the untalented mistress of the questionable source of the finances (mob money). The issue of how much one is willing to compromise in order to see one's vision on celluloid (parallel to the theme of Woody Allen's *Bullets over Broadway*) is the core of *Mistress*. It's a powerful medium, but so too the ego of the director. He is willing to compromise because he wants to be a director more than he is looking for a forum for his ideas. Naturally, it's all about compromise and ego and self-delusion, but the arc of transformation for the main character is more akin to the level of desire one associates with a last chance. The main character makes his choice, makes his compromises, and lives happily ever after with his delusions.

Albert Brooks' *The Muse* (1999) focuses not so much on a last chance as upon the ego of the players. Brooks portrays Steven Phillips, a successful screenwriter who suddenly faces rejection of his new proposals. Whether he has lost his touch or whether the industry has shifted to a younger generation of writers, he sees his house being repossessed, his family in rags, and himself a nerve-wracked failure. When a friend suggests he needs a muse, Steven is ready for anything. He meets Sarah (Sharon Stone) and agrees to all of her outlandish and expensive requests. And since this is a situation comedy, it works. He is not destroyed as is the writer in *Sunset Boulevard*. On the contrary, superstition is a valid career maker in *The Muse*. This is, after all, a situation comedy. The implication is again that ego will take you to strange places, particularly in Hollywood.

The third example of the comedy approach to Hollywood and its participants is Steve Martin's *Bowfinger* (1999). Here Robert Bowfinger, the main character, is a cheap porno director who has a cast of marginal actors and crew whom he calls upon. Bowfinger is the classic manipulator. He pulls together a production on the basis of having a star, Kit Ramsey (a neurotic Eddie Murphy). But Ramsey doesn't know he's in the film. As the crew films him without his knowledge, they create a story that will take advantage of the distant travelling shots they've been able to film without revealing themselves. The director finds Jiffernson, a stand-in who looks like the actor to portray the other narrative sections where he appears (Murphy plays the naive amateur as well). The film within the film is made with the requisite results—it's a great film!

Martin explores the behavior and the culture that lives at the margin of Hollywood: those who want to be stars. Because this is a comedy, judgment about the morality of their behavior is replaced by a romantic elevation of desire as a justification for questionable behavior. Although this is a film about exploitation of stars and want-to-be stars, Martin focuses more on their desires. Thus we are charmed by the inventiveness that desire promotes, and we downplay the moral lapses in the behavior of the characters.

When we turn to more serious story forms, the same actions are assessed rather differently. In Paul Thomas Anderson's *Boogie Nights* (1998), the main character, Eddie Adams (Mark Wahlberg) is offered a chance to be in adult films. The producer, Jack (Burt Reynolds), recognizes something in Eddie, something he wants to exploit. Eddie changes his name to Dirk Diggler and a career is launched. The melodrama treatment will follow the rise and fall of Eddie as a porn star in late 1970s Hollywood. The adult industry, as it's called, is happy to use up Eddie. For the industry, he's just a performing body rather than a person. Anderson's treatment of celebrity, ambition, and the industry is, as we expect, a personal tragedy for Eddie and for *so many of the* people he works with. This frame has been used with a boxing backdrop (*The Harder They Fall* [1956]), a waterfront backdrop (*On the Waterfront* [1954]), and a labor strike backdrop (*Matewan* [1987]), and in each case the arc is similar: the powerless person fights the power structure for power, and something is lost in the struggle. By the end of *Boogie Nights* the character is faced with the fact that he's not a celebrity, he's just meat.

No film about Hollywood has been as critical of its values as has Robert Altman's *The Player* (1992). Here the character we follow is a studio executive. The form the writer Michael Tolkin chose for his novel and screenplay for *The Player* is the genre Altman favors, the satire. Like the attack on television in *Network* and on the medical system in *The Hospital*, the approach in *The Player* is to attack the values that Hollywood represents. This time the main character is not an actor as in *Boogie Nights,* or a screenwriter as in *Sunset Boulevard*. Griffin Mill is a studio executive. He wants to keep his job and more. He wants to move up. But he faces a number of threats to his ambition—a rival at the studio and a menace outside the studio. Someone is sending him threats. Griffin believes it's David Kahane, a disgruntled writer, whom he begins to follow, making a point of confronting him in a parking lot outside a cinema. In the struggle that follows he kills Kahane. Not satisfied with that victory, Griffin also begins to pursue June, the writer's girlfriend and strikes up a relationship with her, pretending to console her about her loss. Although Griffin is a suspect in the killing, he is cleared by the end of Act II because he is not identified as the suspect in a police line-up. The police think he did it. So does the head of security at the studio. But this is a satire on values, the values of Hollywood, so he gets away with it. He also defeats his rival at the studio. At the end he has the girl, the job, the power. The message is that you have to be a killer to succeed in Hollywood. And so our executive is a success.

Altman and Tolkin have not romanticized Griffin's victory. It is a dark victory, and the film in its narrative arc succeeds in portraying a community with values that are immoral. A corollary has been made and Hollywood has been skewered. The Hollywood dream has become the American nightmare.

Turning to the most powerful medium, television, we find a diverse but creative set of films that caution us about what is real and what is manufactured, in life and on television.

We begin with Paul Thomas Anderson's *Magnolia* (1999). *Magnolia* is a narrative with nine characters whom we follow. Two of them, Stanley Berry and Frank

Mackey, are subjects in television. Stanley, a young boy, is a participant in an "intelligence" show for students. Will he be nationally recognized, as the show has the capacity to do for you if you win, or not? Frank Mackey, a facilitator played by Tom Cruise, is a celebrity who celebrates men and masculinity. Mackey is the subject of an investigative TV documentary. The black woman who interviews him is challenging, looking for ways to deflate this aggressive male promoter for manhood.

Both of these narrative lines explore issues of celebrity, the promise that TV can confer fame and fortune—or destruction. On the other side of the equation Anderson places the human values. Both Stanley and Frank have to deal with demanding, difficult, and conditional fathers (win and I will love you; be what I want you to be and I accept you). Again public life and personal life are in conflict with one another. Anderson is not definitive about the medium of television, but he is very critical about its exploitative quality. It makes us be what we're not. Or it punishes us for being who we are. In both of the characters' stories, he is critical of the intentions of the medium.

A parallel narrative to Stanley's story in *Magnolia* is the narrative of Robert Redford's *Quiz Show* (1994). Redford's narrative is based on television's early, ignoble, and influential history. *The $64,000 Question* was one of the most popular television shows of the 1950s. However it proved not to be real-life quiz show but rather entertainment. It was discovered that the show coached its participants in their answers in order to stage the creation of the winners, whom the producers felt were the heroes the public wanted to embrace.

Redford interweaves three story lines. Two of the stories follow the two antagonists in the great TV contest. Herbie Stempal is a working-class Jew, intense and difficult. Charles VanDoren is a blond, likeable, upper-class Brahmin, a Yale professor of English and the son of a highly regarded professor. The third story line follows Dick Goodwin, a Washington investigator looking into corruption charges about this famous show. When the story lines merge, the champion, the blond Brahmin, will be discredited for being coached. But more importantly, the film as a whole is a caution that what you are watching may engage real people, but the medium that presents them is an entertainment medium. It's about ratings and dollars, not about truth and justice. Redford presents the narrative as that moment when the public lost its innocence about television. He also implies that television never had any innocence. It was always about a bigger revenue stream.

If *Quiz Show* is a cautionary tale, *Galaxy Quest* is an homage to the power of television. Framed as a situation comedy, *Galaxy Quest* is based upon the phenomenon of *Star Trek*, one of the most enduring legends of television. The narrative focuses on the cast of the show *Galaxy Quest*, which has been cancelled but is seen in perpetual reruns. The actors are a grumpy lot signing autographs in shopping malls and at trade shows—in uniform, of course. Jason Nesmith, the leader of the pack, based on Captain Kirk of *Star Trek*, is an egocentric drunk, and he goes downhill from there.

Enter a plot. A group of aliens who have studied the TV show, *Galaxy Quest*, feels the crew is the answer to their situation—they are being subjugated by the ugliest, most aggressive creatures television could conjure. But now it's for real. They try to convince the captain and crew to lead them, to rescue them from the tyranny of the tyrants. Because Jason is bored and in need of the adulation offered, he agrees and the group travels into outer space. The machinations of the plot will lead them through a lot of the old plots and resolutions, but gradually they accept that it's all for real, and save the civilization through the canny wiles dreamed up in a TV series.

As a situation comedy, *Galaxy Quest* fulfills the requisite fusion of television and reality. In this case television enables "reality," the civilization that was threatened, to survive. Indeed, the civilization is improved because of their knowledge of television. Of course this is a fantasy notion, charming in its delivery and romantic in its benign approach to the medium. This is what we expect in situation comedy.

The same cannot be said for the hyperdrama *The Truman Show* (1998), Peter Weir's vision of a future where the highest rated show is the created world of a young man named Truman. From his birth the public has watched his every move. They've lived with him in his hometown, with his wife, and his family. What we discover, however, is that it's all fake—the wife, the family, the town, all except Truman. He's for real. He is the subject and the victim of the Truman show. At the end of Act I he discovers it's all artifice, and he spends the balance of the narrative trying to get out of this unreal world. What he's trying to get to is the real world. And in the end, he breaks through the set and reaches the real world.

The moral of this tale is that if we don't suspect manipulation in our life we will be manipulated. It's a narrative that implies that paranoia, when it's real, is a virtue. On another level it's a cautionary tale about the power of television to invade our lives. It's too powerful, too invasive, too likely to promote artifice as opposed to human and humane values. On yet another level, the film advises us not to believe what we see on this medium. All of the above suggests how very powerful television is perceived to be.

In this chapter we have looked at the media as a powerhouse in globalization as well as a character contributing to that globalization. Filmmakers such as Peter Weir have taken a direct frontal approach to the media in films such as *The Truman Show*. Others, such as Krystof Kieslovski, have taken a more philosophical approach in a film such as *Red* (1994). Here a young woman communicating via modern telecommunications with her fiancée has poor human communication with him. On the other hand, her personal encounter with a local judge who has cut himself off from personal relationships (he has abusive telephone relations with neighbors) has a meaningful personal exchange with this young woman. They meet when she injures his dog while driving. Their personal relationship, initiated because of the dog, grows and compensates for the failures of modern technology, i.e., telephone relationships with a fiancée or a neighbor, both more natural relationships for each of them.

In Kieslovski's eyes, the media is omnipresent, a way of perceiving and communicating rather than a direct character. Whichever the approach, the media has become an active character in the internationalization of storytelling.

15

THE CENTRALITY OF
METAGENRE

In order to speak to and reach their national audiences, national cinemas have favored particular genres. The United States has used the western and the gangster films to explore its national mythology with an historical palate, the western, and a modern palate, the gangster film. Germany has preferred melodrama to explore contemporary themes and science fiction/horror to explore mythology in the future or the past. Italy has preferred the comedy/satire as an outlet for optimism and the melodrama as a lament about the past. These genres have been useful to speak to national audiences. To reach an international audience, the metagenre has become far more important.

Metagenre, or the genre that transcends specific genres, can be categorized as melodrama, hyperdrama, docudrama, and experimental narrative. These are the basic genres whose qualities one finds in various formulations in each of the genres. For example, there is a level of melodrama (the struggle of the powerless person for power from the power structure) in the gangster film, the biography, the epic, the war film, science fiction, the action-adventure, film noir, and the horror film. The degree may vary, but melodrama is a presence in all of these genres. In the case of docudrama, we are talking about the voice or the point of view of the writer-director. It may be present in a more pronounced manner in the war film than in film noir, but it is nevertheless present. In docudrama, it is simply the most overt element of the genre. In the case of hyperdrama, there is a relation to voice as in docudrama. But in hyperdrama, voice is affiliated with a moral lesson or fable that represents the point of view of the writer-director. In the use of experimental narrative, style is more pronounced than narrative content; here the medium, the style, is the message. In those genres where style is critical, the experimental narrative provides the edge that influences how the narrative will be presented.

Why has metagenre become more important now? To understand this development, we need to look at the current shift towards the internationalization of storytelling. In other words, what is it about these genres that makes stories more accessible to an international audience?

The easiest genre to see in terms of its usefulness in international storytelling is the melodrama. Not only is the melodrama the fundamental layer of so many genres, bit it is also the genre that deals with believable characters in credible or recognizable situations. When an Iranian filmmaker makes a film about a young boy who doesn't accept his stepfather (his father died in the war), an international audience will immediately understand the feelings of a powerless boy looking for power in a world dominated by adults (*The Father*, Majid Majidi, 1991). His rivalry with his new father for the loyalty of his mother is a universal theme. Whether the character is from Northern California or Southern Italy or from Iran, you and I understand him and empathize with his dilemma. This is the core issue for the contemporary viability of the melodrama. It deals with real themes of the day that cross cultures. Another example is director Amos Gitai's *Kadosh* (1999), which is set in the orthodox community of Jerusalem. The main character is a woman, and the story is about her inability to bear children. Although her husband loves her, he has to divorce her due to familial pressure to marry someone who is fertile. This narrative is about the rights of a woman in a man's world. *Bandit Queen* (1994) in India, *Elizabeth* (1998) in England, *Girlfight* (2000) in the United States—all of these films are about the same narrative arc. They may have different plots, but all are melodramas about women today. And wherever you live, you can recognize and relate to this struggle. This is the strength of the melodrama in international storytelling.

In the case of docudrama, the increasing exposure of the international audience to the broadcast documentary makes the docudrama an increasingly recognizable shape to an international audience. But more important is the affiliation of this genre with political, social, economic issues of the day. This feature of the docudrama also derives from the broadcast documentary. The form gives the narrative gravitas, weight, just as the documentary does. The issue of voice, so increasingly important, is also facilitated in the docudrama. All of these factors have made the docudrama more important and available to the international audience.

Hyperdrama, whose sole purpose is to convey a moral fable to its audience, is particularly well suited to an international audience. Morality tales are about the Ten Commandments. But they can also be about issues of faith in a faithless age, or about more philosophical or existential issues such as immortality, or about the major struggles of our time, such as technological progress and its price. The world of biotechnology is rife with moral issues. Political, social, economic life, each is rife with moral issues, and so they too provide material for the hyperdrama.

What's important to say is that these issues cross national boundaries very well. Moral fables are nationless, they are genuinely international, and so hyperdrama has become particularly important in this era of international storytelling.

Finally there is the issue of experimental narrative, the last of the metagenres. We live in a world of many languages. The common language of film is the visual. Of all the metagenres, the experimental narrative tends to be the least dependent upon dialogue and the most reliant on the visual. This nonverbal quality makes experimental narrative travel quite well in the global village.

MELODRAMA

Stories about recognizable people in believable situations, the struggle of a powerless person looking for power from the power structure, these are the key qualities of the melodrama. A melodrama such as Robert Redford's *Ordinary People* (1980) was effective because it dealt with a primal issue—how do we deal with loss in a family? In that story the loss was a brother, and the narrative, although told from the point of view of the younger brother, also focused on the impact of the loss on each parent and on the family as a unit. In this chapter we want to understand why melodrama now has made films more available to an international audience. To explore why melodrama and why now, we need to burrow into a spectrum of very different melodramas. What elements of these stories help the stories travel well around the world. We begin with an unlikely candidate.

Phillip Haas' *Angels and Insects* (1995) tells the nineteenth-century story of a young scientist, William Adamson, who has made his scientific reputation in South America, but he now tries to make a life for himself in the home of his sponsor, a rich scientifically minded Englishman, Sir Harald Alabaster. William comes from a middle-class background; he is educated, well-mannered. Sir Harald offers him a home in which to progress in his scientific work, particularly in his work on butterflies. The complication in the narrative is that the scientist falls in love with one of Sir Harald's daughters, Eugenia. She is for him like a butterfly—beautiful and rather inscrutable. He is very tolerant of Eugenia's volatility and her seeming vulnerability. The relationship progresses through the efforts of William to be accepting of Eugenia. She is constantly distracted (it seems her fiancé had committed suicide prior to their wedding). William proceeds, and much to his surprise and pleasure she accepts his affections and they will marry. Sir Harald is agreeable, but his brutish son, Edgar, Eugenia's brother, objects on the basis of class. The marriage goes forward. Eugenia is a surprisingly agreeable lover, but the first child doesn't look like William nor does the second. By the end of Act II, William discovers that she has been having an ongoing incestuous affair with her brother, Edgar. The children, without a doubt, are not his. In the end, William leaves the estate together with Matty Crompton, the tutor for the younger daughters of the family. Matty, plain but passionate and talented in science, shares the morality of William, and we suspect they will be a far more appropriate match than his first.

What makes this melodrama a period film that resonates today is the core issue of family values, so often a topic of social and political life in North America. In *Angels and Insects* we have a classic melodramatic arc: William, the scientist, the powerless person, attains or tries to attain power by marrying into an upper-class family. He has crossed the great divide in his society. True, he brings education and intelligence into the new relationship, but will these new or modern values (representing a power grid we today value) be enough? The answer is no. But not for failure on his part. The family that betrays family values is in fact the family that represents the power structure. The upper-class family has members who are willingly incestuous, certainly in Edgar's case. Nor is Edgar intelligent, in fact he is uneducated and disinterested in what has drawn his father to this scientist. Nor is Eugenia very interested in the future, or in progress. She is only interested in satisfying her desires, carnal or otherwise. She and her brother represent the "dinosaur" qualities in their class, while the scientist and the tutor represent something vibrant, alive, curious and future-oriented. And so family values, or the hypocrisy about family values, is the dimension of *Angels and Insects* that speak to international audiences today. The issue of class and class boundaries also speaks to audiences today. Finally, Matty, the powerless woman from a class perspective, but bright, observant, and talented, is the other character in this narrative who resonates for women who recognize her situation in their everyday lives. Men and women can celebrate that she frees herself from that situation.

Turning to a more contemporary film, we see the interesting role ethnicity plays in the melodrama. Karyn Kusama's *Girlfight* (2000) tells the story of a young Puerto Rican teenager, Diana Guzman, who chooses to advance her life by becoming a boxer. Her character is following the immigrant up the acceptance ladder of mainstream American society via sports. The film takes up its plot line from such boxing films as Reuben Mamoulian's *Golden Boy* (1939), Abe Polonsky's *Body and Soul* (1947), Martin Ritt's *The Great White Hope* (1971), and Martin Scorsese's *Raging Bull* (1980). The ethnicity is different in this case, as is the gender of the main character. Both of those qualities make this film speak to a diverse international audience. As those other films, however, we see the deprivations and tragedy in her family life; we see how she is an outsider in the conventional track to success, the educational setting; and we see how her anger at her life circumstances fuels the aggression so useful to all these characters in the ring. But it is the ethnicity and the gender of the main character that speak loudly to a world where ethnic difference is embraced proportionately to the level to remind us— we live in one world.

Turning to another recent, independently produced melodrama, we note another feature of internationalization—the dominance of economics. Ben Younger's *Boiler Room* (2000) is about a young, ambitious man, Seth Davis, who is entrepreneurial. He runs a gambling casino in his house, and he makes money. But his father, a judge, doesn't want his son involved in illegal activities. So Seth trains to make millions as a stock trader. The company he works for is even more illegal than the gambling casino, but in a world where money talks, Seth wants a loud voice, and this is a way to get rich fast and impress his father. It doesn't quite happen that way, and Seth ruins himself and almost ruins his father. Echoing films such as *Wall Street* (1987) and its values ("Greed Is Good"), *Boiler Room* captures the amoral and immoral pursuit of riches by a young generation that sees wealth all around them. This is an international phenomenon for the twenty-something generation—a world of unprecedented wealth. The narrative poses the question of values and ethics in such a material world. Seth Davis wanted power, as the young often do; and as tends to happen in the melodrama, the effort has tragic consequences.

These last two films point out another phenomenon of the melodrama in international storytelling. Both main characters are young people trying to make their way in a world where adults have all the power. This tendency to focus on young main characters is the other quality dominant in current melodrama. This makes sense when we acknowledge that the market for film is dominated by an audience that is twenty-five and under. No recent melodrama focuses on this age phenomenon more effectively than Gus Van Sant's *Good Will Hunting* (1997). Here the main character, Will Hunting played by Matt Damon (who with Ben Affleck cowrote the screenplay), is a kid from the other side of the tracks. The place is Boston, a city dominated by more universities than any other city. One might call higher education the company town motto. Will is a mathematical genius who isn't formally trained. Working on the janitorial staff at M.I.T., he spends his working hours sweeping up and correcting or completing mathematical problems on classroom blackboards. Quickly, Gerald Lambeau, a math professor is on to him and works hard to psychologically and educationally bring this outsider into the power structure. In the end, Will Hunting does follow his own dream, in this case, Skylar, a privileged young woman, rather than his professor's dream. The melodrama succeeds with audiences because the main character and the audience share age and aspiration. They want power but on their own terms.

Less conventional melodrama has also been appealing to the same young international audience. The use of multiple main characters and a more open-ended conclusion mark Paul Thomas Anderson's *Magnolia* (1999) and Atom Egoyan's *The Sweet Hereafter* (1997). A shift in tone from realism to a heightened realism makes Pedro Almodóvar echo the stylized realism of the Douglas Sirk melodramas of the 1950s. And the mixing of melodrama with satire, a most unlikely pairing, makes the character layer of Mendes' *American Beauty* a narrative and emotional surprise.

I suggest that its narrative nature, as well as its tremendous malleability as a story form, has made melodrama particularly attractive today. Its dominance in certain national cinemas, such as Iran and Denmark, highlight the universality of melodrama and imply the reason for its resurgence in this era of international storytelling.

DOCUDRAMA

No cluster of films has used the characteristics of the docudrama—with its aura of actuality, its emphasis on style, and its relationship with the broadcast documentary—to greater effect than the Dogma 95 films from Denmark. *The Celebration* (1998), *Mifune* (1999), *The Idiots* (1998), each has the feel of the docudrama, but in fact they are not about actual people in real life events. The films are actually melodramas that present as docudramas. There is little doubt that these films are more sculpted, more performed, more directed than films such as Ken Loach's *My Name Is Joe* (1998). But these films that have adopted the style of docudrama have had a tremendous impact around the world. And they represent a new chapter in the story of the metagenre, docudrama: the expansion of its role beyond a political or social goal.

The power of television, particularly the style of the broadcast documentary, has broadened the experience of dramatized narrative to be experienced in as vital or immediate a manner as the traditional docudrama. The subject matter of the docudrama no longer needs to confine itself to biographies of significant international personalities—royalty or leaders in the political or economic realm. The characters of *The Celebration* are presented with a level of veracity and importance equivalent to the story of Princess Diana. Whether this is a democratization of narrative or a tribute to the power of a style, I leave to you to decide. What we do see is that the scope of narrative material addressed within the umbrella of docudrama has broadened considerably. And it is to this broadening that I now turn.

Mary Harron's *I Shot Andy Warhol* (1995) is a portrait of Valerie Solanas, the woman who shot Andy Warhol at the height of his fame. The shooting frames the narrative beginning and ending the film. In between we have a portrait of Valerie, as well as a portrait of the 1960s New York art and independent film scene surrounding Andy Warhol. Perhaps a half-dozen characters from Warhol's coterie, including Candy Darling, Paul Morrissey, and of course Warhol himself, are focused on in the narrative. What is critical about this narrative is that it presents a portrait of Solanas clearly establishing her marginal position in the circle around Warhol. It also portrays Valerie Solanas' growing paranoia as it leads up to her attempted murder of Warhol.

Solanas herself is portrayed as an intelligent, aggressive feminist whose sexuality (lesbian) and whose politics (anarchistic) found a ready outlet in the freewheeling, free-basing New York art scene of the 1960s. Valerie wrote a manifesto called *Scum*, an anti-male, anti-capitalist diatribe that she sold on the streets of New York. She also wrote a play, *Up Your Ass*, which she promoted for production through Warhol. Although the play was deposited with Warhol, it was dismissed by him and the copy was never returned. This act on his part, together with a publication contract signed with a slippery French New York-based publisher of alternative material, drove Valerie to the attempted murder. Whether this was a byproduct of her growing paranoia or her desperation for celebrity or both, the narrative depicts her instability and her asocial character as factors.

Harron gives us home movies, a direct performance of *Scum* (in black and white), as well as snippets from Solanas' life. Clearly a desperate person, Solanas is a street peddler, a panhandler, a vagrant, a prostitute, and a political activist. Harron takes no authorial position because she is trying to portray the 1960s art scene in New York as a haven in which all these qualities are valued, where eccentricity is a prerequisite to the creation of art, rather than a judgment on character. The result is a narrative that has all the features of docudrama: veracity, a feeling of being there, and the referent points of documentary—the on-air interview and the documentary home movie footage. And yet it is also a film that creates a sense of time and place where madness, such as the madness of a Valerie Solanas, is not seen as madness but rather eccentricity and art. Harron plays down her own voice in order to give voice to a sense of this era. The result is a portrait of Valerie Solanas, would-be killer and artist, and of Andy Warhol, pop artist and pop icon. Mary Harron's *I Shot Andy Warhol* is a docudrama that presents a portrait without judgment. By subsuming her voice, Harron presents a portrait as unsettling as the characters and period.

Frederick Fonteyne's *An Affair of Love* (1999), known as *A Pornographic Affair* in Europe, is a Belgian docudrama about an affair. A forty-something woman advertises in the newspaper. She is looking for a man who has certain qualities, described, with whom she can have casual sex. They meet in a restaurant. He is Spanish. And they proceed to a local hotel and have sex. She insists on no names, no history, no biography, just sex. Since the sex is good for both, they agree to meet again, and this becomes a regular event. The complication is that a man down the hall has a heart attack, and they take him to the hospital. They comfort his wife. The man dies. And unwittingly what each has resisted happens. They have humanized each other and they fall in love. Each is prepared to make a commitment to the other, but somehow in the conversation a defensiveness enters and they agree to part. This inability to commit, and the relationship as a whole, is then examined sometime later by a camera crew. Each is interviewed about the affair, about the other. This interview forms the leitmotif of the narrative, an investigation into love, as it were. But there are no answers here.

Fonteyne has created a very orthodox investigation into an accident—falling in love. It's as if the interviews will provide the answer: how to avoid the accident that has befallen these two people. What we learn is that the science, the sexual act of making love, has a chemical component, and that chemistry is inexplicable and unpredictable.

As in *I Shot Andy Warhol*, Fonteyne approaches his material without editorializing, and the result is structurally an investigation but experientially a mystery and a discovery. There is a dominant docudrama, almost talking-heads style. There are only four characters, but Fonteyne has used docudrama to give an air of authenticity to his investigation. Like *The Celebration*, the style lends gravitas to the script. The result feels important as docudrama does, but it has a less aggressive case structure that is central to the power of this metagenre.

Kore-eda Hirokazu's *Afterlife* (1998) is a docudrama about a way station between earth and heaven. When people die they go to the way station. While they are there they have to decide on a single memory that they will take with them to heaven. Hirokazu interviews many of the people at the way station, the old and the young. He also interviews the people who work at the way station. The structure of the film is as one expects—arrival, stay, departure—and each is treated in the manner one expects in the documentary, with a focus emphasizing a sense of actuality. Only the last part of the film, the recreation of the fantasy of a worker at the station, takes us out of the sense that the narrative we are experiencing is a docudrama. At this moment the fantastic tone takes over and the narrative becomes a memorial to first love as the memory the character will keep. This shift in tone is reminiscent of the shift of tone in Von Trier's *Breaking the Waves* (1996), from realism to the fantastic. But in the Von Trier film, there is more preparation for the narrative and tonal shift. Although there is humor and wry observation in the Hirokazu film, nothing has quite prepared us for the poignant leap into the fantastic. Hirokazu has used the docudrama to explore deep interior, metaphysical issues about life and death in *Afterlife*. This is a long way from the external, political, and passionate voice of Peter Watkins in *Culloden* (1964), the more typical terrain of the docudrama. Hirokazu, in *Afterlife*, has broadened the palate for docudrama, just as Fonteyne and Harron have. Each of these shifts has made docudrama more accessible, less predictable and more plausible to filmmakers searching for an international audience.

HYPERDRAMA

Hyperdrama is the genre of moral fables for adult audiences. As I mentioned earlier, in this shifting world rushing toward technological solutions to every human problem, there is an exponential number of issues suitable for treatment in hyperdrama. We've moved from a Frank Capra view of the world in *It's a Wonderful Life* (1946), where the issues of happiness, responsibility, and disappointment were at the heart of the narrative, to a meditation on the value of each human being no matter how gifted or limited, as in Robert Zemeckis' *Forrest Gump*. Hyperdrama can have a political moral to the tale, as in Schlondorff's *The Tin Drum* (1979), or it can have a spiritual moral, as in Phil Adlen Robinson's *Field of Dreams* (1989).

Contemporary hyperdrama, as with melodrama and docudrama, has broadened its palate to deal with issues resulting from globalization—the loss of individual identity, the challenge to national identity, the struggle for spiritual values in an increasingly materialist world. An atavistic hyperdrama that is reminiscent of Charlie Chaplin's work in *Modern Times* (1936) is Roberto Benigni's *Life Is Beautiful* (1998). The hyperdrama as we've known it in the past has not been forgotten. But first we turn to hyperdrama that is addressing globalization—Andy and Larry Wachowski's *The Matrix* (1999).

The Matrix, a plot-intensive narrative, focuses on a world where there are two powerful forces struggling with one another—the first force represents those in power. The characters who represent that force are technological, powerful, knowing, and controlling. The second force is presented as something of a rebellion, with an endangered but clever smaller group led by Morpheus (modeled after John the Baptist). He and his representative, Trinity, try to convince the main character, Thomas Anderson (computer name, Neo) that he is "the One"(modeled after Jesus Christ). As Morpheus explains, they are the humans and the other side in power is a by-product of human ingenuity, AI or Artificial Intelligence. Sixty years earlier (1999), AI took over their world. Now they use humans for energy or a power source. They have enslaved the human world and they use the Matrix, a neural-simulation computer-generated dream world, to keep humans under control. This matrix or illusion of computer-generated residual images of a world imprisons humans. And Morpheus views Neo as the One who will lead the humans back to freedom. To do so he has to defeat the Matrix and its AI representatives.

Whether this is a metaphor for computerization and its dangers, the plot, Neo's revolt against AI, is the narrative arc of *The Matrix*. In a series of ritualized fights Neo tries to conquer AI's "top man." When he succeeds, human values will be able to reemerge, and human beings will no longer be victimized by the computer and its technological outputs, AI.

At times a computer game, at other times science fiction, and at times a western, *The Matrix* uses all of the qualities of the hyperdrama—plot, lower involvement with the main character, and ritual—to convey a moral caution about our growing reliance and optimism about computers and their implications for a more positive future. By echoing the Christ parable of 2000 years ago in the present, the Wachowski brothers are making every effort to create a modern parable with equivalent implications. It is not surprising that as a result *The Matrix* had a far more powerful reception internationally than it might have had if it were simply a science fiction film. Its use of hyperdrama with its modern lesson broadened the accessibility of *The Matrix* for audiences.

David Cronenberg's *Existenz* (1998) takes the notion of a computer game and creates a whole world extended out from the game. Here the creator of the virtual reality game, Allegra Geller, is threatened by a "true believer," someone who objects to her power. The narrative opens at the introduction of the new game, and ends when the world has in essence turned into her game. So here the struggle is not so much control of the world, as it was in *The Matrix*, but rather control over what is real. If the higher reality is the virtual reality game as opposed to "reality," the world is ordered by a new reality. Cronenberg's narrative is a caution about the power of games. It's as if he is saying that bad things happen when video games take over your life. Is this an indirect plea for a return to literature as in *Fahrenheit 451*? Whether or not it is, Cronenberg is clearly presenting a dire, dangerous image of a world dominated by illusion.

The narrative has Allegra and her assistant entering Existenz. There they encounter helpers who become harmers and harmers who are helpers. It's a world where you can't trust what people first say or do. Everyone is misleading. Indeed, the assistant whom Allegra inducted to help her ends up being one of those threatened by Allegra. She ends up having to kill him—after many allusions to their being a good, appealing match. *Existenz*, as we might surmise, freely mixes reality and fantasy. It's as if Cronenberg wants us to end at the point where we accept paranoia as a realistic response to the situation in his narrative. Plot and character keep us at arm's length. Irony is a presence, and in the end we are left with Cronenberg's chilly message about the consequences of taking video games too seriously. If you do, you lose touch with reality. This is the caution in Cronenberg's hyperdrama.

Neil Jordan's *The End of the Affair* (1999) is a far more hopeful melodrama, but it evolves half-way through into a hyperdrama. Jordan has flirted with this shift in *The Miracle* (1991), but there he stays with the melodrama. He also flirts with this shift in *The Butcher Boy* (1997), but again stays with the melodrama with an exceedingly unusual tone. In *The End of the Affair*, however, Jordan lets go and makes the change in story form.

The narrative is simple: during World War II a writer, Maurice Bendrix, has an affair with the wife of a friend, Henry Miles, a man in government service. Maurice is totally obsessed with Sarah Miles. He becomes jealous, and destructively so. They part because of a particular incident. One afternoon when they are finished making love, there is a bomb alert. Rather than go to the basement for shelter they dawdle in bed. The bombs come closer. He goes out into the hall to check on the passage down the stair to the basement. At that very instant a bomb blast shatters the window behind him and Maurice is thrust into the stairwell. He falls. The blast appears to be severe enough to kill him. At the bottom of the stairs he awakens, returns battered to the bedroom where he finds Sarah praying. She ministers to his wounds, dresses, and leaves him. The affair is over.

Two years later Maurice sees Henry who invites him home for a drink. Henry expresses concern about Sarah, her distraction. Maurice recommends a detective. Sarah returns, and for the first time in two years they see one another. Maurice is brusque, hurt, and leaves. On his own Maurice hires a detective to follow Sarah and discover if she has a lover. When Sarah calls him a few days later they meet, and they are observed by the detective, Mr. Parkis, and his son, Lance (a young apprentice). The meeting is brought to a close abruptly. Sarah says with regret that it is over. She leaves, upset. Proof of an affair is provided to Maurice. He himself is part of the proof. Maurice challenges the other piece of proof—a man. When he uses Lance as part of a ruse to confront the man, we discover that this supposed other man is a Catholic priest. He knows who Maurice is. The ruse has not worked. We notice, not for the first time, that Lance has a very large birthmark on the left side of his face.

We then shift to Sarah's version of the end of the affair. That day of lovemaking and bombing is repeated, but this time from her point of view. And this time Maurice dies from his wounds. This is certain because Sarah tries to resuscitate him but cannot. She then prays in the bedroom, saying if God will let him live, she will give up the affair forever. Now we understand why Sarah is so short with Maurice and her renouncement of the affair takes on a new meaning. It is about faith. The narrative continues from Sarah's perspective. This time we see her encounter with Lance, outside the priest's home. She is kind to the boy. She takes him to the train station and there she kisses his face. She kisses him on his birthmark (this will be significant in the conclusion of the story). Later Sarah takes up again with Maurice. She cannot keep her vow. We now learn she had a Jewish father and a Catholic mother. She leaves Henry and goes off with Maurice to Brighton. There they are observed by Mr. Parkis. Now Sarah is an adulteress.

But there is a complication. Now she is ill. Henry finds them in Brighton to tell her the news of her illness. Sarah will die. Henry proposes Maurice move into their home to care for and be with her. He does, and Sarah dies. The priest tries to see her, but Maurice angrily rejects him and God. Maurice no longer believes in anything but his anger. At the funeral he sees Mr. Parkis, who has very kind words about Sarah. He tells Maurice that she kissed Lance, and his ugly birthmark has disappeared. We see Lance, whole, unblemished, happy. Maurice is left with a second expression of her love—the cured blemish and his life reclaimed from death. The film ends with Maurice struggling with his beliefs.

Jordan has used the melodrama form to use the affair as an exploration of faith. In her world faith, belief had restorative powers. This isn't the rational world of the writer, a world where love meant jealousy. Jordan has posed a deeply religious question: What do we believe in?—in this narrative. *The End of the Affair* could also be called the beginning of belief. Graham Greene, the writer of the novel on which the novel is based, so often struggled with this issue of belief and its importance in his work. Here, Neil Jordan, using the hyperdrama, has posed an answer to Greene's questioning.

Finally, we turn to the example of Benigni's *Life Is Beautiful* (1998). This story is a love story about a man in love with life. Guido finds its expression in Dora. They marry. They are happy. And then World War II occurs. They are Jews, and with their young son they are transported to a concentration camp. There the boy is with Guido, who wants to withhold this ugly side of life from his son. He does so by creating another world, a fantasy world where there is laughter and joy. In order to sustain his son's life, Guido sacrifices his own. When Italy is liberated and mother and son are reunited, the boy holds on to the memory of happiness created by his father. He and his mother go forward positively with the life view created by Guido.

Benigni is using the Holocaust to say terrible things happen in the world, but what is critical is that life be viewed in as positive a way as possible. Benigni feels this is critical, especially for children. This is the world of *Life Is Beautiful*. Although controversial in its use of the Holocaust as a metaphor, Benigni is trying to powerfully create a world view that will help prevent future human catastrophes. Hyperdrama is the form that he finds most appropriate for his fable.

EXPERIMENTAL NARRATIVE

The experimental narrative is more about its style than about content. It tends to rely not so much on character and plot but rather on what the writer-director is trying to say. Its nonverbal quality makes it ideal for crossing national boundaries more easily than dialogue-intensive narratives. What must also be said is that experimental narrative, because it presents more as a puzzle than an assertively charming character or plot narrative, is a much more difficult form for audiences. Consequently it is a metagenre that has a limited audience. All the more surprising, then, that this form has had an appeal in international storytelling.

Perhaps the most successful example of this genre is Tom Tykwer's *Run Lola Run* (1998). The narrative is simple. A man calls his girlfriend. He has a problem. He collected a large amount of money for his employers; they are the mob. He lost the money on the subway. Could she get the money from her father the banker and rescue him? He's in a phone booth. He needs the money in twenty minutes. If he doesn't have it he will be killed. What follows is her run to rescue him. The story is repeated three times. The first sets a time frame. The second version is two seconds earlier; the third is seconds later. The time shifts alter the outcome.

Essentially we have a problem followed by a chase. Tykwer uses references to cartoons and video games and exercises a sense of irony in the last episode. Consequently the tone varies from episode to episode, as well as produces different outcomes. The result is a nonlinear meditation on the influence of time. We don't get to know the characters beyond a flat stereotypical view, and so we are fascinated by Lola's run, its urgency, but not about the person for whom she is running. Empathy doesn't enter. And after the first version of the story, we are more engaged by the tonal element than the outcome. What I'm suggesting is that neither the plot nor the character engages us, but voice and structure do. And so we're left with a meditation on time in *Run Lola Run*.

Mike Figgis has made two experimental narratives, *The Loss of Sexual Innocence* (1999) and *Timecode* (2000). The first, *The Loss of Sexual Innocence*, is about a feeling, desire, that transcends race and nationality. It's also about the fine line between white European first world people and dark-skinned African third world people. In one story, a kind of creation myth, the two characters, Adam and Eve, are young and desire dominates. In the second story with different characters, there is a dependence of first world people on the third world, with the implication of class and exploitation being at the root of the relationship. This relationship inevitably ends in violence, the opposite of the first narrative. The two stories are interwoven, each unfolding with its own arc and inevitability. Perhaps Figgis is trying to say that these two worlds cannot coexist. Or perhaps he is trying to illustrate what one world loses when it is out of touch with the senses and the sensual world. Whatever Figgis' goal, there is a powerful sense that growing up, as a person or as a culture, implies a loss of innocence. He is also implying the Rousseau-like notion of the nobility of the primitive and the opposite about barbarity of the "civilized." In *The Loss of Sexual Innocence* we can see how broadly the experimental narrative lends itself to interpretation. The nonverbal dominates the form, leaving considerable space for interpretation.

Figgis' *Timecode* is consciously nonlinear. Four stories proceed simultaneously and are merged in a large single image. We see all four stories unfold, and we can choose which story to follow. There are also relationships between the stories. The actress in one story is the mistress of a producer in another story. The mistress' lover will kill the producer at the end of the narrative. Another narrative is about the producer's wife. So the characters will enter each other's stories. Set in Hollywood, each is the story of career and love. No character can have both—this is the throughline of the collective narrative. Each has to choose, or a choice will be made for him or her. As in *The Loss of Sexual Innocence*, the characters are shallow and caught up in a simple arc. Each story adopts a real time frame, so we are watching ninety minutes in the life of four characters. The events themselves are everyday events (except for the shooting). The style implies the linkages between these characters, and the common themes of love and work and the notion that you can't have both links the stories to one another. The style is the novelty of *Timecode*, and the style rather than the characters keep us engaged with the simple narrative.

Again, the strengths of experimental narrative is its nonverbal quality, and when it is effective, we are very attuned to the voice of the writer-director.

Whether it's the use of experimental narrative or hyperdrama or docudrama or melodrama, the use of these metagenres is a critical factor in the effective outreach for an international audience.

16

BIG ISSUES PLUS
NATIONAL STEREOTYPES

There are global issues that increasingly are attracting writers and directors from various parts of the world. Feminism infuses the British film *Elizabeth* (1998), the Canadian-Indian film *Fire* (1997), and the Dutch film *Antonia's Line* (1995). Each treats the national stereotypes about men and women through a feminist filter.

The challenge to the dominance of the male is the focus in the British *The Full Monty* (1996), the Japanese *Shall We Dance* (1996), and the French *French Twist* (1996). Each screen story plays with the national stereotype and bends it. In this chapter we will look at these films and others to test a premise about contemporary success in the international market. That premise is that you take big issues plus national stereotypes, explore them, expose them, and the result is international success.

The stereotypes we will look at in this chapter are ideas about the roles of men and women in specific cultures. We are not looking to ridicule those stereotypes but rather to examine how filmmakers who use and challenge those powerful stereotypes have in turn created powerful and accessible narratives for an international audience.

What is important to say about this phenomenon is that the filmmakers in every case have chosen realistic genres for their narratives: the melodrama and the situation comedy or a mixture of both. To choose this narrative route, the writers and directors are looking to make their films accessible to the largest possible audience, for these are the two most popular genres, the genres that understandably dominate television. Both genres are dominated by their character layer, although they can have a plot as well. And both genres have characters who are believable, for they echo recognizable people in human proportions as well as recognizable situations. As we look at each of these films, then, we will examine how the filmmaker humanizes or makes accessible the character, and then look at the dramatic arc and how it bends national stereotypes.

THE CASE OF *ELIZABETH*

Shekhar Kapur's *Elizabeth* (1997) is the story of Elizabeth I, whose fifty-year reign as Queen of England was a golden age. But the film focuses on the period prior to her becoming queen, and on those early years when her crown was anything but secure. The plot layer of the film follows this arc. At the outset she may be killed by her sister Queen Mary who is Catholic. If she ascends the throne, the monarchy will shift to Protestant control, and so those who oppose her within her court and outside Spain and France are Catholic. The plot layer ends when the plotters are put down and she is secure on the throne.

It is the character layer of the narrative that pivots on the feminist issue and consequently resonates for an international audience. Elizabeth is a monarch and a woman. A monarch is a powerful figure, but a woman in a male-dominated society is powerless. And so we have the arc of the melodrama. A woman who is powerless because of her gender aspires to be the monarch, a powerful position. But the men, whether they be kings, dukes, noblemen, advisers, or lovers, all attempt to manipulate her because she is a woman. The issue for Elizabeth is that it is increasingly clear that you cannot be both a woman and a monarch, and that she must make a choice. If she chooses to be a woman she will be controlled by her lover or her advisors, who recommend a marriage with a prince of France (a Catholic). There is also no guarantee that this choice will secure her crown. The alternative, the choice that Elizabeth finally makes, is to set aside the lover and her traditional advisors. She sides with one advisor, Walsingham, against all others. But to be a monarch is to renounce her womanhood. As she puts it, "I will be married to England." Thus by choosing the monarchy she gives up her feminine side and becomes "The Virgin Queen." This choice marks the conclusion of the narrative.

England in the Renaissance was not simply a society that was male-dominated in its monarchy. Henry VIII, father of Elizabeth, had moved through numerous wives, beheading the out-of-favor in order to have a male heir. He dissolved the relationship with the Catholic Church and established the Church of England in order to secure a marriage that might enable him to sire a male. Such was the view of woman as potential monarch. Elizabeth's half-sister, Mary, was the first Queen of England, and Elizabeth was the second. This only happened because Henry's sole male heir died in adolescence. I mention all this to contextualize the narrative of *Elizabeth*. But the history only provides a picture of what Elizabeth faces as she ascended to the throne. The story of Elizabeth has been the subject of numerous narratives. Bette Davis alone played Elizabeth at least twice. She is a character in a dozen films, and each takes a reading on her character and on her relationships that is different. But no reading has been as specifically feminist as the Kapur film.

Granted, the writer, Michael Hirst, wanted to make the story modern; granted, the activity around the Royals today; and granted, the Protestant-Catholic rift is as powerful as it was and lives on in Northern Ireland. But the most critical element is the feminist frame of his narrative. In North America the sexual revolution brought forward a litany of stresses and strains between men and women. The adjustment is not so much power sharing, as it is a constant tug of war for economic, social, and political equality. In Europe, issues of equity, first addressed in Eastern Europe, are a powerful force that is growing. And in Asia, the sleeping tigress is beginning to stir. This feminist nerve is in the public consciousness, and so the Hirst-Kapur reading in *Elizabeth* is a modern reading of a Renaissance story. That reading makes this story available and meaningful to today's international audience.

THE CASE OF *FIRE*

Deepa Mehta's *Fire* (1996) is set in modern Delhi, in an educated middle-class family. There are two main characters, both women. The film opens with Sita, the younger of the two women, marrying into the family. The second, Raga, has been married for some time to the older brother. They live together with the son's mother and a servant in an apartment over a prosperous food and video business.

Both women have a problem with their husbands. Sita's problem is that her husband didn't really want to marry her. He did so under pressure from his older brother. Since the older brother was not going to have children, the future of the family depended upon the younger brother. In fact, the younger brother has a mistress whom he loves but who didn't want to marry. He maintains the mistress even after the marriage. His devotion to her becomes more intense in proportion to his resentment toward his young wife. Sita is baffled and hurt.

The problem for the older woman is even more complex. Her husband follows a guru who requires support, money, and a belief that abstinence from sex will purify the person. There will be no children in this marriage because there is no means.

In Act I, then, we have the portrait of two modern, attractive women trapped in the institution of marriage in a society that is male-dominated in an exceedingly selfish fashion. These two men care for themselves and for the concept of family, but they are indifferent and even cruel to the women, their wives who must serve them.

Deepa Mehta's exploration of this contemporary dilemma for women takes a surprising turn at the end of Act I. Sita, instead of crying because she hates the marriage, cries because she loves Raga. She confesses her love. Act II then becomes an exploration for each woman of their relationship with one another versus the relationship each has with her husband. Act II ends with the choice. For Sita, the choice is clear, to leave her husband. She proposes to leave with Raga. For Raga the decision is more difficult. But in the end the two women meet at the appointed place to go off and begin a new life. Throughout Act III there is an air of violence in the anger of the two men and we anticipate tragedy. This is the reverberation of the freedom of action the men have exercised vis à vis their wives in the earlier portion of the narrative.

However we interpret this narrative—two women looking for passion in their lives; passion absent in each of their marriages; and passion only available within the narrow confines of the family unit—the story focuses on the powerless finding a solution that is available. Mehta creates great empathy for each woman by making the men unappealing in their selfishness and immaturity. Then she proposes the solution of lesbian love as a positive solution.

Understandably, Deepa Mehta has generated great controversy in India with this story. India is a deeply conservative, religious society. Elsewhere, however, in Europe and in North America, the narrative has struck a cord. What makes this film work so strongly is that it offers a modern solution to an old problem in a traditional society. Because of its modernity, it is a threatening and dangerous solution—it challenges tradition. It challenges the national stereotype of women, and it challenges the national stereotype of men. It argues for dropping the double standard. Why should only a man be allowed to follow his desire, any desire, inside and outside of marriage? And it accepts love, gender-blind love, as a basically good thing for the two people who were victims of marriage. This positive take on love regardless of gender, and the notion that they deserve love, is the radical idea that has helped *Fire* travel so well around the world.

THE CASE OF *ANTONIA'S LINE*

Marlene Gorris' *Antonia's Line* (1995) is even more assertively feminist in its position on the relationship between men and women. *Antonia's Line* is a lifecycle story of four generations of Dutch women. The line begins with Antonia's mother and stretches to her great-granddaughter Sarah.

The narrative begins on the day of Antonia's dying and will return at the end to her death, surrounded by the people she loves and who love her. In between, the story of the four generations is narrated by the great-granddaughter.

The chronicle begins when Antonia and her daughter return to her village for the funeral of her mother. The time is the end of World War II. Not to her surprise, Antonia finds her mother not quite dead, spewing venom about her dead abusive husband. This sets up an ongoing theme, that men are useful for procreation, but not good for much else. After her mother does die, Antonia decides to settle in the village. She has a number of friends, male and female, but for the most part she recognizes the anti-female behavior in most of the men of the town. There is one man, the farmer Bas, a widower with five sons, who offers to marry her. She tells him she doesn't need what he offers, but she invites him to lunch on the farm in return for practical help on her farm. These lunches form a leitmotif, a continuum through the balance of the narrative. They represent stability and a collective solidarity for the participants.

The story then proceeds along two arcs, the communal behavior of Antonia and her daughter toward the rejected, the limited, and the outcasts of the community. Indeed, they make these outcasts part of their family. Antonia punishes a boy who is cruel to a mentally retarded male worker. The man, Loony, joins her. Antonia's daughter Danielle rescues a retarded woman being raped by her brother. The woman, Dee Dee, joins the family, and in short order she and Loony marry and become a subset of Antonia's family. When Danielle announces that she wants to have a baby, her mother takes her to the city where they meet Lette, who is at a hostel. She volunteers her brother to service Danielle, and Danielle becomes pregnant. She gives birth to Therese. Eventually Lette will arrive, two children in tow, also joining the growing family. Eventually Theresa will give birth to

Sarah. At all times Antonia stands for female solidarity. She accepts Danielle's female lover. She accepts Therese's special gifts intellectually and her limitations as a mother emotionally. She is aggressive and menacing when the local bully rapes Therese. Antonia represents in every sense an idealization of female strength, independence, and nurturance.

The second narrative arc has to do with men. They are cruel, like Pitte, the bully who rapes his sister and later Therese. They are hypocritical and cruel toward women, as in the case of the town priest. Or they are passive and depressed, as in the case of Antonia's friend, Crooked Finger. But the portrait is not entirely grim. They are useful in having babies, as in the case of Lette's brother for Danielle and Simon for Therese. And they are useful as an occasional companion, as Bas is for Antonia. But the portrait of men here is definitely in the category of temporary usefulness.

By using a chronicle of women over four generations, and by presenting it from a position of choice, Marlene Gorris is making a powerful statement about the relations between men and women. These women are strong, not victimized by social position and family organization as in Deepa Mehta's *Fire*. Nor are they hampered by the politics of male-female relationships and the nonsharing of power between men and women in *Elizabeth*. The women in the Gorris film are the opposite of the weaker sex. As Antonia says late in the film, "Life wants to live." She sees women as the life force. This is not so much about which sex is smarter or better or more powerful. *Antonia's Line* is a portrait in which women choose to take power from the male power structure. There is no question that they succeed.

THE CASE OF *ALL ABOUT MY MOTHER*

Pedro Almodóvar's *All About My Mother* (1999) is a feminist narrative about family, about the roles of men and women, and about the question of gender identity and gender blurring. This story comes out of a culture with very powerful notions about masculinity. This is a country of demonstrable masculinity—bullfighting, heated and rivalrous notions about regionalism, and about hierarchy. But the hierarchy is always established in verifiable and conflictual terms. Testosterone rather than diplomacy is the national masculine stereotypical behavior in Spain. This is the context in which to consider the radical reordering of the importance of men and women in Almodóvar's story.

Since we discussed the narrative itself in Chapter 12, "The Search for New Forms," we can now turn to how Almodóvar plays with national stereotypes, as well as how this play transforms *All About My Mother* into a meditation on men and women and the recasting of their roles in a broader definition than the constraints of the national stereotypes allow. I suggest that it is this recasting that has transformed *All About My Mother* from a Spanish film into an international phenomenon.

Just as women proved to be best for other women in Gorris' *Antonia's Line*, the same is true in *All About My Mother*. Almodóvar has the main character, who has lost her son in a hit-and-run accident in Madrid, return home to Barcelona. There she searches for the boy's father, an actor, who has now become a transvestite—in effect a man with breasts. As her companion to live with, she chooses her close friend, an actor who has become a woman and therefore is now an actress. Thus we have two men who have been transformed into women. To flesh out the family, the main character essentially adopts a pregnant nun, a woman of privilege, whose conventional family has acted all too conventionally and rejected her. The blame is cast against the father (an untransformed man). He is ungenerous and aggressive. When the nun dies in childbirth, the main character and her companion (the man who became a woman) have a family again. It's as if the baby is a replacement for the son she so tragically lost.

In *All About My Mother*, the only good man is a man who has become a woman. Those men who remain men are not terribly useful to children or to the creation of a positive, emotionally nurturing family life. This is a long way from the national stereotype. Almodóvar is suggesting that transformation can only take place when the man is literally transformed into a woman. Almodóvar's position is not very far from Gorris' in *Antonia's Line*.

THE CASE OF *FRENCH TWIST*

Josiane Balasko's *French Twist* (1997) works with a particular dimension of the national stereotype, that Frenchmen are notorious lovers and serially unfaithful in their devotion to lovemaking. This aspect of the French male, when contextualized in marriage, means at the very least a mistress. But in the case of *French Twist* it means a husband out of control. He is consistently and unambiguously devoted to as many daily conquests as possible. In *French Twist*, he is married to a Spanish woman who is passionate and beautiful. In this situation comedy her nature is supposed to suggest to us that he is also somewhat foolish.

The main character in *French Twist* is the Spanish wife, Loli. She is not unhappy, but she is frustrated by the "busyness" of her husband. His excuse is business, but we know otherwise. He is devoted to validating his masculinity. The twist of the title is the arrival of a woman, Marijo, whose van breaks down in front of the house of the principals. Loli, being welcoming, invites Marijo in, and before too long the guest has made advances to Loli. Although Loli is heterosexual, she is flattered by the attention. She is certainly not getting attention from her husband. Before long attention has become affection, and affection turns to sex. The choice is now a male husband or a female lover, an inattentive partner or a partner overflowing with passion.

Once the husband learns that he is being thrown over for a lesbian, he is crazed. His masculinity has been insulted. First he tries to be indifferent to his competitor, and then he turns violent in his jealousy. To no avail. In the end, Loli does take the husband back, but not before he has been seriously humiliated and chastened. He must give up his wandering ways and be devoted to his wife. In the end the oversexed sex hound turns into an obedient puppy. This is the transformation for the French male in *French Twist*.

Balasko has attacked stereotypes about French men, Spanish women, and about lesbians. Her goal is to poke fun in order to lessen the hostility to same-gender love by illustrating how cross-gender love can be very demeaning to the woman involved. Since the position taken is framed in a situation comedy the situation is enabling for the character, and Balasko hopes it will be for her audience as well. Her work echoes earlier gender narratives such as Doris Dorrie's *Men* (1985) and Maggie Greenwald's *The Ballad of Little Jo* (1992). All are narratives that try to promote tolerance toward gays and/or lesbians. Films such as Mike Nichols' *The Birdcage* (an American remake of Edouard Molinaro's *La Cage aux Folles* [1978]) set in Miami, attempts to do the same. But rather than simply dealing with the gender issue, the Balasko film uses powerful national stereotypes in order to heighten the power of the narrative.

THE CASE OF *SHALL WE DANCE*

Masayuki Suo's *Shall We Dance* (1996) is a situation comedy focusing on the behavior of Japanese men and women and upon the difficulty of showing affection or feeling toward one another in public. There are no samurai or aggressive business types here, just a repressed, hard-working Japanese man. This is a man who is responsible at home with his wife and daughter, and responsible as the head of the accounting department at the large company that employs him and holds his mortgage. His wife suggests to his daughter that he's depressed, but actually he's a man looking to break out.

One evening coming home from work via the subway, the train is stopped. Mr. Sugiyama looks up and he sees on the second floor a school of ballroom dance, at the window, Mai, a beautiful woman. He sees Mai again the next night. At home he reads about dance, but he hides the book from his daughter. The next time he gets off the train; he is not confident or expressive, but he commits to begin dancing lessons. Whether the subtext is to blossom or to pursue this dream woman-dance instructor, or both, is the balance of the story.

In fact, most of the characters, men and women, in *Shall We Dance* are stymied about their comfort with themselves. They're unhappy, and each turns to the dance floor to rise above their life problems. The main character's colleague from work dons a wig and becomes John Travolta on the dance floor. At work he is eccentric, unappealing to his colleagues, a sad balding man. Another man taking lessons is overweight and unappealing to women. A fourth is short and so on. The men presented here are not comfortable in their skins.

The women are no more expressive. An inappropriately expressive woman works four jobs in the daytime to make the money for lessons. Although she has a daughter, she's lonely. For her the dance is about being appealing rather than dour. Even Mai, the dream woman, the lithe instructor who becomes the love object for the main character, is depressed. A championship ballroom dancer at Blackpool, the international competition, she fell during the semifinals. She blamed her partner and returned to Japan depressed and no longer hopeful. For all these characters, the dance is more than a hobby. It's a way of transcending cultural or personal inhibitions and to experience joy, grace and a liveliness absent in their everyday lives.

The plot is simple. Mr. Sugiyama begins not to come home until late each Wednesday. He is taking dance lessons. His wife, Masako, thinks he is having an affair. She hires a private detective who begins to follow the main character and discovers he's taking dance lessons. The private detective evolves into a marriage counselor and a dance fan. He suggests to the wife he's not having an affair and maybe the dance lessons are a good outlet for a personal unhappiness. Mother and daughter as well as the detective and an associate attend a dance contest where the main character is competing. The detective by now is a real dance enthusiast. Masako, however, feels left out, even rather abandoned. Mr. Sugiyama, when he sees his wife and daughter, trips over his dance partner. He quits dance as a result, but the daughter plays peacemaker and asks that the parents dance together for her. The wife not only accepts his dancing, she encourages him to attend a going away party for the dance instructor. (She has recovered her will to dance after training the main character and seeing his joy and his entering into a real, supportive partnership with his dance partner.) There he dances with Mai. Their grace and happiness conclude the narrative.

Shall We Dance is strongly character-driven. Just as the main character cannot be himself in regular life, so too the other characters. Only on the dance floor do they shed their cultural inhibitions and experience a wider band of feeling and joy. They overcome their sense of shame about expression. In a sense this triumph of feeling over reticence and restraint challenges the national stereotypes about the public behavior of men and women in Japanese society. This is Suo's goal in *Shall We Dance*. By making the challenge to national patterns of behavior his goal, Suo has moved the story from the nation-specific to the universal. Many cultures are conservative in their expectations of public behavior. *Shall We Dance* conveys the message, Lighten up—a message wrapped in the pleasure of dance. The message travels well across national boundaries.

THE CASE OF *THE FULL MONTY*

Peter Cattaneo's *The Full Monty* (1977) works with national stereotypes about men and women in contemporary British society. One of the points I'm trying to make in this chapter is that it isn't enough simply to refer to national stereotypes. Success lies in challenging, deflating, and reversing those stereotypes. But it does begin with putting those national stereotypes front and center in the narrative. The stereotypes being put up in *The Full Monty* are as follows: British men are the breadwinners in the family. British men are repressed, unexpressive, and most of the time, downright deceptive. Because of all these qualities, they are self-defeating, and certainly a disappointment when it comes to being fathers or husbands. As for British women, they are more pragmatic—as mothers or breadwinners. They'll be strippers if they have to, to support their families, but if they are, it's a practical decision rather than an issue of desire. So British women are practical whereas the men are not. It's beginning to sound like the makings of a screw-ball comedy—which is precisely the basis for the narrative of *The Full Monty*.

The setting is Sheffield in the industrial north of England. Unemployment is high. The problem for Gaz, the main character, is that his ex-wife wants to diminish his access to his son. Gaz is a bad influence. And since he is so behind in his child support, he is clearly an irresponsible father. His wife sues for sole support. The pressure then on Gaz is not only financial, it's also about his sense of self as a father.

Before I go into the plot, what's important to reiterate is that the critical moment suggests that men are no longer the breadwinners, the women are. The catalytic event is the observation that women in the town pay to see men strip (the implication is that in past times when men worked, men paid to see women strip). The notion of Gaz's friend is, why don't we do the same? The economic situation is dire, and so the enabling plot for a main character whose goal is to be a father to his son and therefore a man, is to form a group of male strippers. If Gaz can organize such a local group, he and his colleagues will be fathers, husbands, and earners, men who have recovered their dignity as men because they are making money. The irony here, and the source of the humor, is that they have to do what women have always had to do when faced with economic hardship—view their bodies as a commodity and sell it. For Gaz, if he and his colleagues can succeed by emulating women, he will be able to remain a father to his son, and he will be able to regain the dignity he has lost since Sheffield's steel industry went down the tubes.

The team that Gaz assembles is a cross-section of dispossessed men. They include labor and management, heterosexual and gay, white and black, lean and stout. This is a truly representative cross-section. Cattaneo and writer Simon Beaufoy make sure that we have a background story for each of these characters so that they are not simply stereotypes. It should be said, however, that since the narrative is plot-driven, the characterizations hover closer to stereotypes than is typical in British films. The diversity of the men and their focus on a shared goal, however, make the impact of the story far more about men in general than it would have been experienced if the focus had remained on the main character. Because it is a diverse group of six men, *The Full Monty* becomes far more about challenging to the stereotypes about men and women. As in the case of *Shall We Dance* and *French Twist*, the situation comedy story form provides not only a positive outcome, but the more overt position that challenging national stereotypes about men and women is the core purpose of the narrative. And as in those other films, *The Full Monty* wants to change those stereotypes about men and women.

The idea of this chapter has been to look at recent films that have challenged national stereotypes about men and women and how that idea has led to narratives that not only travel well across national borders but, because of the centrality of the relations between men and women in modern life, have also achieved international success. In essence, each of these films reminds us of the kinds of stories that speak to audiences around the world. In the next chapter, we elaborate on the issue of searching for subject matter that is global.

17

THE SEARCH FOR THE
GLOBAL TALE

In Part III of this book I have been exploring those elements of storytelling that together suggest how the internationalization of story has proceeded, particularly in the last decade. Clearly every filmmaker wants to see his or her story succeed with audiences all over the world. Now there is a pattern emerging that suggests there is a kind of story that does succeed with audiences all over the world. One component of this pattern is the cultural diversity of writers and directors who are making films in cultures other than their native culture. Ang Lee, Agnieska Holland, Michael Radford, and Shekhar Kapur have joined Bruce Beresford, Peter Weir, and Phil Noyce from Australia, Roland Emmerich and Wolfgang Peterson from Germany, Paul Verhoeven from the Netherlands, Roman Polanski from Poland, and many others making films in another culture. So often these storytellers using their own voice alter the balance of plot and character, and although their films are set in a particular culture other than their own, the new perspective—their voice—transforms the story from a regional film to a universal story.

The other component of this search for the global tale is revealed when we look at the kind of story these filmmakers are telling. They have to choose a large theme as their subject matter—the fate of the family, for example—and we will look at how these filmmakers have treated material that will travel globally. There are basic universal elements that transcend national boundaries: relationships, the individual in society, the influence of politics on the individual, and the family. To create a coherent examination of how international storytelling has proceeded, a focus on one issue will help, and for that one issue I will look at how family has been represented.

The context for this chapter is how the family has been represented in the past. The melodrama has always been the basic story form for family stories. However, when the writer and director wanted to make a larger statement about society, for example, they resorted to another genre; but this too has everything to do with the prevailing values of the day, of the culture, and, of course, what the writer and director want to say. We begin with the 1940s.

The value of the family unit and the dissolution of the family unit due to economic change is at the core of John Ford's *How Green Was My Valley* (1942). Set in

Wales, Ford's family is an ideal. Respect, affection, and identity all accrue from this family. So too the family in William Wyler's *The Best Years of Our Lives* (1946). Set in postwar middle America, the Stephenson family, represented by Fredric March and Myrna Loy, is an ideal of a different kind. The parents love each other expressively, and they are not so much idealized authority figures as in the Ford film; they are flesh and blood. They are decent, thoughtful, and fair-minded. As a loan officer at a bank, Al Stephenson gives a loan to an ex-soldier who is a farmer because he's fought with men like him, rather than refuse him because he has no collateral. The Stephensons have decency and fairness in their blood and in their personal conduct, inside the family and beyond the family. These are solid, feeling, and generous individuals, and this is the image of family that they project. In Europe, destabilized by six years of war, the family also remains the core of decency and feeling. In Vittorio de Sica's *The Bicycle Thief* (1948), Antonio, a father, jobless because of the theft of his bicycle, steals another bicycle not out of outrage but out of economic necessity to support his family. He is caught, and observed being caught by his son, Bruno. Although it is Antonio who is humiliated publicly and embarrassed because of Bruno's knowledge, it is Bruno who accepts the father. The tolerance and the dignity between them is painful, but it projects the same image of family as we see in the Wyler film.

The preservation of family changes somewhat in the 1950s. In George Stevens' *Giant* (1956), a sense of dynasty and acquisitiveness is not enough to fracture the Benedict family. Leslie, the mother has to protect the kids, Luz and Jordan, from Jordan, the father, in order that they can live their lives rather than their live father's version of their lives. This disillusionment with father only gets worse in Nicholas Ray's *Rebel Without a Cause* (1956). Adolescents blame their parents for being conformist, and they turn their backs on the parents and look to the peer group for identity and individuation. This is not the portrait of family projected in Sajayit Ray's *Pather Panchali* (1952). Here, economic hardship challenges the integrity of the Ray family, but the unit is fundamental and powerful, even though it is under attack and eventually eroded. Ray's portrait, however, echoes the old-fashioned family idealized in Ford's *How Green Was My Valley*. The family remains the ideal, the safe haven from the dangers and threats of the real world.

If the children were having the identity crisis in the family films of the 1950s, it's the adults who are having the identity crisis of the 1960s. In the 1960s families were not only not supportive havens, they had become the enemy. A kind of paranoia had set in. In John Cassavetes' *Faces* (1968), a longstanding marriage collapses, and the film chronicles how Richard and Maria Forst seek solace from inappropriate outsiders. It gets even worse in Roman Polanski's *Rosemary's Baby* (1968). Here the husband, Guy Woodhoouse, makes a pact with the Devil. In return for help in furthering his career as an actor, he facilitates his wife, Rosemary—without her knowledge—being host for the Devil's baby. This horror film implies that the Ford family is dead and that a wife is a material means to self-promotion. The me-generation had arrived. It gets no better in Italy, where Michelangelo Antonioni's *Red Desert* illustrates marital ennui and wanderlust that doesn't promote a sense of well-being but seems to fracture the identity of the main character, the woman in the marriage, even more.

The 1970s revisits family as an ideal and a haven. In Francis Ford Coppola's *The Godfather* (1972), the family is the reason Don Corleone takes up the family business, criminal acquisition of material goods and power. The family is quite central to the rationale for the behavior of the Don, and throughout the narrative he tries to inculcate family values among his children (with mixed success). Because *The Godfather* is essentially an immigrant-makes-good story in a gangster film form, family is contextualized as an immigrant and pre-World War I phenomenon. As we see in *Godfather II*, which focuses on Michael Corleone, the film opens with brother Fredo aiding assassins to attempt to kill Michael, and it ends with Michael having Fredo killed for doing so. The view of the family as ideal does depreciate with the future generation.

Paul Mazursky continually examined the modern family in this period. Could the family manage the pressure of an open marriage is the subject of his *Bob and Ted and Carol and Alice* (1970). Could the family handle the pressure of infidelity is the subject of *Blume in Love* (1973). Not well, but still hanging in was the answer. But not for long. By the time he made *An Unmarried Woman* (1976), the family-unit was broken and he was advising, fend for yourself. The cause in each case is the same: a self-obsessed character, particularly a husband, who needs to be unfaithful. These selfish characters were a negative for the concept for the family. But they did fit right in on the continuum of the me-generation that flourished in the 1960s.

Power is at the core of Luchino Visconti's Aschenbach family in *The Damned* (1969). The fusion of Nazi power and the political and financial rivalries and ambitions in this powerful family is the drawing force of the narrative. The consequence is to break down every taboo within the family: a mother sleeps with her son; brother kills brother; and brother-in-law kills them all. Visconti's portrait of family is as a cancer that destroys. Not a very appealing presentation of family!

The 1980s opens with Robert Redford's *Ordinary People* (1980), which portrays the Jarrett family not as ideal but as all too human. Here families are made up of individuals, and individuals don't always pull together. The consequence is a vulnerable group of family members who can help or harm each other.

Family becomes far more vulnerable in Bob Rafelson's *The Postman Always Rings Twice* (1981). Here a husband, Nick Papadakis, is a barrier to the desire of his wife, Cora. A younger stranger, Frank Chambers, will provide Cora with the means to get rid of the barrier so she can have Nick's finances and the younger Frank as well. Here the selfishness of the Mazursky films' characters and the Polanski film's husband echo through, but this time the woman is the frustrated catalyst for the destruction of the family, in line with film noir expectations. We see this impulse come up again in in Polanski's *Chinatown* (1973) and Kasdan's *Body Heat* (1981), both film noir.

The same corrosive selfishness and destructiveness permeates the southern Provence family in Claude Berri's *Jean de Florette* (1986). It also destroys the family in Bille August's biography of the parents of Ingmar Bergman in *The Best Intentions* (1992).

Although we will focus on a number of films made in the last decade, there are other benchmark films of the 1990s that should be mentioned. Joel and Ethan

Coen brothers are obsessed with family values in their mixed-genre films *Raising Arizona* (1987) and *Fargo* (1996). In *Raising Arizona*, Hi and Edwina McDonnough, want-to-be parents, kidnap a baby from Nathan Arizona, a rich businessman who has quintuplets. In *Fargo*, Jerry Lundegaard has his wife, Jean kidnapped to extort money from his father-in-law. In *Fargo*, a trail of death is the upshot. Neither film portrays family as solid, but rather as a social structure for the sake of appearances. Beneath the surface, venality, selfishness, and cruelty abound. The Coen brothers make family and family values a primary target for examination. They want us to get past the surface social rhetoric. They want us to see the pathology.

The family doesn't get much better in Michael Mann's *Heat* (1995). Husbands and wives have problems, and the kids pay a high price (a suicide attempt). In this gangster film, the family is a collective of individuals. Families break down and reconstitute, but not very securely. The family here is a loose federation of individuals, and not a very effective federation. All the individuals suffer as a result.

It doesn't get much better in James Gray's *Little Odessa* (1994). In this gangster film Joshua Shapira reenters his family's life and neighborhood, the Russian area of Brooklyn (he's on assignment for the Mob). But he can't prevent the destruction that is inevitably the upshot of family tensions in the gangster film. His younger brother, Reuben, dies. A similar fate is in store for Danny, the younger brother in Tony Kay's *American History X* (1998). As hate has played a role in the identity of Derek, the eldest son of a family, a younger brother emulates his idol. The single mother is incapable of managing herself, let alone her children. No matter how hard this family tries to be a unit, it is always invaded by outside influences, and destruction is the upshot in this melodrama. In both of these films there is a nostalgia for family, but what stands out most is how the family cannot protect its most vulnerable members from harm. The family is a sociological phenomenon, but it's not an effective, stable influence in the lives of its members.

A question lingers. Is there any place in the world where the family is portrayed as a more positive or strengthening influence? In Clara Law's *Floating Life* (1997) the family is a source of strength, but the majority of the narrative focuses on the diaspora, the leave-taking of a single family from Hong Kong to Australia and Germany and its consequences. Those consequences are considerable. Zoncka's *Dreamlife of Angels* focuses on a temporary, reconstituted single family of two young women. But it is a temporary stopgap. The family in Thomas Vinterberg's *The Celebration* is the cause of the death of one child (a victim of incest) and the neurotic behavior of all the other children of the father whose sixtieth birthday is the plot of *The Celebration*. Families are not doing very well in the 1990s. This is the impression given by so many of the film stories of the period. To get more specific, we now turn to a number of these films.

THE CASE OF AGNIESKA HOLLAND'S *OLIVIER OLIVIER*

Although Agnieska Holland has dealt with family often in her work, nothing in her work quite prepares us for *Olivier Olivier* (1992). Her film *The Secret Garden*

(1993) dealt with loss and the effort to restore family in order to contain being overwhelmed by that loss. Whether children or adults fare better faced with loss is a legitimate question in that narrative. Holland's *Washington Square* (1997) based on the Henry James novel, is less fair-minded. The blame for the insecurity and poor judgment in Catherine Sloper, a young woman of means, is laid squarely at the feet of her father, Dr. Austin Sloper. His blame of the daughter for the death of his beloved wife has poisoned his relationship with Catherine and given her an unquenchable thirst for his approval and the affection of Morris Townsend, a would-be suitor. In both of these stories, psychopathology runs rampant in "parental" behavior with devastating consequences for children.

Olivier Olivier (1992) tells a very particular story about the relations between children and parents. The narrative hinges on the disappearance of the beloved younger child Olivier when he rides his bicycle to his grandmother's to deliver lunch to her. He never returns. His older sister, Nadine, jealous of the attention Olivier gets (and she doesn't) is self-punitive. The mother, Elisabeth, who was high-strung in any case, is inconsolable. The father, Serge, is angry and looking for someone to blame. An investigation follows with no result. The family falls apart. The father leaves to work in Africa.

Seven years later a boy is found in Paris by the police. He claims to be Olivier. He has a similar scar from a childhood operation. He returns and the family heals. Only Nadine knows this is not Olivier. Serge returns. Elisabeth is almost happy. And then a body is found. The new Olivier admits he is not the real Olivier. A neighbor is accused of killing the real Olivier, and he confesses. The mystery is over, and now the question is whether the family will fall apart again.

Olivier Olivier is a rather toxic view of family. The individuals are high-strung and not together. They argue and fight for attention, and the mother is a millimeter from collapse. This is not an appealing portrait of family. Indeed, Holland implies a porous view of family, where strength ebbs under any pressure. There is no leadership only will in this family. It's as if the tragedy victimized a family that was already a group of victims. Each individual was suffering prior to the disappearance of Olivier. The disappearance merely gave them a focal point for their anguish.

THE CASE OF MIKE RADFORD'S *IL POSTINO*

In the case of Mike Radford's *Il Postino* (1994) the family again becomes an ideal, a source of strength for the main character. But in this narrative the problem is that the main character is too shy to make the first step in family life: to attain a wife.

The main character, Mario, is not only shy, he is lacking in confidence. His gentility could easily be mistaken for weakness, but it is not weakness. He is encouraged by his family, but the more important catalyst is delivering mail to the island's new inhabitant, Pablo Neruda. The postman has seen Beatrice, the woman of his dreams; she works in the town pub. For the postman she is an ideal—beautiful, sensual, and unattainable.

Neruda is expressive, self-assured, and sensual. He also welcomes the post-man and becomes his mentor. He will help the postman be expressive, and the vehicle will be as it has been for Neruda—poetry. Through the tutoring he receives, the postman takes the chance and the young woman is surprised by his approach. She agrees to see him. Coached in a poem by Neruda, the postman goes to the sea with the young woman and wins her with his words. This victory sets up the transformation of the postman from a shy individual to an active family man.

As Mario marries, has children, and has a family, his continued transformation under the tutelage of Neruda deepens. From being a poet he becomes a political activist. This clearly presents family as strengthening the individual member of the family. This extremely positive view of family harkens back not to the ideal-ized family of John Ford but rather the family as a stabilizing force as portrayed in De Sica's *The Bicycle Thief*. It is also the view of the family in Visconti's *Rocco and His Brothers* (1962), Paulo and Vittorio Taviani's *Good Morning Babylon* (1987), and the view of family in the recent Benigni film, *Life Is Beautiful*. Indeed this view of family as a stabilizing influence on its members is echoed in the films of tradition-rich cultures from India (*The Apu Trilogy* [1952, 1956, 1959]), Japan (*Tokyo Story* [1953]), and China (*To Live* [1994]).

This is a markedly different portrait of family from what we find in American films, where the picture has been far more malleable, ranging from the idealized view of family in John Ford and Frank Capra (*It's a Wonderful Life* [1946]), to the demonized view as represented in the work of the Coen brothers and Paul Schrader (*Affliction* [1997]). We turn now to current views of the American family.

THE CASE OF ANG LEE'S *THE ICE STORM*

We saw in Tod Solondz' *Happiness* a nonlinear treatment of contemporary subur-ban life. (See Chapter 11, "The Ascent of Voice.") Applying an MTV style, Solondz created a disturbing disconnect on American family dynamics. The same subject set in the 1970s rather than the 1990s is the basis for Ang Lee's film *The Ice Storm* (1998).

The Ice Storm takes place over a Thanksgiving week in 1973. It is set in New Ca-naan, Connecticut and focuses on two families, each having two near-adolescent or adolescent children. As a nonlinear story, however, the narrative focuses on the points of view within one of these two families, the Hoods: the parents, Ben and Elena, and the two teenagers, Paul and Wendy. The narrative unfolds through each of their points of view. The second family, the Carvers, is very im-portant because each of its members has a relationship with a member of the Hood family. Their lives are essentially sexual, and the implications of those rela-tionships bears on the view of family that Ang Lee and writer James Schamus want to articulate.

What must be said about the Hoods is that they are overtly successful, that their children seem more morally centered than the parents, and that the parents, Ben and Elena, are individually unsatisfied and as a couple are dysfunctional. She seems depressed, and he seems false and insincere. Verification of this view of the marriage is found in his unfaithfulness—he is having an affair with Mrs. Carver—and by her dalliance with a hippie priest.

In both cases sexual expressiveness has become the replacement for a reaching out and communicating with the other. These parents have a serious communication problem, and the example they set is not lost on Paul and Wendy. They too strive for sexual validation to be "with" their peers.

The Hoods, however, are the best communicators of the bunch. The Carvers are in breakdown. The wife is angry and disinterested in the family. She is a furious narcissist. The husband is unavailable. He's out to work in every sense. The younger son likes to blow up things and is sexually obsessed and intimidated. And the older son is simply out of it. He has a drugged sensibility about him. We know he is unpredictable, dangerous, and in danger. He is the one who dies the night of the ice storm. His death is an expression of all that is wrong in all these families.

Rather than being a stabilizing force, the view of the family in *The Ice Storm* is that of toxicity. The social organization of a family houses a group of individuals with their own needs and desires. Family gets in the way and more. It disables its members, and it destroys its weakest members.

Although *The Ice Storm* is set in the era of Watergate, it is also set in affluent America. Yet the affluence isn't enriching the spiritual lives of its members. Sex has replaced feeling. Wife swapping has replaced reading a book. These people are bored, self-absorbed, and miserable. They are in therapy, in self-help groups, and they read the wellness diets. And yet they continue to die spiritually. This portrait of the family is dark and disturbing. It's a long way from Frank Capra's family. It's no wonder that the Hood daughter is so contemptuous of the politics of the day. Her dissatisfaction and her involvement in the world beyond herself (the position her parents represent) is the only hint of optimism in *The Ice Storm*. For the rest, it's family life through the prism of a Love Canal.

THE CASE OF SAM MENDES' *AMERICAN BEAUTY*

Sam Mendes' *American Beauty* (1998) shares a philosophy about family with *The Ice Storm*. This time the story is from the point of view of one character, Lester Burnham. He narrates the story from the perspective of the last year of his life. He tells us at the outset that he will die, in effect, at the end of the story. The time is now, the place suburban Southern California.

Within his family Lester is viewed as the emasculated male. He has a job, but clearly it is his wife Caroline who is the breadwinner. He is without respect from his wife or his teenage daughter, Janie. He is cynical about all aspects of life, including work. It is clear that he doesn't care for his job, and that the job he has as a media writer in advertising is under threat. (He does lose his job before the midpoint of the narrative.)

The view of the woman, Carolyn Burnham, in the family is little better. She is materially successful but doesn't feel she is a success, and so is driven with all her energy to seek out "success." Her lack of feeling successful bleeds over into her feelings about her husband and her daughter. She denies herself a sexual life until she begins to have an affair with her successful rival in real estate. But even there she can only feel sexual because being with him means affiliating with a materially successful man.

The daughter Janie is very alienated from each parent. She seeks solace in self-assured friends, such as Angela, who will become the love object for her father (the catalytic event of the narrative) and her new eighteen-year-old neighbor Ricky, who becomes her own love interest.

As in *The Ice Storm* there is a second important family, the Fitz family, who move next door. The son, like Janie, is the product of an eccentric family, and he's come to an accommodation with his parents. He lies. He earns a living dealing drugs, yet in his manner of communication with Janie, he seems by far the best-adjusted character in the story. His parents, however, are quite another story.

Mrs. Fitz seems utterly absent, whether because she is constantly medicated or simply because she is a person who has escaped into herself in order to live with the reality of the family. Ricky at one point of the story advocates denial as a management strategy. Mrs. Fitz is the best example of this. She works so hard at denying that she's barely there.

As to Colonel Fitz, he introduces himself as a marine to two gay neighbors who arrive at his doorstep to welcome his family. His rudeness to them illustrates his homophobia. His paranoia is so great that he insists on drug-testing his son. He is also physically abusive, beating his son when he catches him videotaping his environment next door at night. Colonel Fitz is an angry bundle of contradictions. Together, the Fitz family is an even less attractive family than the Burnhams. In fact, the Fitz family represents the pathology of family and the Burnhams merely represent the dysfunction.

The plot of *American Beauty* follows Lester's efforts to secure his version of the American Dream—the American Beauty of the title, Angela Hayes. For Lester, Angela, who is youthful, blonde, and beautiful, represents the opposite of what his marriage has brought, material well-being and misery, resulting in Lester's cynicism. Angela represents hope, and once he fastens on to her as a goal, vitality reenters his life. He's pleased to lose his job. He begins to stand up to his wife (much to her chagrin). And when he overhears Angela talking about him sexually with Janie, he adopts a new goal. He exercises, running with his gay neighbors with the goal, "I want to look good naked." He is preparing to make a conquest. When he finally does get the opportunity to sleep with Angela, a moment of honest communication occurs. Angela confesses she is a virgin. Up to this point she has boasted loudly about her many conquests. And Lester becomes protective, fatherly, and age-appropriate with Angela. Rather then the self-absorbed dysfunctional male he has been, he becomes a real person with Angela. This two-way communication is healing for each of them, and in a sense it is one of the few moments of hope in the narrative. Shortly thereafter Lester is killed by

Colonel Fitz who, in a state of homophobia, has interpreted Lester's naked exercising in his garage as a come-on to him. The colonel reveals his own homosexuality and self-loathing. He shoots Lester. Having found almost a state of grace, Lester becomes a victim of another dysfunctional family—his neighbors the Fitzes.

In many ways *American Beauty* echoes the view of family proposed in *The Ice Storm* and in *Happiness*. There is simply too much self-absorption and not enough recognition of the other, whether it be wife, husband, or child, to help each other. The result is a focus on materialism as a replacement for affection and support, and on pathology, where the family is victimized by the lack of honesty, inability to communicate, and the inability to accept the self. Here the family creates victims. No longer is the family seen as a stabilizing force or an idealized focal point to project powerful and decent social values. The family in these films is a toxic zone. In order to understand this family pathology more precisely I turn to a film that focuses on the individual. When the cult of the individual becomes an obsession, strange things happen to families.

THE CASE OF MARY HARRON'S *AMERICAN PSYCHO*

Mary Harron's *American Psycho* (2000) is based on Brett Ellis' controversial novel of the same name. But Harron gives the story a particular reading that yields some insights into the dysfunctional characters of Ben Hood in *The Ice Storm* and Colonel Fitz in *American Beauty*. Both of these men are family men, but they are also self-absorbed men, over-concerned with how they are perceived by others, their peers particularly. Because they live too much in their heads and they are ruled by the conflict between desire and duty, they are confused, troubled men. This is the notion of character that Mary Harron works with in *American Psycho*. She simply takes the character to another level. The operation of this character, however, will yield insight into why so many of the recent portraits of the American family are so critical.

American Psycho focuses on a single character, Patrick Bateman, a young business executive who is successful, concerned with appearances, competitive, and acquisitive. Set in the 1980s, *American Psycho* also focuses on a character who feels empty inside, and lives too much in his head. And what Patrick imagines in his head is murder. If he could he would challenge convention and not simply best his rival at work, he'd butcher him. And in terms of women he wouldn't go after conquests alone. He would have two women at once. He'd pick up women. He'd buy women. And then he would make love to them violently, and then he would do away with them violently. In his head he sees himself as a man out of control. Once he actually gets a taste of killing, he feeds on it and his killings grow exponentially.

At the end of the narrative we learn that all this killing has simply gone on in the main character's mind. In fact, his life is empty in direct proportion to the degree he has filled it up with violence.

What Harron has done is to give us a portrait of the end-game in self-absorption. The result is emptiness, unhappiness, and a wave of resulting hostility that is large enough to fill a small town morgue. This is the pathology that is crystallized by Ang Lee in *The Ice Storm*, by Tod Solondz in *Happiness*, by Sam Mendes in *American Beauty*. This is the caution each of these filmmakers puts forward: an excess of self-interest poisons the members of families. Do so and you imperil your society. These filmmakers, from Taiwan in the case of Ang Lee and from England in the case of Sam Mendes, are using their critiques of the American family to say something about families the world over. Radford suggests that the Italian family, a traditional family, is a stabilizing force in the life of his main character in *Il Postino*, the husband and father in that narrative. The choice is ours. Which is it to be? Families and filmgoers the world over ponder the question as they engage with these stories.

SCRIPT TREATMENT

TREATMENT SAMPLE

<u>RAW MATERIAL</u>*

An original story for the screen

by Kenneth Dancyger

© Kenneth Dancyger

Tentative Title: <u>RAW MATERIAL</u>

CHARACTERS

<u>ERIC FLOCATI</u>, a bounty hunter, he tracks men for the reward
they will bring him. He is not a hateful man, but a man who has
a certain lifestyle to support. He works for the money. He is of
middle height and weight. His hair is short and dark. His most
distinguishing features are his dimples, when he smiles. He is in
his late 30s.

<u>MARIA FLOCATI</u>, an attractive woman who has borne children,
but whose figure belies the fact. She is demanding and whatever
the circumstances feels Eric spends too little time at home.
Maria is a sexy woman of 35.

<u>JEREMY RUSSELL</u>, is a caustic, quick-witted newspaperman.He
is bright-faced, a complexion that suggests his attraction to
drink. He is in his 40s and looks as if nothing could dispel the
bags under his eyes. He is aggressive and, to many, offensive,
as a result.

<u>EMILY RUSSELL</u>, is blonde and tall. She looks almost too much
for baggy-eyed Jeremy. Her appearance placed her high on the
social register. She looks more like a peer of her children than
their parent.

<u>EMIL HASSARD</u> is a policeman. Jeremy's good friend (one is
reluctant to say best friend, because seeing Jeremy, one
suspects he keeps everyone at some distance). He is a gritty cop
who looks honest. He worked his way up from the bottom. Now
he is a lieutenant in the homicide squad. Rough-eyed, Hassard is
blunt, to the point, a trait that prevents him from rising higher
in the force. He is not political.

MORENO FASCI is the assassin. At 35, he looks very athletic. He is always silent. He always smiles. He is dark, and his face has a scar on his forehead. His hair is long.

KENYON ALDRIDGE is the District Attorney. He looks youthful, cleancut. But beneath his exterior of clever mediocrity, is a drive for power that is insatiable.

STUART CASE is the head of a multinational corporation. Their primary market is copper products and aluminum products, but they also own finance companies and insurance companies. Case is a conservative, crusty man in his late 50s. He is the opposite of the pot-bellied company man. He is fastidious in his attention to detail, nothing happens in his company without his knowledge.

FRANKLYN DOUGHERTY is the highup in the Export-Import Bank. A former banker, his appearance belies the past. He is short, ugly, but has an agile mind. He is a political animal, because of the nature of this position.

BLAKE is a vice-president of the above multinational corporation. He is troubleshooter for the company dealing with political to criminal problems. He is a company man, very fascist in his outlook. Yes or no is all he understands. He is slick and unfeeling.

JOHN FIBER, a nervous customs official, very high up. He clears any problems the multinationals may have importing goods. He is an addict and is controlled by the Corporation. He is unpleasantly fat.

CHASEN LEE, an old fat cat politician. He sweats profusely and always talks as if he were on a platform making a speech. He is in the pay of the Corporation. He is one of the lobbyists who press on behalf of the multinationals.

MICK FITS has red hair and a stocky build, He could easily kill barehanded, he has that sort of appearance.

RAW MATERIAL

Scene 1. Prologue

We see a vast landscape of unsettled country,
beautiful, rugged, It could be a hundred years
ago, there are no signs of civilization. In the
distance a wolf is devouring a small animal.
From far off, we hear a low level unidentifiable
sound. The whirring noise is getting louder. A
man with a rifle is running. There is very little
foliage for him to hide behind. He rests behind
a rock. He is dressed like a cowboy, jeans and
boots; he has lost his hat, He looks dusty from
running for a long time. He is desperate.
In the horizon we see what he is running from,
a helicopter. From his point of view it looms
and grows larger, looking as if it will soon
envelop him. The helicopter begins to descend.
The point of view changes to the interior of the
helicopter. There, the pilot and the sole occupant
resemble astronauts, a complete contrast to the
man below them. The occupant is Eric Flocati. He
stands poised watching as his prey runs from
behind the rock. The man turns and fires at the
helicopter, but again it looms terrifyingly over
him; it is descending to land. He turns and runs.
The helicopter lands. Folcati exits and unholsters
a large revolver. He takes aim with a calm

self-confidence; he fires at the fleeing cowboy.
The cowboy falls.

Flocati carried the bloodless body to the
helicopter. We next see Flocati drop the body
on a counter, like a slab of meat. Surprisingly
the cowboy is gaining consciousness. Flocati
tells the policeman behind the counter the
cowboy will be in no shape to escape for a while.
Flocati gives the policeman his address; he tells
the policeman the authorities can forward him the
money at that address after the trial and conviction
of the cowboy. Flocati leaves. A cab takes him to
the airport. His plane sets down. He is greeted by
a woman, his wife Maria. They embrace. They drive
off in a station wagon; they drive home to the suburbs.

Scene 2. Credits

Credits appear over shots of Eric Flocati
puttering in his garden. We see him jogging
around a track, we see him shower. He eats
breakfast with his children and he makes
love with his wife.

Scene 3. The Flocati Home

Eric Flocati is putting on the lawn; his wife
exits the house and tells him he has a call.
He goes to the phone, it is Lt. Emil Hassard
calling about a job. Hassard asks to meet him
at a bar they both usually frequent.

MASTER SCENE FORMAT

RAW MATERIAL*
An Original Screenplay
by Kenneth Dancyger

*Copyright, Kenneth Dancyger
Registered with The Writers'
Guild of America

BEFORE THE MAIN TITLES A LONG SHOT of a vast
unsettled country, desolate, uninviting. There
are no signs of civilization. It could be a
hundred years ago, The mountains in the distance
seem almost to separate this land from the rest
of the world. The heat seems to rise from the
land assuring us that little if anything could
grow or live here.

CUT TO A CLOSE SHOT of a wolf devouring a small
animal. The wolf looks up and stares. We hear
a low level unindentifiable sound; it seems to be
far away.

A CLOSE SHOT of a pair of feet. THE CAMERA tracks
low behind a man running. We see only his cowboy
boots. His foot movements are uneven. He is a
tired, desperate man. His hand and rifle bounce
into frame periodically.

CUT TO A FULL SHOT of the man from the front.
THE CAMERA tracks in front of him. The whirring
noise is getting louder. He stops behind a rock.
He is dressed in jeans and a cowboy short. His
hair is unusually close cropped. He feels for
his hat. He has lost it. He curses as he looks
to the sun. The dust on his face almost obscures
his facial features. He is angry, dry, and tired.
In the horizon coming over the hill, we can see
a shadow of what he is running from—
a helicopter.

CUT TO A SHOT from behind the helicopter. It is
coming closer and closer to him.

CUT TO the point of view of the cowboy who watches
transfixed as the helicopter begins its descent.
At this point the helicopter is a thousand feet
in the air and about a mile away from him.

CUT TO A TRAVELLING SHOT of the shadow of the
helicopter. The shadow becomes larger and larger
as the helicopter descends to the ground. It
takes on the appearance of a monster that will
devour the cowboy, a quality accentuated by its
rapid movement.

A LONG TRACKING SHOT of the cowboy. He turns
and runs from the helicopter. The helicopter
is in the foreground of the shot and the
framing suggests the futility of the cowboy
running from the machine that will easily
catch him. The cowboy jumps into a hollow
depression, and turns his rifle in the direction
of the pursuing helicopter. THE SHOT continues
to follow the action as the helicopter lands, 200
feet from the cowboy. The noise from the
helicopter has become almost deafening. Now
the helicopter cuts its engine.

A CLOSE SHOT of the cowboy eyeing the helicopter
through the sight of his rifle. The only sound
is the cocking of the trigger.

A MID SHOT of the helicopter from the cowboy's
point of view. A telephoto lens almost flattens
out the perspective on the helicopter, a view
that fills the frame, giving it a tranquil,
beautiful appearance.

A LONG SHOT of the helicopter and the cowboy.
They stand glaring at one another in silence.
One is struck by the classical poetry of man
versus technology sitting in the baking sun, as
if in repose.

A CLOSE SHOT of the door of the helicopter as it
is violently and loudly opened, THE CAMERA pulls
back quickly to the man exiting from the helicopter. He jumps to the ground, a case in hand.
He quickly unbuckles the case.

CUT TO THE MID SHOT of the helicopter from the
cowboy's point of view (TELEPHOTO LENS USED).
This time the cowboy's pursuer is also visible.
The cowboy fires continually raising dust all
about the helicopter. He does not hit his
pursuer, who is busily putting up reflectors
in front of himself. Because of the position
of the sun, the cowboy can now see only the
upper 2/3 of the helicopter; the lower 1/3

3

is straight glare. The cowboy fires more rapidly.
He shoots continually.

A CLOSE SHOT as the cowboy stands up. He looks
about for his pursuer, firing above the reflectors
now.

A LONG SHOT. The cowboy has stopped firing and
is looking toward the helicopter for his pursuer.
He sees nothing but as he turns to his right, a
shocked look comes to his face as he sees, not a hundred feet
away, his pursuer staring, smiling,
pointing a large pistol at him.

A MID SHOT of the pursuer as he take aim with
his large revolver. The use of a WIDE ANGLE LENS
here would make the gun seem even longer than it
really is. He fires. The gun shot is more a thud
than an explosion.

A LONG SHOT of the cowboy as he falls. His
pursuer walks toward the body. The pursuer
is ERIC FLOCATI. He is wearing a flight suit.
His facial features are pleasant but unremark-
able. He looks to be of European origin, Northern
Italian. He has black hair, close-cropped, an oval
face, and an innocence and charm that only large
dimples can suggest. FLOCATI is 6 feet tall, and
is slightly paunchy at the waist.

A MID SHOT as FLOCATI stands over the body. He
stares at the cowboy.

                    FLOCATI
            Dwayne, you're a schmuck.

FLOCATI bends down to pick up the body. He carries
the bloodless body to the helicopter.

CUT TO A CLOSE SHOT of the body as it is dropped on a counter.
THE CAMERA pulls back. FLOCATI
unzips his flight suit. He opens the bag he has

at his side and takes out a shirt and tie. He
is changing clothes as the officer at the desk
is taking information from him. We are surprised
to see the cowboy regaining consciousness. A
detective walks in with a female purse snatcher
and books her at the next desk.

                    DETECTIVE
        Book Freda on a 502.

                    CLERK
        This is her third offense, they'll
        go hard.

                    DETECTIVE
        I just bring 'em in. Judge got to
        earn his money too!

                    FREDA
        (to clerk)
        Come to my cell tonight.

The CLERK begins to fill out the paper work on
FREDA.

                    FLOCATI
        He gave us a good run. He'll be in
        no shape to escape for a while.

                    SERGEANT
        Where should we send the money,
        bounty hunter?

                    FLOCATI
        Mr. Eric Flocati
        1244 Meadowvale Avenue
        Orange Heights, California
        02215

FLOCATI turns and leaves.

5

CUT TO FLOCATI, as he gets into a taxi. From
the little we see of the town, it looks like
a smaller town in Arizona.

> FLOCATI
> (to the taxi driver)
> The airport.

CUT TO A SHOT of the plane setting down.

CUT TO the air terminal. FLOCATI is greeted by
a woman. They embrace, She is a good looking,
sexy woman of 35. Her black shoulder length
hair makes her look younger. Her oversize glasses
lend her a fun air.

CUT TO A LONG SHOT as FLCOATI and his wife get
into a large station wagon and drive off.

CUT TO A HELICOPTER SHOT of the car on a freeway.
They turn off onto a ramp and get onto another
freeway. They travel only a short distance before
they turn off another ramp.

CUT to an interior SHOT of the car. FLOCATI and
his wife look very happy, they are silent. They
look at one another. As they drive over the ridge
we can see they are driving into a suburban
development. There are houses street after street.
Their similarity, one to the other is startling.
There are your trees planted symmetrically on
the boulevards of each street. They do nothing
to cut down the glare of the sun that de-beautifies
everything. FLOCATI smiles at his wife. They drive
into their driveway. They are home, in the middle
of this suburb, home, at last.

THE MAIN TITLE START.

UNDER THE MAIN TITLES we see SHOTS of FLOCATI'S
activities about his home in the suburbs. He
cuts the grass. He tends his small vegetable
patch in the backyard, just beyond the swimming
pool. We see FLOCATI as he jogs around the
track in early morning. We see him shower. He

eats breakfast with his children; he washes his
car; he reads the newspaper on his front stoop.
And he makes love with his wife.

END OF TITLE SEQUENCE, as FLOCATI'S WIFE, MARIE,
exits the house to interrupt him as he is putting
on the lawn.

> MARIA
> There's a call. It's Hassard. Tell
> him if he takes you away for long,
> he can start fucking himself.

> FLOCATI
> Yes, dear!

FLOCATI enters the house and takes the telephone in the kitchen.

> FLOCATI
> Emil, you're bothering me in
> my leisure. This had better be
> worth it. . . . . O.K.
> I'll meet you in an hour.

1   INT. IRISH BAR   AFTERNOON

The low-lit bar is very fashionable. The
waitresses are provocative and flirtations
as they serve food and drinks wearing nun's
robes. Their serving trays are in the shape
of enlarged green four-leaf clovers. A trio
wearing heavy beige woolen turtlenecks are
singing. Their outfits are totally ludicrous
in the tropical climate of this part of
California.
FLOCATI is wearing a washed out grey suit and
tie.
EMIL HASSARD is a thin intense man, very tall
with curly hair. There is nothing remarkable
about his looks, but he has an excellent sense
of humor. He wears and open-necked shirt and
an unfitted sports jacket.

INDEX